Closer *to*
FREEDOM

Closer *to* FREEDOM

Enslaved Women
and Everyday
Resistance in the
Plantation South

STEPHANIE M. H. CAMP

The University of North Carolina Press
Chapel Hill and London

Designed by Jacquline Johnson
Set in Minion
by Keystone Typesetting, Inc.

The paper in this book meets the guidelines
for permanence and durability of the Committee
on Production Guidelines for Book Longevity
of the Council on Library Resources.

Portions of Chapter 2 appeared earlier, in
somewhat different form, as " 'I Could Not Stay
There': Enslaved Women, Truancy and the
Geography of Everyday Forms of Resistance in
the Antebellum Plantation South," *Slavery and
Abolition* 23, no. 3 (December 2002): 1–20. It is
reprinted here with permission of the publisher
(<http://www.tandf.co.uk>). Portions of
Chapter 3 appeared earlier, in somewhat
different form, as "The Pleasures of Resistance:
Enslaved Women and Body Politics in the
Plantation South, 1830–1861," *Journal of Southern
History* 68, no. 3 (August 2002): 533–72. It is
reprinted here with permission.

Library of Congress
Cataloging-in-Publication Data
Camp, Stephanie M. H.
Closer to freedom : enslaved women and
everyday resistance in the plantation South /
Stephanie M. H. Camp.
p. cm. — (Gender and American culture)
Includes bibliographical references (p.   )
and index.
ISBN 0-8078-2872-6 (cloth: alk. paper)
ISBN 0-8078-5534-0 (pbk.: alk. paper)
1. Women slaves—Southern States—Social
conditions—19th century. 2. Slaves—Southern
States—Social conditions—19th century.
3. Passive resistance—Southern States—
History—19th century. 4. Sex role—Southern
States—History—19th century. 5. Plantation
life—Southern States—History—19th century.
6. Freedom of movement—Southern States—
History—19th century. 7. Landscape—Social
aspects—Southern States—History—19th
century. 8. Human geography—Southern
States—History—19th century. 9. Slavery—
Southern States—History—19th century.
10. Southern States—Race relations. I. Title.
II. Gender & American culture.
E443.C36   2004
306.3′62′0820973—dc22   2003024975

cloth   08 07 06 05 04   5 4 3 2 1
paper   08 07 06 05 04   5 4 3 2 1

CONTENTS

List of Illustrations *vii*

Acknowledgments *ix*

Introduction *1*

CHAPTER ONE
A Geography of Containment:
The Bondage of Space and Time 12

CHAPTER TWO
I Could Not Stay There:
Women, Men, and Truancy 35

CHAPTER THREE
The Intoxication of Pleasurable Amusement:
Secret Parties and the Politics of the Body 60

CHAPTER FOUR
Amalgamation Prints Stuck Up in Her Cabin:
Print Culture, the Home, and the Roots of Resistance 93

CHAPTER FIVE
To Get Closer to Freedom:
Gender, Movement, and Freedom during the Civil War 117

Postscript *139*

Notes *143*

Bibliography *175*

Index *203*

ILLUSTRATIONS

Slave pass 21

Slave harness 23

Hauling Cotton to the River 29

The Plantation Patrol 31

The Sabbath among Slaves 66

The Festival 67

A Live Oak Avenue 70

A Negro Funeral 73

The Country Church 74

Am I Not a Woman and a Sister? 110

Mother Separated from Her Children 111

Abolition Hall 113

Practical Amalgamation 114

Illustration from "Les esclaves et la proclamation du président Lincoln" 121

The Escaped Correspondent Enjoying the Negro's Hospitality 137

ACKNOWLEDGMENTS

This book began some years ago as a dissertation at the University of Pennsylvania, where I had the good fortune to study with the support of the department's pedagogical and financial generosity. The dissertation from which this book grew (and strayed) benefited from the attention of a few extraordinary professors. Drew Gilpin Faust gently guided the dissertation, drafts of which she read—and marked with comments—with a speed that I have yet to hear of replicated by anyone else. Drew's example of grace in teaching and love of learning continues to inspire me. Carroll Smith-Rosenberg directed me to a number of anthropological and literary scholars whose work set many key ideas into motion. And Farah Griffin was a supportive and honest third reader. I was privileged to be able to study at Penn at all because of a Fontaine Fellowship that supported the first few years of graduate work, while a Mellon Dissertation Fellowship funded a year of writing. Research trips were supported by the Virginia Historical Society, the Library Company of Philadelphia, and the Huggins-Quarles Award of the Organization of American Historians.

In Philadelphia I met other excited graduate students with whom I had stimulating conversations about history and politics, and to whom I could often turn for a read of my work. While it is impossible to thank everyone who contributed to this genial intellectual climate, I owe special thanks to Anjali Arondekar, Ed Baptist, Kali Gross, Elisa von Joeden-Forgey, Russ Kazal, Kostis Kourelis, Jeff Maskovsky, Darrell Moore, Eve Oishi, Matt Reuben, Liam Riordan, Marc Stein, Jennifer Uleman, and Rhonda Williams. Vassar College's Minority Scholar in Residence program allowed me to finish the dissertation while also getting a feel for teaching (with a very kind load). The hospitality of Vassar and its faculty, especially Miriam Cohen, and the beauty of the mid-Hudson valley, made the process of finishing almost bearable. Since graduate school, Herman Bennett, Christopher Brown, Vince Brown, Sharla Fett, Sally Hadden, Walter Johnson, Barbara Krauthamer, Jennifer

Morgan, Dylan Penningroth, and Stephanie Smallwood have taught me a great deal about slavery studies and also made conferences a lot more fun.

After neglecting the dissertation (now a "book manuscript") for a year, I plunged back in ready to make some big changes. This was easier said than done, but detailed feedback about the project's strengths and weaknesses made the process an adventure. Every time that Doug Egerton read the manuscript (which he did three times), an article draft, or a conference paper, he found something new, tough, and brilliant to say. It may sound like hyperbole to state that Doug embodies the ideal of scholarly collegiality and generosity, but in fact it may be closer to understatement. Nell Irvin Painter's thoughtful, multipage comments revealed what the dissertation was really about and transformed my thinking as I inched toward "the book." Her e-mailed citations and ongoing interest in the project meant more than she can know. Suzanne Lebsock gave astute lessons on language in response to a near-final version and sage advice on the profession during my first five years at the University of Washington. Julie Saville read the whole manuscript twice, asked keen questions, and pointed me in some very productive directions, prompting a new set of realizations well after I thought I had nothing left to give the book. I am profoundly indebted to each of these scholars for the interest they took in reading drafts of this project and for the time they took to make this book better than it would have been without their input.

Others have also been liberal with their time and thoughts. For comments on portions of the book, I owe thanks to Houston Baker, the Brown Bag Seminar of the McNeil Center for Early American Studies, "Daughter of HRG," Margit Dimenti, James Gregory, Lani Guinier, Shan Holt, Diannah Leigh Jackson, Bethany Johnson, Moon-Ho Jung, Jeannine de Lombard, Tracy McKenzie, Uta Poiger, Bill Rorabaugh, Andrea Simpson, Nikhil Singh, Carroll Smith-Rosenberg, Matthew Sparke, Carol Thomas, Priscilla Wald, Kathleen Woodward, and the anonymous reviews of the *Journal of Southern History* and *Slavery and Abolition.* Lynn Thomas cast her judicious and insightful eye over papers and an article and helped me to clarify and improve my arguments. As commentators and audience members, Ed Baptist, Timothy Burke, Miriam Cohen, Richard Dunn, Steven Hahn, Wanda Hendricks, Evelyn Brooks Higginbotham, Stephanie McCurry, Steven Stowe, Priscilla Wald, and Richard White asked questions and made comments that have helped me to think through the issues explored here. Sandra Joshel's pen proved acute at the page proof stage.

Under the dexterous coordination of Robert C. Stacey, former chair of the Department of History, leave time was granted so that I could accept a Ford Foundation Postdoctoral Fellowship, a fellowship with the Society of Scholars at the Walter Chapin Simpson Center for the Humanities, and a Junior Faculty Development Award. Research trips were facilitated by the Philadelphia Library Company, the Virginia Historical Society, the Royalty Research Fund at the University of Washington, and the Gilder-Lerhman Center for the Study of Slavery, Resistance, and Abolition at the Yale Center for International and Area Studies.

During research trips, I was fortunate to work with talented archivists at the Library Company of Philadelphia, the Southern Historical Collection at the University of North Carolina, the Special Collections Library at Duke University, and the Virginia Historical Society. I especially appreciate the tips that William Erwin, Phillip Lapsansky, and Frances Pollard gave. Tatiana van Riemsdijk and Hampton Cary extended their personal hospitality to me in Richmond and shared what they were learning about Richmond archives. Ed and Stephanie Baptist and the Neville family made me feel at home in North Carolina. To such hospitable friends, my credit card and I say "Thank you." Closer to home, Theresa Mudrock has expedited research from a distance by winning grants to purchase microfilm. Anthony Blackburn and Alicia Woods were meticulous research assistants. Moon-Ho Jung and Jeannine de Lombard very kindly shared notes from their own research, and Leslie Rowland sent an unforgettable e-mail detailing methods for approaching the formidable holdings on the Civil War in the National Archives and at the Library of Congress. Kate Torrey ushered the book through publication with efficiency and took the time to instruct me on the process every step of the way.

I am grateful to Marie Camp and Don Camp for encouraging the creative life, and to Dorothea Camp for the sense of perspective that her dark sense of humor brings to our conversations. Marc Mariani repeatedly took time out of his hectic schedule to read the manuscript and, by his example of discipline and ardor at work, kept me to my task. Best of all, he put a little sugar in my bowl and is the sweetness in my soul.

Closer *to*
FREEDOM

INTRODUCTION

*All margins are dangerous. If they are pulled this way
or that the shape of fundamental experience is altered.*
—Mary Douglas, Purity and Danger

In the past three decades or so, the question of slave resistance in the United States has won the attention of dozens of historians. Beyond only historians of slavery, even scholars of the Old South not specializing in the topic have given thought and space to the issue in their books. It was, after all, the existence of slave resistance and the study of it that helped to move American scholarship on slavery from the plantation nostalgia of the late nineteenth and early twentieth centuries and the "Sambo" theses of midcentury to the impassioned "accommodation versus resistance" debate of the past few decades. This argument has shaped the contours of much of what we have learned about life in the Old South.

A cursory review of the literature would suggest that the argument revolved around such either/or questions as Did enslaved people identify with their owners, or did they infuse their lives with independent religious and cultural meanings? Were their families destroyed by the slave trade, or did they rebuild, remember, and endure? Did they submit to slaveholders' authority, or did they condemn it as immoral and unjust? On closer inspection, scholarship from approximately the 1970s through the end of the twentieth century was rarely so simply framed, and much of it provided the foundation for recent work that explicitly dissolves dichotomous choices. Some scholars of slavery now consciously explore the contradictory and paradoxical qualities in bondpeople's lives: for instance, the ways in which they were both agents and subjects, persons and property, and people who resisted and who accommodated—sometimes in one and the same act.[1] Enslaved people were many things at once, and they were many things at different moments and in various places.[2] They lived multiple lives, some visible to their owners and to the archival record, some less visible. Side by side, public and hidden worlds coexisted in the plantation South; their black and white inhabitants shared space, agreed on its importance, and clashed over its uses.

While studies of resistance are easily and often accused of naïveté, of romanticizing bondpeople and of underestimating the extent and subtlety of their owners' power, it seems that the opposite is also often true: these very studies offer a keen appreciation of the forms of abuse and exploitation against which the enslaved struggled and to which they often submitted. Slave resistance was a fact of life throughout the Americas, constituted not in the trends and opinions that shape academic discourse but in the slavery experience itself. The fields, auction blocks, chains and jails, disease-ridden swamps, whips, damp and drafty residences—these were the settings and instruments that ensured the coexistence of misery and dissent in the quarters. Slave resistance in its many forms is a necessary point of historical inquiry, and it continues to demand research. Yet *how* resistance is studied has changed and must continue to do so; complicating the questions that inform the study of resistance need not mean abandoning the category altogether. Indeed, doing so would cost us insight into essential parts of the history of slavery. For all that we now know about slave resistance, many of its dimensions remain opaque. Assuming that few new sources will come to light, we need innovative ways to read our existing ones.

Theories of everyday forms of resistance, those small acts with sometimes outsize consequences, have opened enormous possibilities for understanding the meanings of actions that might otherwise appear to be little more than fits of temper. Theft, foot dragging, short-term flight, and feigning illness were commonplace acts in the Old South and are widely understood to be everyday forms of resistance—hidden or indirect expressions of dissent, quiet ways of reclaiming a measure of control over goods, time, or parts of one's life. But what are we to make of the larger significance of such opposition?

Though it is possible to understand such acts as "safety valves" (that is, as individual expressions of dissatisfaction that released anger and frustration but posed no danger to the system), such an interpretation loses sight of their importance to slaves and slaveholders. Neither accommodationist nor a direct attack on slavery, everyday resistance occupied, as political scientist James Scott has argued, the wide terrain between consent, on one hand, and open, organized opposition, on the other.[3] Before the rise of a strong, centralized state in the United States after the Civil War, conflicts between people over everyday practices and more were especially important. On antebellum plantations, where elite slaveholders had many of the powers later ascribed to the state, it was in the daily tug-of-war over labor and culture that power and its assumptions were contested from below—not in formal institutions such as courtrooms or political organizations. In such a context, the everyday is a particularly salient category of analysis. The day-to-day resistance of slaves demands to be understood in multiple ways. To a degree, day-to-day acts of opposition were the result and expression of the dialogic of power relations between owner and owned—part of quotidian plantation relations characterized by a paternalistic combination of hegemonic cultural control and violent discipline that was supposed to extract not only obedience but even consent from enslaved people. To a larger extent, however, this framework fails to explain everyday slave resistance sufficiently. The paternalist model offers an apt theory of plantation management but an incomplete perspective on plantation, and particularly black, life.[4] Sustained, collective rebellion was almost always impossible under the level of slave control that permeated antebellum southern culture. Most opposition was, of necessity, masked and short lived; in itself, this is a measure of the force (not the hegemony) to which enslaved people were subjected.

Turning our attention to the everyday, to private, concealed, and even intimate worlds, is essential to excavating bondwomen's resistance to slavery because women's history does not merely add to what we know; it changes what we know and how we know it. The valorization of the organized and the visible veils the lives of women, who rarely participated directly in slave rebellions and who made up only a small proportion of runaways to the North—the kinds of slave resistance that have been most studied within the United States. It is, therefore, particularly important to look to the subtler forms if we are to understand women's lives in and resistance to slavery. In turn, these add complexity to our knowledge of American slavery itself. Studying bondwomen's opposition has demanded creative approaches: a shift from the visible and organized to the hidden and informal, as well as rigorous attention to personal topics that, for enslaved women, were also political arenas.[5] *Closer to Freedom* proceeds from the conviction that dichotomies such as personal/political, material/symbolic, organized rebellion/everyday resistance, accommodation/resistance obscure at least as much as they reveal.

The attenuation of classic social scientific dichotomies, then, is one of this book's themes. Understanding resistance mainly as a "public" phenomenon (visible, organized, and workplace oriented) and as less significant in "private" places limits our understanding of dissent and distracts us from interesting connections. Overlooking the links between the public and the private—between material or political issues, on one hand, and cultural or intimate (emotionally and physically) issues, on the other—limits our understanding of human lives in the past, especially women's lives.[6] For bondwomen, even more than for enslaved men, intimate entities, such as the body and the home, were instruments of both domination and resistance. Enslaved women's bodies were exploited in the fields and sexually violated in the quarters. Although enslaved women were hardly housebound in the way that antebellum white women of means, trapped by the "cult of domesticity," often were, they nonetheless were burdened by a disproportionate share of household labor. The body and the home were key sites of suffering but also a resource in women's survival.[7]

To think about women's bodies and their distinct forms of labor within the home is to think about the spatial history of American slavery, a topic we have only begun to investigate and that is this book's second theme. Social relations and social values are constituted and reflected in the design of the built environment and in the distribution of people in space. The architecture and peopling of places of work, amusement, intimate life, and public interaction all help to shape and reveal details of wider social life. As geographer David Harvey has written, "temporal and spatial organization . . . serve to constitute the social order through the assignment of people and activities to distinctive places and times."[8] Take, for instance, the transformation of Virginia's wealthiest farms in the late seventeenth and early eighteenth centuries. Until about the last quarter of the seventeenth century, the main dwelling house on such farms was often a ramshackle construction situated as one among other buildings. Farm buildings and the fields and gardens that skirted them were laid out in a random if not haphazard manner. Tobacco and corn crops were sown between the trees and stumps of uncleared land as well as in fields, and livestock grazed freely across unfenced pastures, woodlands, and fields. To travelers in eighteenth-century Virginia, these farms looked, one historian has reported, like "slovens."[9]

By the mid- to late seventeenth century, however, a small group of elite families (about twenty-five family lines) had acquired large landholdings and great wealth. A fashion-conscious clique, they looked to England for the latest in clothing and architecture. These stylish fat cats were, by the early eighteenth century, in the grip of the Georgian style of architecture. This good taste, they hoped, would illustrate their rank and their difference from the riffraff with whom they lived in the colony. Order, symmetry, and harmony were characteristic of the Georgian style, as was the incorporation of classical details such as pediments and columns. Great houses, built not of rickety and impermanent wood but of brick, were carefully sited on their estates among formal gardens and parks that conspicuously displayed ornamental, nonfunctional use of land. Avenues approached them in a linear manner to highlight the centrality of the great house. Offices, outbuildings, and slaves' quarters were sometimes arranged on a grid and always in a predictable and balanced manner around a main residence that was occasionally elevated above the other buildings. The built relationship of these great houses to their "dependencies" was clearly one in which "a strong sense of gradations of dominance and submission was expressed."[10] The Georgian design of house and estate showed planters' mastery of nature and their prominence in society.[11]

Gender roles, like class rank, were constituted in space. Harvey was again instructive when he wrote that "the body, the house, gender relations of reproduction as well as gender roles . . . all become caught up in a wider symbolism constructed around space, time, and value."[12] As historian Stephanie McCurry has shown, the prestige and power of property holders in South Carolina was linked to the marking out of boundaries of landownership. In 1827 the South Carolina legislature amended a 1694 statute on fences, revealing a shifting attitude toward what needed to be enclosed and for what purpose. The 1694 law had mandated six-foot fences around "corn and other provisions" in order to prevent "evilly minded" small farmers from craftily enticing free-foraging livestock over short fences and onto their property, where they could then claim them as their own. The 1827 law, on the other hand, had very different intentions and, McCurry noted, "encoded a markedly different landscape." Instead of being designed to prevent the theft of mobile livestock by small farmers, fences in the 1827 law were to enclose and protect the crops of property holders, including crops grown for the market by larger farmers. Whereas the 1694 law tried to deter a form of theft but continued to uphold common rights to land, the 1827 law initiated a "slow and steady" erosion of common rights in the antebellum years.[13]

The "boundaries of power" created by fences consolidated white patriarchal authority over both large plantations and self-working yeoman households, McCurry has demonstrated. The Fence Law and the rulings for which it provided precedent in the following decades slowly eroded common access to land, waterways, and roads. Neighborhood residents who might have previously enjoyed decades of public passage on a road, for example, could find it suddenly—and legally—fenced off and impassable. Certainly the hunting and foraging that was permitted on unfenced land (even if privately owned) stopped when a fence was encountered. Over the antebellum period, South Carolina's jurists created "a plantation landscape dominated by fenced enclosures" that guaranteed property holders the "exclusive use" of their land. Inside fenced boundaries, property rights were sacrosanct. Moreover, property holders were acknowledged to be not merely heads of households but masters of them and of all the dependents (free women and enslaved people) within. Fences had become symbols of the Old South's gender, race, and labor relations within the household.[14]

This project builds on these histories of the relationships between space, social relations, gender, and power in the Old South. It gives less attention than other studies to the built environment and more to the peopling of plantation space—to the containment and movement of enslaved women and men. It argues that the broad operation of politics in the Old South was profoundly invested in black and white uses of space. Space mattered: places, boundaries, and movement were central to how slavery was organized and to how it was resisted. This project explores planters' attempts to confine slave activity to specific places, the ways enslaved women evaded that captivity, and the perpetual conflicts that arose as a result of these differing ideas about how space was to be used. Geography has provided both a way of seeing new aspects of enslaved women's lives and the language to describe those sights.

By the antebellum period (beginning around 1830) laws, customs, and ideals had come together into a systematic constriction of slave movement that helped establish slaveholders' sense of mastery. Planters presided over controlled and controlling landscapes dictating the movements of their slaves into the fields or yards and back to the quarters, with carefully considered breaks and holidays. Morning reveilles, slave patrols, curfews, and laws requiring passes and banning independent travel or meetings were all instituted to limit and control slave movement in both space and time. Enslaved women and men were bound by this "geography of containment," but women in greater numbers and with greater consistency were confined to southern plantations; as a group they enjoyed much less mobility than did men.[15]

In violation of slaveholders' orders and the state's laws, though, enslaved people left the quarters at night. "Watching every step that they take for the guard or patrol," slaves "venture[d] out" at night to the very woods and swamps that were intended to distinguish legitimate and illicit plantation space.[16] "All margins are dangerous," Mary Douglas commented. "If they are pulled this way or that the shape of fundamental experience is altered. Any structure of ideas is vulnerable at its margins."[17] Again and again, enslaved people ran away and created other kinds of spaces that gave them room and time for their families, for rest from work, and for amusement; on occasion, women moved forbidden objects into their quarters to worrisome effect. As they moved about, those who had the gift read the sights and sounds of the natural environment—the events of the skies or the squawks of birds—for signs of opportunity or trouble. Others simply looked for the landmarks—distinctive trees and shrubs or outbuildings—that could guide their way along clandestine trails to secret meeting places.

In short, bondpeople created a "rival geography"—alternative ways of knowing and using plantation and southern space that conflicted with planters' ideals and demands. The term "rival geography" was coined by Edward Said and has been used by geographers to describe resistance to colonial occupation.[18] I have adapted the term for the slave South, where the challenge for enslaved people was not one of repossession of land in the face of dispossession but of mobility in the face of constraint. Thus the rival geography was not a settled spatial formation, for it included quarters, outbuildings, woods, swamps, and neighboring farms as chance granted them. Where planters' mapping of their farms was defined by fixed places for plantation residents, the rival geography was characterized by motion: the movement of bodies, objects, and information within and around plantation space.[19]

The rival geography did not threaten to overthrow American slavery, nor did it provide slaves with autonomous space. Much of the rival geography, such as woods and swamps, was space to which planters and patrols had access, and other parts, including quarters and outbuildings were places over which they also had a large measure of control. Nor was there anything safe about bondpeople's illicit movements or the temporary spaces they created; to the contrary, these activities and areas were truly dangerous. The rival geography did, however, provide space for private and public creative expression, rest and recreation, alternative communication, and importantly, resistance to planters' domination of slaves' every move.

Just as slave resistance was forged in the conditions of enslavement, it gained some of its significance from that same source. The importance of slave resistance cannot be separated from slaveholders' concerns about social control and plantation efficiency and attributed solely to its value to the enslaved. Enslaved people's many forms of resistance were struggles for life without reference to their owners as well as responses to their owners' efforts to deny them, for instance, access to their families or time alone. It is planters who attest to how much slaves' search for space and time to themselves mattered *in their own time*; slaveholders' violent actions and their words illustrate the extent to which some slave activities cut them to the quick by challenging their authority and, they feared, by making their plantations less efficient. That enslaved people were willing to risk gruesome punishments for the sake of a degree of mobility speaks volumes about its importance to them.

Space and the control of bodies in space were important to both slaveholders and enslaved people, and they were major points of conflict. Studying the rival geography requires a leap of the imagination, for it was space charted by movements that were, by design, hidden, and as a result, little documented. Mutable and secret, the rival geography was far less institutionalized than the black public sphere of the postemancipation years, and probably less so than the "invisible institution" of slave religion.[20] What follows is an exploration of this unstable underground, of women's participation in it, and of planters' outraged responses to it. *Closer to Freedom* explores the entanglement of gender, race, space, and slavery in the American South. Not limited to the antebellum years, the relevance of space in the formation of race and place runs throughout American history, including the postemancipation years. Indeed, in light of the findings here, the rise of segregation in the late nineteenth century seems less like a new solution to an old "negro" problem and more like a fresh expression of deep-rooted investments in the placing of black and white people in space and society.

A few words on method are necessary. Though spare, documentation comes to us consistently from both the upper and the lower South in slaveholders' diaries, journals, and correspondence; in state legislative records; in nineteenth-century autobiographies by ex-slaves; and in twentieth-century interviews of the formerly enslaved. All of these sources present difficulties, and alone none tells all we might want to know. For all of the problems of plantation records and legal sources, however, historians of slavery tend to focus their methodological critiques on the interviews of ex-slaves. The criticisms contend that the interviews collected by the Works Progress Administration (WPA) were conducted decades after emancipation, after too much had happened in the lives of the informants to make their recollections creditable. Many of the interviews were also done by whites, further warping the information respondents gave. I do not dispute the problems inherent in the WPA interviews, but I do not conclude from them that these sources are unworkable.[21] Gathering material from a variety of sources (which are black and white, contemporaneous and subsequent, written and oral), this book builds a story out of their agreements and common accounts, as well as from the insights offered by their differences.

Variations among locales were important and, when the sources allow it, are explored. Overall, though, *Closer to Freedom* studies bondwomen across the South, and not only for reasons of evidence. Many recent studies on American slavery focus on a region, a crop, or a county.[22] This trend has deepened our understanding of the variations of work and culture in American slavery, it has furthered our sense of important differences among enslaved people, and it has added texture and detail to our picture of day-to-day life in bondage. At the same time, for all of the important variations attributable to crop, region, and local demographics, American slavery was, above all, a system of economic exploitation, racial formation, and racial domination that, when studied in a broad geographic range, reveals strong continuities as well as differences. Studying slavery across the South remains a valuable practice, as recent works on the slave past have demonstrated.[23] We have much to learn about the interplay of local and individual experiences of enslavement, and much also to learn about slavery as a system and resistance to it as a practice with patterns and trends common in different states and subregions. Everyday forms of resistance and competing moralities regarding the uses of plantation space were an issue everywhere in the slave South.

I make no attempt to catalog all forms of illicit movement. Readers interested in fugitives, slave religion, *marronage* (the establishment of independent societies), theft, and other related topics that have been closely examined elsewhere will find references in the notes.[24] Even less does this book cover the many forms of resistance in which bondwomen engaged. This work studies women's lives in and resistance to bondage and those aspects of motion and space most pertinent to women: the short-term movement of the body and the uses of the home. Like many other recent histories of women, this book does not and cannot exclude men from the story, for enslaved women's lives were in many ways entangled with the lives of their men. Bondwomen did not inhabit a "separate sphere" from their male relatives, lovers, friends, and neighbors. At the same time, women's experiences of slavery were in significant ways distinct from those of bondmen, and this book gives most of its attention to them.

Change over time is central to the study of history, as is attention to the pace of change itself, which also varies. No moment in the life of the world is ever static, but if words such as "revolution" and "transformation" mean anything, they imply that change is faster and more profound in certain times than in others. The Civil War years were the time of greatest flux during the period under study here. The power and control that planters had enjoyed was, at different rates in various places, eroded by Union soldiers who disrupted the local status quo, by the demands of Confederate armies who overrode the autonomy of individual planters, and by the actions of enslaved people who, more openly than they ever could before, broke rules, spoke their minds, and ran away to the Yankees. The war years saw revolutionary change that had been in the making, as we shall see, for decades preceding the conflict.

This book, then, is thematically and not chronologically organized. Two themes run through the following chapters. The dissolving of common distinctions—between individual and collective (Chapter 2), pleasure and politics (Chapter 3), private home and public matters (Chapter 4), and day-to-day resistance and mass action (Chapter 5)—is the first theme. Motion, the key element in the rival geography, is the second. The first chapter establishes the spatial framework for the book, tracing how containment was a core part of American bondage. Planters went to great trouble to control the movements of the people they owned, and Chapter 1 investigates why such minute control was meaningful to planters at the time, and why it is an important part of the history of American slavery now. The next three chapters focus on patterns of barely discernible activity that were carefully hidden on plantations across the South. Chapter 2 looks at the practice of truancy, an intentionally temporary escape. In addition to engaging in absenteeism a good deal more than they ran away, women were also key to enabling the short-term flight of others. Women, then, were users and makers of slaves' rival geography and were instrumental in facilitating an endemic labor problem in the Old South. Chapter 3 explores bondpeople's secular hidden institution: the illegal party. This chapter argues that women created "third bodies" that were sites of pleasure and resistance. Chapter 4 is a close reading of two incidents involving bondwomen who acquired abolitionist materials and posted them on the walls of their homes. In these instances, slave cabins were linked to a national readership of abolitionist print culture and an illustration of the advancement of abolitionism into the South. They were the meeting ground of everyday plantation resistance and high national politics.

Investigating everyday forms of resistance does more than draw us into secret worlds; it alerts us to the hidden origins of the most dramatic historical events. Revolutionary moments may make spectacular breaks with the past, but they also are formed by them, spilling over from the old constraints and making the most of new opportunities to do visibly what formerly had been cloaked.[25] Chapter 5 analyzes the moment when the hidden was made visible, when covert resistance moved out of the underground and into the light of day. In this chapter I look at enslaved women's and men's motion from a perspective somewhat different from that of earlier chapters. During the war thousands of enslaved people escaped slavery by running to Union army camps. This migration from bondage to freedom was shaped by antebellum gender patterns that deepened during the war, and it was made possible by the knowledge antebellum slaves (especially men) had acquired about plantation and extra-plantation space and the value that all had placed on its use. The relative openness of flight during the Civil War made slaveholders—and the records they left behind—more informative about slaves' illicit movement than they had been before. At the same time, the activities of women remained more difficult to locate than those of men (in whom the Union army was very interested and about whom they wrote a good deal; war, it is clear, was men's business). The effort to find and write about black women during the Civil War continued to require resourceful reading of the material.

During their enslavement, women and men—in fear, rage, indignation, and desperation—fled some of the worst moments of their bondage. These escapes were not palliatives but were of value to enslaved people and offensive to planters. They were also part of a long-term freedom struggle that ended with emancipation and the Confederate surrender in April 1865, only to begin once again at those same moments. The unmaking of the slavery regime was in process throughout (at least) the antebellum period, in the hands and feet of those who would live to exploit national crisis to bring about their own liberation.

A GEOGRAPHY
OF CONTAINMENT

The Bondage of
Space and Time

THE PRINCIPLES OF RESTRAINT

At the heart of the process of enslavement was a spatial impulse: to locate bondpeople in plantation space and to control, indeed to determine, their movements and activities.[1] Enslaved people in the nineteenth century were trapped in more than an exploitative labor relation; they were the captive losers in a battle for power that had begun centuries earlier in the Atlantic maritime world. As outsiders, heathens, perhaps even beasts, Africans were, unlike Europeans (no matter how debased), viewed as fundamentally enslaveable by the European merchants, planters, travelers, and adventurers who traversed the Atlantic world. Once enslaved, Africans were considered more like the captives of war to whom they were compared in the early, formative years of American slavery than to the indentured servants to whom they are sometimes compared now. In the minds of the earliest participants in and witnesses to the African slave trade, as historian Winthrop Jordan has put it, "enslavement was captivity."[2]

Slavery's roots as a form of captivity lived into the nineteenth century. Enslavement in the American South meant cultural alienation, reduction to the status of property, the ever-present threat of sale, denial of the fruits of one's labor, and subjugation to the force, power, and will of another human being.[3] It entailed the strictest control of the physical and social mobility of enslaved people, as some of the institution's most resonant accouterments— shackles, chains, passes, slave patrols, and hounds—suggest. These effects were as much a part of abolitionism's image-based protests against bondage as were depictions of the lash, the auction block, or stooped slaves in the field.

These same images have persisted into our own visual culture of bondage, testaments to slavery's denial of a medley of freedoms.

By the nineteenth century, lawmakers and slaveholders had laid out, in their statutes and in their plantation journals, a theory of mastery at the center of which was the restriction of slave movement.[4] Passes, tickets, curfews, and roll calls all limited slave mobility. In his remarkable memoir of life in bondage, Charles Ball called the legal and day-to-day regulations that governed black movement "principles of restraint." "No slave dare leave" the plantation to which she or he belonged, Ball wrote, not for a "single mile" or a "single hour, by night or by day," except at the risk of "exposing himself to the danger of being taken up and flogged."[5] Bondpeople everywhere were forbidden by law and by common practice to leave their owners' property without a pass, and slave patrols attempted to ensure obedience to the law and to plantation rules. Formerly enslaved people compared bondage to another form of confinement: "I was a slave," Henry Bibb wrote in his autobiography, "a prisoner for life." Fountain Hughes agreed, saying of enslavement that it was a "jail sentence, was jus' the same as we was in jail."[6]

Antebellum principles of restraint rested on a legal bedrock laid in the colonial and early national periods. Between the seventeenth and the early nineteenth centuries, as colonists and settlers seized and organized land that would become states, elites passed laws to govern the people who populated these new societies. Slaveholders everywhere in the slave South shared a common interest in constricting black mobility; intraregional differences of crop, demographics, and culture modulated but did not fundamentally alter this investment.[7] Virginia was the first colony to pass laws governing bondpeople's behavior. Among the colony's earliest slave laws was the act of 1680 "for preventing Negroes Insurrections." The concerns expressed in this ordinance indicate a sense of urgency in regard to controlling black mobility. To prevent "Negroes Insurrections," the colonial legislature prohibited enslaved people from possessing weapons and, in the same breath, from leaving their place of work without a pass, or "certificate." The law read: "It shall not be lawfull for any negroe or other slave to carry or arme himselfe with any club, staffe, gunn, sword or any other weapon of defence or offence, nor to goe or depart from of his masters ground without a certificate from his master, mistris or overseer, and such permission not to be granted but upon perticuler and necessary occasions." Judging independent slave movement to be akin to the possession of arms, the Virginia legislature banned both. This law also established the punishment for errant movement away from the "masters ground:" "twenty lashes on his bare back well layd on."[8] From fairly early in colonial history, slaveholders' control depended on the confinement of slaves.

Distinct kinds of runaway activity demanded recognition of their differences. Between 1748 and 1785 the Virginia Assembly passed a number of laws prohibiting and punishing "outlying" and "outlawed" activity.[9] In 1748 Virginia's lawmakers distinguished between outlying runaways (short-term runaways, those historians now call "truants") and outlawed escapees (now known as "runaways" or "fugitives"). Surprisingly, it was not the outlawed that most concerned the assembly, but the outlying. In that year, in response to the "injuries" that lurking truants were said to cause, lawmakers went so far as to make outlying a capital offense. Revealing the anxiety that truants caused them, Virginia's elite authorized local authorities who captured outlying runaways to "dismember" and even to "kill and destroy" them.[10] In 1772, on the eve of the American Revolution, lawmakers reconsidered. Punishments such as these were inconsistent with emerging theories of humanity, and "doubts have arisen" about the "method of proceeding against outlying slaves." Moreover, dismemberment or execution of the many outlying bondpeople meant financial loss for their owners who then clamored for compensation. For these reasons, lawmakers rescinded the blanket policy, authorizing death only when it could be demonstrated that the truant had been "doing mischief." Legislators also clarified the question of compensation: "The owner . . . of such slave shall not be paid for such slave by the publick."[11]

A significant proportion of South Carolina's earliest slaveholders had migrated from Barbados, and when they established the colony in 1670, they founded a slave society slightly different from the rest of the U.S. South. Following a Barbadian legal grammar, in 1690 the colony began to regulate slave activity, implementing pass laws modeled on the Barbadian "ticket" prototype. The 1690 law prohibited slave owners and managers from allowing bondpeople to "go out of their plantations . . . without a ticket" on pain of a forty-shilling fine. Enslaved people were permitted to move from one place to another only when they carried such a ticket or when "one or more white men" were "in their company." The ticket, lawmakers dictated, must "expre[ss] their names and numbers, and also, from and to what place [they] are intending for, and [the] time" granted by their owners.[12] In 1690 permissible punishments for repeat offenders included whipping, burning "some place" in the face, and slitting the nose. "For the third offence" death or "any other punishment" was permitted. In 1712 lawmakers repeated that it was "lawful" to "beat, maim or assault" as well as to kill anyone who "refuse[d] to shew his ticket."[13] The 1712 law also illegalized the harboring of runaways and required managers to search bondpeople's cabins "diligently and effectually, once every fourteen days" for escapees and weapons.[14]

Within this familiar framework, the young colony showed its Caribbean roots. South Carolina's rice planters became the wealthiest in the British North American colonies and the owners of a usually large retinue of household laborers. To expedite the work of these domestic bondpeople (and perhaps to distinguish them from others of their caste even further than the livery they were expected to wear already did), in 1690 lawmakers made an exception from the ticket laws for those who "usually wait on [the] persons" of their owners.[15] In 1712 legislators reminded colonists that every other "negro or slave that shall be taken hereafter out of his master's plantation, without a ticket, or leave in writing . . . shall be whipped." Again, those who "wait[ed] upon" their owners "at home or abroad" or wore "livery" were exempted.[16] By that same year lawmakers had become displeased with the amount of ticket writing, and they banned issuing a ticket to anyone on a Sunday and added more precision to the temporal and spatial contours of the few tickets that had to be granted on Sundays for unavoidable business.[17] Tickets in general, for all days of the week, it was also stipulated, "shall particularly mention the name of every slave employed in the particular business, and to what place they are sent, and what time they return."[18] Much of this formula became characteristic of ticket form. Elite South Carolinians were a metropolitan group who preferred to live in Charleston and leave their country estates to black and white management, an arrangement unique in the North American colonies. Consequently, some of South Carolina's earliest slave laws focused on Charleston, while the problems of urban slavery were of relatively little interest to most other colonial legislatures.[19]

South Carolina's particularity coexisted with the values it shared with the rest of the slave South, where common principles of restraint wove a continuous thread through the variations of regional space. Bondpeople everywhere were prohibited from leaving their workplaces without the knowledge and written consent of their owners and managers. Tickets were enormously powerful in South Carolina and elsewhere. No mere scraps of paper, passes and tickets were animated by the power of absent owners and overseers; they spoke for slave managers and acted on their behalf, directing and overseeing the movement of enslaved people.

Throughout the early nineteenth-century South, the control of slave movement continued to be an issue of paramount importance. More than any other single slave activity—such as trading, learning to read, consuming alcohol, acquiring poisoning techniques, or plotting rebellions—slave movement was limited, monitored, and criminalized. Even topics such as the conditions and administration of manumission, sale, inheritance, and taxation received less attention than black mobility. Everywhere, enslaved people were barred from gathering for assemblies and from leaving their places of work for any reason. When they went, as Louisiana put it, "beyond certain limits" enslaved people were invariably required to obtain and carry written permission to do so. Lawmakers mandated that these written passes indicate the date of departure, the person's destination, and the date of his or her expected return. As the state of Georgia put it when it amended its patrol law in 1839, "written permits" must "set forth the time allowed for their [slaves'] absence, and distinctly designate the place or places where such slaves . . . desire to visit." North Carolina went so far as to sketch the route that enslaved travelers were to take when it demanded that the bearers of passes "keep the most usual and accustomed road."[20]

Furthermore, legislatures defined and redefined types of runaways,[21] outlined and revised minimum punishments for violations,[22] drafted whites into compliance and enforcement,[23] and occasionally devised ingenious punishments for runaways, such as putting them "in labor on the streets of said cities or towns, and on the highways and bridges adjacent," as frontier Mississippi did in 1829.[24] Legislators also outlined procedures for capturing and returning runaways[25] and enjoined blacks and whites alike from harboring them.[26] Short- and long-term flight were not the only forms of movement that legislatures forbade. For instance, lawmakers commonly banned and reiterated bans on independent gatherings of bondpeople,[27] and in some places enslaved people, except for boat and dockworkers, were strictly barred from traveling by water. In Georgia black sailors were "quarantined" after 1829 and were officially barred from setting foot on shore.[28]

Legal tinkering with pass laws slowed dramatically during the antebellum years, though it did not cease. Until the eve of the Civil War, lawmakers occasionally experimented with variations in language and content, perhaps hoping to find the right combination that would make the law's word stick. In 1856 Virginia warned whoever listened that enslaved people "found strolling" without passes would be "dealt with according to the law."[29] Lawmakers created the state-backed principles of restraint that criminalized and enclosed slave movement, and slaveholders joined them in this work.

GEOGRAPHIES OF CONTAINMENT

Antebellum slaveholders put the principles of restraint into practice in everyday life, adding to them their own plantation rules and building "geographies of containment" on their farms. Place functioned both metaphorically and literally in the Old South.[30] Enslaved people's inferior and subjected position within the framework of antebellum southern society, their social "place," was reflected and affirmed by white control over their location in space, their literal place. Place, metaphorical and literal, came alive in the memories of slavery that some people carried with them in freedom. Only so long as "slaves stayed in deir places," Harriet Miller recalled, were they not "whipped or put in chains." As Andrew Boone said, "If you wus out widout a pass dey would shore git you. De paterollers shore looked after you. Dey would come to de house at night to see who wus dere. If you wus out of place, dey would wear you out."[31] Slaveholders' power to define bondpeople's proper location illustrated slaveholding authority, and it did the same for the subjugation of the enslaved. By dictating bondpeople's locations, slaveholders made their plantations controlled and controlling landscapes that had a distinctly nineteenth-century cast.

In the decades after the Revolution, proslavery ideology shifted subtly from the patriarchalism of the colonial period to paternalism, a form of social control more consistent with the humanitarian ideals of the age. During the colonial era, planters had not sought to convince enslaved people of the legitimacy of bondage. Before the success of the Revolution, elites had scarcely bothered to justify what seemed only natural, namely, hierarchical societies. Even if planters had desired control of the hearts and minds of African slaves, they could not have won it: language, meaning systems, and values all stood in the way. Rather than seeking to educate and convince their subordinates of the rightness of their world—as paternalist planters would do later—patriarchs sought simply to maintain their place in the social order. Their culture and politics expressed the established social values of the ruling elite; they did not seek to impart those values to the lower classes and to the enslaved or to coerce these populations into sharing their assumptions and priorities. Political discourse and everyday culture (for instance, architecture and dress) expressed but did not justify social place.[32]

By the antebellum years, a number of factors had combined to shift the tone of slaveholding ideology. The American Revolution, with its triumph over aristocratic rule and forced dependency, introduced a conflict between the new nation's ideals and its continuing reality of inequality. Whereas patriarchal slaveholders in the colonial years had hardly needed to defend their ownership of people, such a defense now seemed crucial. But the call for a rationalization of slavery came from more than revolutionary politics; it came also from two waves of abolitionist activism, one at the turn of the eighteenth century and a more militant one in the 1830s. Where patriarchal slaveholders had viewed bondage as a "necessary evil" and demanded obedience while expecting resistance and opposition, antebellum paternalists argued that the institution was a "positive good," beneficial to both the master and the slave. In addition to obedience paternalists demanded loyalty and at least the appearance of consent.

Paternalist slaveholders' impulse to convince the enslaved that they were better off in bondage may have been shaped by another characteristic unique to the nineteenth century. During the first decades after the turn of the century, the population of enslaved people leaped from just under 700,000 in 1790 to almost 1.2 million just twenty years later—an increase of more than 70 percent. Growth continued apace, and the slave populace had tripled by the beginning of the Civil War in 1860, when it numbered almost 4 million.[33] Antebellum planters needed to believe that all of these people were content with their station. Hence, unlike colonial planters, antebellum elites were often surprised, even shocked, by the occasional acts of organized rebellion, such as Nat Turner's 1831 slave revolt, or the escape of thousands of enslaved people during the Civil War.[34]

Paternalism was also influenced by the early nineteenth-century ideal of affectionate family life and placed possessive and demanding fathers at the head of the plantation household. Planters desired the affection and allegiance of their underlings, imagining an intimacy with their slaves that patriarchs had not. This sense of intimacy partnered with a strong sense of license, and paternalist planters often intervened in the lives of their slaves. With paternalism came great attention to black bodily minutiae; nutrition, dress, hygiene, bodily functions, pleasure, and family and intimate relations all became the targets of planter meddling. Advice manuals proliferated to guide slaveholders in their treatment of somatic details, and some planters studiously recorded their efforts in farm journals.[35] The most paternalistic planters added carefully considered food and clothing allowances and decent quarters in the hope that these measures would help to create a "settled arrangement." Paternalism's imagined "mutual obligations"—protection for loyalty, care for obedience—were designed, in part, to make the slave "as comfortable at Home as possible, affording him What is essentially necessary for happiness" so "as to make it unnecessary for a negro to leave it."[36] Paternalists hoped that their manipulations would enable them to master bondpeople and to make them stay in their place.

John Blount Miller personified the paternalist paradigm of his class and historical moment. Miller codified his ideal of slave behavior when he wrote the "rules for government" applying to his "Negroes." Miller mandated that his bondpeople "work for themselves," that their "Conduct" be upright ("be kind to each other"), their "Words" virtuous ("no lying or profane language to be used"), and their "Morals" "honest in word and action & conduct & in all things." At least as much as with the manners and speech of his enslaved people, Miller concerned himself with their various forms of movement. One of the chores that Miller instructed his bondpeople to do for themselves was keep a garden. But Miller also carefully noted that when they raised excess produce, he would "sell it for them," rather than allow them to leave and sell it themselves as some enslaved people were allowed to do in South Carolina if they had a ticket. In a similar vein, Miller banned attendance at black religious gatherings. Slave religion inspired spiritual strength and rapture, and it demanded autonomy (and mystery) of movement. Participation in the black church required congregation, whether or not owners were informed or willing. So Miller made his position on slave religion plain: "Meetings religious: None at night. Not to go from home to them at night."[37] The principles of restraint were elemental parts of Miller's feeling of mastery for reasons that Charles Ball explained. "All over the South," Ball wrote, "the slaves are discouraged . . . from going to any place of religious worship on Sunday. This is to prevent them from associating together, from different estates, and distant parts of the country; and plotting conspiracies and insurrections."[38] Independent movement could take bondpeople in any number of directions, away from the direct command of their owners.

Other slaveholders echoed Miller's orders as they wrote rules (or as one planter confidently called them, "plantation laws") that commonly included prohibitions against leaving plantation space without a pass.[39] When slaveholders gave their expressed permission, they sketched the contours of legitimate travel. For instance, one pass read, "All persons are requested to permit the bearer Adam to go from my house to Mrs. Martha Robert's house and to Mr. Wm. Watkin's in the county of Charlotte, and home again without interruption."[40] In coastal Georgia and South Carolina where work was tasked and where slavery differed in so many ways from the rest of the South, slave managers also frequently banned visiting or leaving without a ticket.[41]

Time, too, was an element of bondpeople's captivity. Recall that Charles Ball's description of the principles of restraint included not only spatial constrictions but constrictions of time as well. In Ball's experience, bondpeople were punished for straying by "a single hour, by night or day" as well as by "a single mile." Expiration dates and curfews further limited the travel of a pass holder. Many passes explained to their reader the spatial and temporal parameters that both legitimated and limited the enslaved traveler. "Edward is sent to Rich[mond] to remain there till Monday next," read one pass.[42] Another pass, dated 31 August 1843, specified that its bearer "has permission to pass from Lynchburg to Thomas L. Spraggins of the county of Hallifax without molestation[.] the said Charly has from this date untill Sept. 1st at 2 oclock."[43] Fountain Hughes detailed the enormous burden these practices placed on the enslaved, and his statement merits being quoted at length:

> Now I couldn' go from here across the street or I couldn' go through nobody's house 'out I have a note or something from my master. An' if I had that pass, that was what we call a pass, if I had that pass, I could go wherever he sent me. An' I'd have to be back, you know, whoever he sent me to, they, they'd give me another pass an' I'd bring that back so as to show how long I'd been gone. We couldn' go out an' stay an hour or two hours or something like. But they'd give me a note so [that] wouldn' nobody interfere with me, an' tell who I belong to. An' when I come back, why I carry it to my master an' give that to him, that'd be alright. But I couldn' jus' walk away like the people does now, you know. It was what they call, we were slaves.[44]

Passes gave some bondpeople permission to go to some places some of the time. Passes also prevented most enslaved people from going to most places most of the time.

Time measured movement, and it regulated work. By the antebellum period, time had become an important element in planters' farming methods, especially on the majority of plantations where work was organized according to the gang system. Influenced by the model of industrial efficiency in northern and English manufacturing, more and more southern planters aimed to increase the productivity of their plantations. The most ambitious of them embarked on what historian Mark M. Smith has called an "age of improvement," an age of progress and modernization. Innovations in the uses of time and timepieces were part of the movement for scientific agriculture. The clock was a tool that promised to somewhat rationalize the agricultural workday, otherwise governed by nature. The beginning and the end of the workday as well as any breaks were increasingly announced by the soundings of bells and horns, what Smith has called "aural time." Rational, planter-controlled aural time joined nature's measure—the tempo of sunrise and sunset and the rhythm of the seasons—to govern antebellum plantation production.[45]

The preoccupation with time was an ideal made into a day-to-day reality by ordinary plantation rules and practices. The formerly enslaved Nancy Young recalled that her owner obligated his bondpeople to march "by the big house" to "call the roll." Each name was called out and responded to, and from there enslaved workers went to the fields. "This was done," Young said, "to let them know who had gone to work on time or who had not gone."[46] Virginia planter Richard Eppes was a diligent student of slave management

Slave pass written by Thomas E. West, 31 August 1843. In this pass "Charly," a bond-man, is given permission to travel. The pass limits as much as it permits Charly's movement. His point of origin and authorized destination are specified, as is Charly's expected return. Mobility and confinement cohabited in slave passes, which were granted to far more men than women. (Spragins Family Papers, VHS)

who studied advice manuals as part of his ongoing effort to improve the "system" of his plantation.[47] One of these emphasized the central role that plantation boundaries of space and time played in the efficacious running of an agricultural machine. "No business of any kind," the book warned, "can be successfully conducted without the aid of system & rule." Indeed, the manual asked rhetorically, "What is management but the carrying into practice of a well arranged system of order and rule?" It behooved "every man who expects to make himself a manager" to make "order" his primary "aim" by adhering to two core "maxims." First, "there must be a time for everything, and everything done in its time," and, second, "a rule for everything, and everything done according to rule." Giving specific guidelines for the application of the first directive, the handbook instructed its readers that "it is strictly required of the manager that he rise at the dawn of every morning; that he blow a horn for the assembling of hands; require all hands to repair to a certain and fixed place in ten minutes after the blowing of the horn, and there himself see that they are present, or notice the absentees."[48] Eppes's advice manual made the location of enslaved people in time, as well as their place in space, a basic component of his farm's "order." These were lessons that Eppes, like his neighbors, put into effect, determining the movement of his bondpeople throughout the day. Dawn, accompanied by the overseer's trumpeting horn, announced the proper location of Eppes's "hands." In the mornings Eppes expected them to be "in the field at sunrise" and to go home to their quarters only "at sunset."[49] Planters in the lower South acted similarly. While working in a planter's home, William Wells Brown was permitted to rise thirty minutes after the "ringing of the bell" that roused the field hands. During that half-hour interval, he "often laid and heard the crack of the whip, and the screams of the slaves" who were slow to rise from their pallets or were delayed in arriving at the field.[50] Sound marked boundaries and sometimes announced their crossing. Truants and runaways might be locked in a metal harness with a bell at the top that rang when they moved, letting everyone know their whereabouts.

No moment in the day, including breaks and meals, was too small to merit attention and direction. As a slave, Austin Steward had to "rise and be ready" in the field thirty minutes after the sounding of the "horn or conch-shell." The bellowing of the shell or horn throughout the day let Steward and his neighbors know that it was time for their thirty-minute morning meal of "a little bread," then their one-hour lunch, and finally the end of the workday. "Woe be to the unfortunate, who was not in the field at the time appointed," for the "overseer was always on hand to attend to delinquents" and "never failed" to make them "feel the blows of his heavy whip."[51] Once in the field, "the fears and labors of another day begin," said Solomon Northup. With little or no rest, enslaved people worked and worried; the bondman "fear[ed] he [would] be caught lagging through the day; he fear[ed] to approach the gin-house with his basket-load of cotton at night; he fear[ed], when he [lay] down, that he [would] oversleep himself in the morning."[52] Waller Holladay instructed his overseer about the precise times individual bondpeople were to arrive at work, making allowances for their various capacities and residences even as he detailed strict temporal expectations for all: "If Alfred & Henry get home by quarter of an hour after sunrise, I will be satisfied. John and Lewis should be allowed at least one hour & ¼ after sunrise; Harry as he is lame one hour; and Iverson, as he has to walk farther than any of the others, and is an old man, two hours after sunrise. Allowances should be made for bad weather, and dark mornings, as they have no time-pieces, and cannot always tell when day breaks."[53] Women's reproductive labor was also made to fit into planters' timetables. As one enslaved person said when a nursing mother went to feed her infant, "She had a certain time to stay; if she stayed over that time she was whipped."[54]

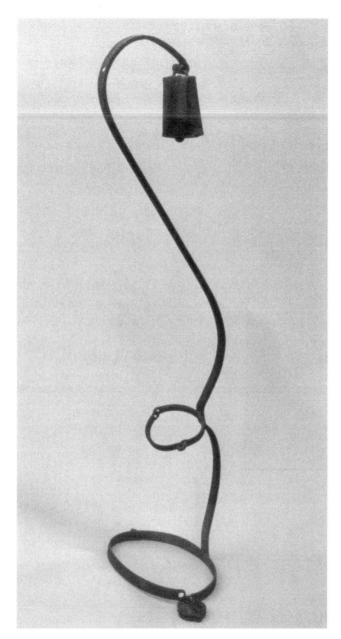

Slave harness, iron and brass, late eighteenth century. Slave harnesses such as this one were more common in the colonial era, but slave testimony suggests that they did not disappear altogether in the nineteenth century. The bell on the harness rang when its prisoner moved—unless it was stopped up with mud. (Courtesy of The Historical Society of Pennsylvania Collection, Atwater Kent Museum of Philadelphia)

Sensing the potential for trouble nonetheless, planters consistently gave special attention to the nighttime. Almost all enslaved people were forbidden to leave the plantation at all in the evenings, and some were prohibited from even stirring from their quarters. Mississippian William Ethelbert Ervin scrupulously combined temporal with spatial control on his plantation. In December 1846 Ervin wrote his ideal of slave behavior. First, he indicated that plantation borders not only marked the edges of his estate but also hemmed in his bondpeople. No one was to "leave the place without leaf of absence." Second, within those spatial borders he added temporal limits that bound enslaved people's movement even more: "At nine o'clock every night the Horne must be blown Which is the signal for each to retire to his or her house and there to remain until morning." Ervin directed his overseers to check on people in the quarters, and if anyone was found "out of their places," they would be "delt with . . . according to discretion."[55] Most often, those who were late to work were "delt with" violently. Another planter banned movement around the plantation at night, insisting that "no one should leave yard at night without my permission."[56] Many others established curfews, sometimes announcing them with the same horns that trumpeted the beginning and end of the workday. Often there was scarcely enough time to hastily gulp down dinner before lights-out. Matilda McKinney occasionally ate in the dark when she was young, for the "curfew horn" had blown, and the candles in her cabin had been blown out.[57] When enslaved people disregarded curfews, they could expect to be thrashed if they were caught. There was no safety in numbers, either, for one planter "whiped half the Quarter last night for being up after 10 O['clock]."[58] While slaveholders might grant overnight passes for specific purposes (such as a visit to family), a great many wrote passes that expired before nightfall, and these made lasting impressions on enslaved people. One bondman recalled only this latter type, saying that "no sun could go down on a pass."[59]

Slaveholders enforced their rules with the lash. When "three women" were caught in the field "sitting down with a pot of their fine cooking" for an early lunch, the overseer "had them punished," a planter woman wrote to her brother. "As you may suppose."[60] The diligent Richard Eppes developed an exceptionally thorough paternalist system on his plantation. He allotted financial rewards and punishments (a yearly "present" of one dollar for good behavior, deductions for "any crimes"); delivered an annual "lecture and exhortation to improve" to those who engaged in "roguery, fighting laziness &c" as well as "crimes coming under the heading of immorality"; and consistently drew and redrew boundaries of space and time. Yet none of these paternalist tools could work without the power of the whip. As Eppes himself noted, "it is not meant by" any of these practices "that the lash is to be abolished, it would be worse than the abolition of capital punishment."[61]

Some rural planters were too distracted, uninterested, lazy, or incompetent to enforce legal ideals or to create plantation rules regarding slave movement. Henry Smith's owner was known as a "negro spoiler" because he allowed his bondpeople to leave his farm at night without passes.[62] Similarly, G. W. Patillo's owner, surnamed Ingram, allowed his bondpeople to go "any place" without passes, and he so resented slave patrols' incursions onto his property that he hammered in signs around his farm warning intruders that "Paterrollers, Fishing and Hunting" were "Prohibited on this Plantation." The result was that whites in the neighborhood referred to Ingram's bondpeople as "Old Ingram's Free Niggers."[63] Elsewhere, those who sneaked out at night were said by the patrollers who tried to catch them to have "too much liberty."[64] For whites in the Old South, the privilege of locomotion was integral to freedom, just as its denial was an element of enslavement.

But planters' greater and lesser commitments to policing black movement in space and time were united by a consensus among most slaveholders that enslaved people's movement must be severely limited. Most acted as judge, jury, and executioner when it came to the violation of planters' rules and society's laws. Still, the participation of every slaveholder was unnecessary, for southern communities organized slave patrols to uphold the principles of restraint, whether or not individual slave owners subscribed to them with the same depth of feeling as their neighbors. With the shift to paternalist techniques of social control among slaveholding elites in the decades after the Revolution came increased policing of illicit slave behavior. The consolidation of patrol activity during the nineteenth century was a part of the violence and coercion that buttressed planter power and complemented paternalism. Whereas slave patrol operations were "irregular" during the colonial years in both the Chesapeake and South Carolina lowcountry regions,[65] antebellum slave patrols were less experimental, better organized, and increasingly regular in their schedules. Informal patrols continued to exist, though, not infrequently as amusement for bands of young men out for the evening. Even ministers were known to help pursue slaves. As one led a group that "gave the chase" to an enslaved person, he shouted "at the top of his voice, with horrid oaths, 'Catch the rascal.'" Such activity was considered a "common amusement" among white men.[66]

Slave patrols stopped blacks on the road and demanded their passes. They entered slave cabins to see that all were present and that no fugitives were being harbored. Patrolmen also lurked around churches and tippling houses hoping to catch people without a pass. Patrols rode the most when they expected higher levels of slave movement, on Saturdays and Sundays, for instance, or during holidays such as Easter, Christmas, or the end of harvest in the autumn. Times of flux, like the hiring season during the beginning of January, were also times of intensified surveillance.[67] But at all times bond-people had to remember the principle regulating their movement: "Got to have paper. Got to carry you paper. Dem patroller put you cross a log! Beat you to death."[68]

Slave patrols shared with planters and slave managers unequal responsibility for keeping enslaved people within plantation space. In part, planters counted on one another for help. When elites going about their business crossed paths with bondpeople traversing roads or estuaries, it was customary for them to demand to see a pass. Once, when James Henry Hammond encountered a neighbor's bondman "at the mill without a pass," he took it upon himself to "flo[g] him" then and there.[69] Planters also relied on overseers and black drivers, whom they directed to assist in administering plantation policies and whom they held liable for breaches. Overseers' reputations as good managers depended on their effective control of enslaved people, including the critical issue of their movement. Overseers who dispensed passes liberally quickly lost their "character"—their reputation for assertive supervision—and could find themselves unemployable.[70] This pressure might combine with an overseer's contempt for his labor force to dangerous effect. One bondman named Moses was caught by the overseer on a neighboring farm retrieving his wife's sister for a "meeting." "Instead of being humbled & asking pardon for coming there without permission[,] he braved instead of begging his way out." Moses paid for his pride and returned home "badly whipped."[71] Black overseers, called "drivers," were also drafted into informal policing. As a means of ensuring their cooperation, drivers were sometimes held to account for the truancy of their charges. As far as one planter was concerned, if his driver allowed a bondman to leave, he would be just as "answerable" for the "absence as the negro would be, did he go away without any permission at all."[72] An overseer's concern for his career and a driver's or ordinary enslaved man's desire to avoid punishment were real incentives to curtail the illicit movement of others.

The agricultural journal *Southern Cultivator* advocated nightly rounds by all managers to ensure submission to plantation boundaries of space and time. An 1840 issue of the periodical recommended that managers begin the day by ensuring that "every negro is out by daylight in the morning—a signal being given by a blast of the horn." It was advised to end the day with a "visit [to] the negro cabins at least once or twice a week, at night, to see that all are in" the quarters. The journal carefully drew attention to temporal boundaries when it insisted that "no negro must be out of his house after ten oclock in summer and eleven in winter."[73] On these rounds, which many planters in fact demanded (at least in their plantation journals), overseers and drivers sussed out "any strange or unlawful visitors or any wrong appearance of things."[74] The most assiduous planters established night watches manned by plantation blacks and whites to enforce nightly curfews. Effective informal policing mechanisms in themselves, night watches also attested to the vigilance of the planter, a vigilance that might underscore his fearsomeness. Bennet Barrow thought so, noting in his journal that "the very act of organizing a watch bespeaks a care and attention on the part of a master, Which, has the due influence on the negro."[75]

Planters commonly viewed adherence to spatial and temporal discipline as essential to overall order. One slaveholder thought that illicit departures were an expression of disrespect and that "Impertinence in any form or shape . . . is the first step to destroying all of the above regulations." In addition to perceiving a slippery slope from impertinence to the dissolution of plantation discipline, this slaveholder feared that unimpeded rule-breaking would "finally lea[d] to dissatisfaction," to a breach of the paternalistic contract.[76] For a planter like Bennett Barrow, there were other issues at hand. Barrow prohibited people, including his driver, from ever leaving the plantation "unless on business"; banned abroad marriages (marriages between people living on different farms); and forbade trading, because doing so gave him unlimited access to their time, their bodies, and their labor. Barrow saw this unlimited access as a matter of both "expediency and right." It was his "right" because he was the master of his slaves. Barrow wrote in his journal that he adhered to the "doctrine that my negroes have no time Whatever, that they are always liable to my call without questioning for a moment the propriety of it." His complete possession of their time was also a matter of "expediency," and the practical considerations were not limited to his access to their labor. They included, as well, the protection of the plantation from robbery or other "intrusions of ill designed persons." "Who," Barrow wanted to know, "are to protect the plantation . . . When evry body is a broad?" Or if a recurrent danger such as fire struck, how "could the flames be arrested if the negroes are scattered throughout the neighborhood, seeking their amusement"?[77] Spatial and temporal order were essential to basic plantation functioning.

But the disciplining uses of space and time did more than maximize efficiency; they reminded black and white plantation residents of the racial etiquette that governed their world. Across the slave South, laws, customs, and ideals came together into a systematic constriction of black movement, a constriction that had both pragmatic material and symbolic social functions. There were differences within the South in the employment of space and time: idiosyncratic differences among planters and, importantly, differences according to the organization of work. More than the gang system, the task system made a distinction between planters' time and the time belonging to the enslaved.[78] Work in the task system was organized more by accomplishment than by time. Bondpeople were given daily work assignments, or "tasks." Once the tasks were completed, typically around midafternoon, bondpeople were permitted to tend to their own gardens, crafts, and other work. Yet even in the South Carolina and Georgia coastal rice plantations structured around the task system, time still had a role to play. Tickets, like passes elsewhere, governed and controlled enslaved people's movement, and planters or managers endeavored to prevent enslaved people from leaving farms without permission. These endeavors had different consequences for women and men.

SLAVERY, SPACE, AND GENDER

The geography of containment was somewhat more elastic for men than it was for women, in large measure because the work that provided opportunities to leave the plantation was generally reserved for men. Male teamsters transported plantation products to town for sale, retrieved purchases made by their owners, and moved the goods that were sometimes traded among neighbors. When notes, letters, and documents needed to be carried to local recipients, it was bondmen who served as messengers. Thus did men at times gain the opportunity to learn the lay of the land, roads, and waterways.[79] These opportunities were denied to women, who rarely received passes for work purposes. Family obligations, too, presented enslaved men with the occasion to leave the farms on which they lived. In abroad marriages it was generally the man who visited his family, in accordance, probably, with both black and white gender ideals.[80] Likewise, during the weeks and months of romancing that would precede any settled relationship and during the heady days of more casual affairs, it was the men who traveled to woo and sweet-talk.

Men who visited their families and girlfriends were far from unlimited in their mobility, although slaveholders were not always in agreement about how tightly passes should circumscribe the bearer's travel. Larkin Hundley wrote a pass that was good for one month, a "general pass," allowing a bondman named Ben to "pass & repass to his wife." This pass was almost certainly understood to be valid only on Saturday afternoons and Sundays until the evening, or perhaps through early Monday mornings.[81] Whatever

Hauling Cotton to the River, from *Harper's New Monthly Magazine*, March 1854. Some men were able to leave plantations when they transported goods to town or port for trade. Other work, such as running errands or delivering correspondence and documents, also gave some men a measure of mobility that far fewer women enjoyed. (Manuscripts, Special Collections, University Archives, University of Washington Libraries, UW 22863)

understanding may have accompanied the pass, it was a rarity in the rural South. Such general passes were more common among urban bondpeople and those who hired out their own time.[82] Most rural planters would have disapproved of Hundley's practice and agreed instead with the slaveholder who believed that "no practice is more prejudicial to the community . . . than that of giving them general Pass'es—to go Where they please." This planter strictly refused to give "general Pass'es" and provided only narrowly written passes. These he only granted when a petitioner "first states particularly where he wishes to go, and assigns a cause for his desiring to be absent. if he offers a good reason, I never refuse, but otherwise I never grant him a Pass."[83] Another slaveholder required any enslaved visitor not only to prove that he had the authorization of his own owner but also to "report himself to the overseer immediately" and ask for "permission" to visit. Should the caller "wish to become a regular visitor," he was required to secure "permission from me."[84] Moreover, bondmen were not always permitted to visit their wives or even to marry women from other farms. Some planters, in search of "perfect order" among their "people," banned such abroad marriages, insisting that their bondpeople were "not to marry from Home."[85]

Even when men who wanted to visit their loved ones asked all the right people and got their documentation in order, there was still potential for trouble. Visiting bondmen had to be extremely careful not to lose their passes, for they could pay dearly for the error. When men were stopped, they were at the mercy of slave patrols who themselves were often motivated by the payment they could gain for capturing a runaway. One bondman, Jim Booker, spent "4 months in jail" when he was "illegally" arrested as a runaway. His owner was outraged by what happened; Booker had shown the patrollers his pass, but one of them "tore [it] up in the presence of witnesses (white) & then took Booker up as a runaway."[86] Passes provided bondmen with a measure of mobility, but that mobility was a mixed privilege.

Because of the allowances sometimes granted men for work and family reasons, the sight of enslaved men transporting letters, messages, goods, and materials and men visiting their girlfriends and families was an ordinary part of antebellum landscapes—as was the mandatory presentation of the pass that legitimated their travel. But their limited travel certainly sparked their imaginations for what lay beyond. The bondman Charly was given written permission to pass between his owner's properties and appears to have made the most of the time he spent on the road. After a few years of moving about for work, Charly was captured as a runaway some five miles from "where he lately lived."[87] Men's dreams of running away could be explored and tried out as they traveled through their neighborhoods and, in some cases, farther afield.

The overall situation was the opposite for women, who were held more firmly than men within plantations. There were exceptions, especially in the upper South. Women who worked as domestics might enjoy the occasional perquisite. For instance, one Virginia planter woman wrote passes for some of the women she owned to take their cotton to "Miss Sally Taylor" and have "simple cloth woven."[88] Women residing in towns or cities, whether permanently or on a yearly hiring basis, might also receive passes to perform their

The Plantation Patrol, from *Frank Leslie's Illustrated*, 11 July 1863. Although some bondmen enjoyed a degree of mobility unknown to most enslaved women, they nonetheless were strictly policed. Patrols, gangs of young white men, and ordinary citizens all could and did demand to see passes. They punished those who lacked the proper papers, as well as those who had them. (Virginia Historical Society)

chores, as the Richmond bondwoman Ann did in order to "pass from my *house* to the *Grocery Store* & return." On another occasion Ann was given permission to "pass from my room on *Bank. St.* to my rented house in the valley untill 9 *O'Clock* to night."[89] Doctor women and midwives necessarily took their skills to different places. For truly special occasions, even field women might find themselves stepping out with the permission of their owners. Virginian Richard Eppes once gave a group of men and women "passes to be baptized in Petersburg."[90] Though more common to the upper South, exceptions were not entirely unique to that section. In Louisiana, Bennett Barrow gave "Lucy Mary O[ld]. Hannah Lucky jenny Lize & Leah" passes to go work on a relative's farm.[91]

The very novelty of such passes, however, only highlights the rarity with which they were given to women. Over the course of their lives, bondwomen would leave their home plantations, with permission, extremely rarely. On Christmas Day 1848, slaveholder Rebecca S. C. Pilsbury granted "all the *Boys*" permission to be "absent" on "holiday." She required that they return the following day but was not entirely confident that they would obey her orders. Pilsbury was alone with her slaves that day and noted nervously in her journal, "not one *white* person have I seen since ten o'clock"; she sensed that without any white men to help her, her authority was compromised. Made "more anxious than usual" by her isolation, Pilsbury undermined her own authority by granting a second holiday against her judgment and in contradiction to the farm's general policy of never allowing bondmen to leave "after sunset." Self-recrimination ensued: "I really believe I should give them permission to run away if they but wished it." Yet her anxious permissiveness did not extend to the bondwomen she owned. Pilsbury granted permission to leave during these holidays to only one woman. After Christmas was over, a woman named Fanny was allowed to go and visit her family.[92] Pilsbury did not perceive her bondwomen as frightening or intimidating. Consequently, her enslaved women did not gain the concessions that could be won from a jittery slaveholder like Pilsbury.

Within plantation boundaries, women sometimes occupied spaces different from those of men. Many women served in the slaveholding homes at some point in their lives, ordinarily during childhood, pregnancies, and again in old age. Women thus found themselves in the yard, kitchen, and interior of slaveholders' homes at intervals throughout their lives. On the rice plantations of coastal South Carolina, gender difference in space was even greater, for rice cultivation was largely female work. While male supervisors regulated the flow of water over the rice, and the rest of the men worked in other crops and on plantation maintenance, women on large rice plantations worked in the fields, planting seeds, hoeing and transplanting seedlings, weeding continuously, and then harvesting mature plants.[93] Men and women who produced rice worked in different fields, occupying different physical locations in the rice swamps.

If gender altered women's locations in some southern spaces, it also configured plantation time differently for women and men. Generally, men and women both quit working in the fields at or about sunset, but women's evenings were less easily "off" time than men's, for they arrived home only to begin their "second shift" of household work. "Women had to work all day in de fields an' den come home an' do de housework at night," one bondwoman recalled.[94] After they had all quit their daily labor in the fields, the women did "dere cookin' at night." To be sure, bondmen also labored for the benefit of their families: they hunted, fished, gathered firewood, and contributed craft work to their households. Together, women and men "attend[ed] to [the] duties of their own dear homes," as the formerly enslaved Thomas Jones put it.[95] Men also sometimes performed extra field work at night, such as burning brush and various chores "'round de place."[96] But women's second shift of labor was a greater and more consistent burden. Most bondwomen arrived at their quarters to cook supper, perhaps with enough left over for the next day's lunch; to clean the cabin; to produce household goods, such as soap and candles; and to wash and mend their own and their family's clothing. They also had to make that clothing, as well as any bed linens, bonnets, or other extras that some enjoyed, and produce textiles for general plantation use.

Enslaved women, then, worked tiring second shifts during which they had to "wash, iron, patch, and get ready for the next day."[97] Women worked these second shifts whether they labored according to gang or task organization, and they were held to similarly high standards by their managers. When one Georgia woman failed to complete her "task of spinning," her manager "called her up," cursed her, "made her strip stark naked," and tied her to a post. Her arms were wrapped around the post and held by her husband while the overseer thrashed her with some seventy stripes.[98] Women's second shifts of work intensified the time-based controls that enslaved people throughout the South experienced. They also compounded women's greater spatial immobility by making escape difficult.

A final distinction characterized women's experiences of the geography of containment: its enforcement. When women were physically punished, the violence directed against them was not infrequently laced with sexual overtones. The hint of sadism charged the atmosphere when women were stripped, tied down, and thrashed. In an infamous passage from the autobiography of Solomon Northup, the author recounted the flogging of Patsey, an enslaved woman who was her owner's unwilling mistress and his jealously guarded possession. When she visited a friend on a neighboring plantation, her owner suspected that she had another lover, and his sexual rage issued in brutality. Patsey was stripped of "every article of dress," laid down "upon her face" completely "naked," and beaten cruelly. "Nowhere on that day, on the face of the whole earth, I venture to say, was there such a demoniac exhibition witnessed as then ensued. . . . She was terribly lacerated—I may say, without exaggeration, literally flayed."[99]

Cruelties that twisted such intimacies as sexual possessiveness, or the private body, into public events and violent acts were familiar features of women's lives in slavery. When women broke the rules and moved out of bounds, they risked and received punishments that were more than physically painful and heartbreaking; some were sexually degrading. Charlie Hudson sensed the sexual overtones in the whippings his overseer inflicted on the bond-women in his charge. The man "had whuppins all time saved up special for de 'omans. He made 'em take off deir waistes and den he whipped 'em on deir bar backs 'til he was satisfied. He done all de whuppin' atter supper by candle light." Hudson could not remember "dat he ever whupped a man. He jus' whupped 'omans."[100] Even if Hudson's overseer did whip men, he evidently did not do so in as memorable a manner. The geography of containment did not hold women and men in the same ways, nor to the same degree, and it did not impose the same toll on all. Neither did it entirely enclose bondpeople of either sex.

I COULD NOT STAY THERE

Women, Men, and Truancy

Like enslaved people everywhere, Sallie Smith was forbidden to leave her home plantation without a pass. But Smith broke the rules and laws that dictated where she ought to be and when she ought to be there. Smith sometimes ran away to the nearby woods, eating what she found, burrowing under leaves and moss to sleep at night, and sneaking to the quarters on a nearby farm for occasional shelter from the cold. Such a life was unsustainable for long, and Smith eventually returned to her owner. When she arrived, her owner had her tortured inside of "a big barrel he kept to roll us in, with nails drove all through it." "Madam," she told the black woman interviewing her in the late nineteenth century, "I thought he was going to kill me." When Smith emerged from the contraption, she "could hardly walk"; but another bondwoman greased her injuries, and she quickly "went to work." Smith's interviewer, Octavia Albert, had been born a slave, but emancipation came when she was still a very young child; she had not yet learned slavery's harshest lessons. Nor had she become familiar with the bitter resilience that some bondpeople had to draw on at points in their lives. "I suppose that was an end to your stay in the woods?" she asked her informer. "No, madam," Smith said, "I did not stay more than a month before I ran away again. I tell you, I could not stay there."[1]

Sallie Smith's persistence was uncommon, but her unwillingness to "stay there," fixed in plantation space, was less so. Smith was like many other bondwomen who, for short periods of time, occasionally ran away from overwork, violence, planter control, and the prying eyes of family and friends. Called "runaways" by antebellum blacks and whites, and "truants" and "absentees" by historians, such women did not intend to make a break for freedom in the

North but sought temporary escapes from the oppressive regimes that compelled them to work as drudges for most of their lives and that intended to limit the time for and meanings of independent activity. (The words "runaway," "truant," and "absentee" are used here synonymously; "fugitive" refers to those who ran to the North.) For periods lasting a night, a week, or several weeks, enslaved women and men ran away to nearby woods, swamps, and the slave quarters of neighboring plantations.

While planters dreamed and schemed about the creation of orderly plantations in which the location of enslaved people was neatly determined by laws, curfews, rules, and the demands of crops, enslaved people engaged in truancy, a practice that disturbed and in some cases alarmed slaveholders. Though common, truancy never became an acceptable part of plantation life in planters' minds. Rather, it was the source of a fundamental conflict of interest between owner and owned.[2] Places, boundaries, and movement were central to how slavery was organized and to how it was resisted. When bondpeople engaged in absenteeism, they withdrew their labor, confronting and opposing the authority of their owners and creating an endemic problem of labor discipline in the Old South. Perhaps most importantly to them, as truants slipped between their own and others' quarters, woods, swamps, outbuildings, and farms, they plaited these diverse spaces into a shared rival geography that provided the space and time not only for relief from exploitation, control, and surveillance but also for independent activity.

GENDER IN MOTION

Women and men alike engaged in truancy, but it held different meanings to each. Compared with their numbers among permanent fugitives, women were much more highly represented among absentees. In different periods and in various parts of the South, women consistently made up a small minority of those who ran away to permanent freedom in the North. Between 1838 and 1860, Virginia's bondwomen were a mere 9 percent of fugitives, while women in South Carolina made up 19 percent of the group. Fourteen percent of North Carolina's and 12 percent of Tennessee's runaways were women. Louisiana had the largest percentage of female runaways, still less than a third (29 percent) of all fugitives.[3] Runaways, it was understood, generally were men. That the greatest American runaway, Harriet Tubman, was a woman has done nothing to diminish the perceived masculinity of fugitive activity. After all, Tubman was and is known as the "Moses" of her people.

Paramount among women's reasons for not running away as fugitives more frequently were their family responsibilities and gender ideals among the enslaved. Women, as a group, were enmeshed in networks of extended family and friends, and they played central roles in the black family. Abroad marriages, the disproportionate sale of men into the slave trade supplying labor to the new cotton lands in the deep South and the Old Southwest, and African cultural legacies resulted in many female-headed families throughout the antebellum South. Such households depended on women for their survival. Many women understood themselves as persons deeply connected to community, and they identified as women, in part, through their activities on behalf of their families. Thus imbricated in dense social relations, women appear to have considered permanent escape to be even more difficult than did many men.[4]

Such day-to-day realities reinforced gender ideals among enslaved people. Community sanctions against women abandoning their children normalized female dedication to the family and were another pressure that limited the number of women who could escape to the North. Invoking a standard of respectable womanhood, Molly Horniblow chastised her granddaughter for even thinking of running away: "Nobody respects a mother who forsakes her children."[5] Taught community ideals, children held their mothers to them. Expressing a feeling of betrayal uncharacteristic of former bondpeople remembering their fathers' escapes from bondage, Patience M. Avery was heartbroken by her mother's escape: "No, chile, I can never fergit dat. You see my mother gimme dem pennies to mek me hush cryin'. Yes, yes, I can 'member dis as good as ef 'twas yestidy; how my mother stole out and lef' me." Avery murmured to her interviewer a plaintive refrain of heartbreaking loss: "I was a po' motherless chile."[6] Women such as Avery's mother who did dare to escape left behind children whose grief would be a lesson to other women who considered running away. Duty, affection, and conceptions of black womanhood tightened and complicated women's attachments to the South.

The point must not be overstated: enslaved fathers were important to their families, as their families were to them. George Ross, a former bondman who was interviewed in Canada during the Civil War, noted that "a man can get off a great deal easier than a woman," but at the same time some men "say if they can't get their families off, they won't go themselves."[7] Ross was willing, if it came to that, to "go away and leave mine" but pledged to return and retrieve his family. Unlike most fugitives, Ross was able to keep his promise: "I studied head work, and got them away very well indeed." William Wells Brown, too, overcame his initial reluctance to leave his family only by planning to work diligently to purchase and emancipate them.[8] Most enslaved men did not attempt to run away at all, partly because of their own roots in their communities, and some women did leave families and lovers to head north.[9]

Nonetheless, gender-specific roles within the family created different responsibilities and conceptions of acceptable behavior for women and men. Even as Ross's interview testifies to the importance of family to enslaved men, it also affirms the distinction between men's and women's family responsibilities and the different pressures those roles brought to bear on them. Ross's leaving slavery and his family behind did not contradict his personal identity as deeply as the same act would have undermined many enslaved women's sense of their womanhood, their obligations to family, and their places in their communities. Gender norms and definitions of female duty helped to shape fugitive behavior by diminishing women's rates of flight.

A final factor preventing women from running away in the same numbers as men was their relative lack of knowledge of geography beyond the plantation. Women did not generally perform the work of transporting people, goods, and messages that took carriage drivers, teamsters, and the runners of errands off farms. Thus women rarely became familiar with neighborhood geography or with water craft. As fugitives, if they abandoned the byways for a main road, they were sure to draw attention—and suspicion. One bondman was a regular truant and very "skilled in running away." He had learned to carry a bridle with him so that "if any body should see me in the woods . . . and asked, 'what are you doing here sir? you are a runaway?'—I said, 'no, sir, I am looking for our old mare;' at other times 'looking for our cows.' For such excuses I was let pass."[10] Such "excuses" were useful for men who performed the greater share of chores off plantations. Conversely, the possible presence of children, with their own demands of needing to be fed, carried, hurried along, and kept quiet, would only have highlighted the conspicuousness of a woman traversing unfamiliar terrain.[11]

The dangers that all women and men anticipated if they thought about escape to the North were fearsome: dogs, patrols, unknown directions, cold, heat, lack of food, the risk of capture, and in that event, certain horrific punishment. All in all, the social and the logistical difficulties were nearly insurmountable for the majority of enslaved people who even bothered to contemplate flight to the North. Even fewer women than men tried it; apparently many women concluded that permanent escape was impossible or undesirable. As a result, they were bound more narrowly to planters' geographies of containment.

Yet enslaved women did not submit to planters' designs for spatial and temporal order by remaining obediently in their assigned places. Instead, like men, they chose truancy, generally by fleeing to the nearest woods or swamps and occasionally to nearby towns. Truancy was particularly important in the lives of enslaved women, but not because it was a "female form" of resistance. It was not; men made up the majority of truants most of the time. Rather, absenteeism is an important part of the story of women's enslavement because women engaged in it more frequently than they ran away as fugitives. Women also played an essential supporting role in the practice of absenteeism by feeding truants. Both of these factors gave gender-specific meaning to women's acts of truancy and to their role in the creation of the rival geography.

Some plantations left documentation that allows us to see how much more frequently women ran away temporarily. In Adams County, Mississippi, John Nevitt presided over Clermont plantation, located on fertile land along the Mississippi River at the state's southwestern border. Nevitt's bondpeople worked Clermont's land producing cotton, tobacco, and rice, which Nevitt easily traded in nearby Natchez, whence it was transported along the river.[12] But the production and sale of these goods was not smooth; rather, it was marred every month by multiple incidents of absenteeism, including many by women.[13] Compared with the number of women among fugitives, women's rates of truancy are striking. When women on Nevitt's estate ran away, they generally represented significant proportions of the total numbers of incidents of absenteeism and of the number of truants: with two years excepted, women constituted from 19 to 41 percent of truants.[14] The differing behaviors of men and women at Clermont plantation are similar to those in other, relatively more opaque but still instructive plantation records. In the summer of 1828, the sole year in which incidents of truancy at the Rockingham plantation in the Beaufort District of South Carolina were documented, 55 percent of the truants were women.[15] During the best-recorded period of truancy at James Henry Hammond's Silver Bluff plantation in South Carolina, the time between his assumption of ownership in December 1831 and the end of his first full and highly tumultuous year, 32 percent of the truants were women.[16] Clearly, at least on these three plantations with distinctive records of truancy, women made up a greater proportion of truants than they did of runaways.

These plantation records come from two lower South states: South Carolina and Mississippi. Excellent evidence also comes from Louisiana, where enslaved people worked in the harsh sugar fields. In general, planters from the lower South appear to have complained about truancy more than slaveholders in the upper South. Or at least they were driven to record their frustrations in their journals more commonly. Both trends suggest that enslaved people in the lower South may have engaged in truancy more frequently and consistently than those in the upper South. Perhaps their great distance from freedom in the North and the near-hopelessness of running away there made flight in other, more local directions for shorter periods of time a more practical form of escape. Yet just as southern states shared a commitment to suppressing black movement, they also shared the problem of absenteeism.[17] While a great deal of evidence comes from the lower South, much planter documentation also survives from the upper South. Moreover, slave testimony comes from both sections. The limited and fragmentary nature of the evidence requires that conclusions about intraregional distinction remain speculative. Truancy may have been more widespread in the lower South, but it was certainly practiced everywhere.

SLAVES JES' RUN

Truancy, like migration, was set into motion by a number of forces, including such "push" factors as labor disputes, violence, and terror, on one hand, and the "pull" of incentives such as reconnection with family and community, on the other. Labor exploitation was, naturally, a source of conflict between slaveholders and slaves, and truancy was one method that the latter used to establish some limits to the amount and pace of their work. In contradistinction to planters' ways of using plantation space to discipline slave labor, absentees sometimes disappeared into the rival geography in search of relief from work. "Sometimes," Lorenzo L. Ivy recalled, "slaves jes' run' 'way to de woods fo' a week or two to git a res' fum de fiel', an' den dey come on back." When bondman Ginney Jerry reported that he was ill, he encountered his owner's suspicions and was told to "go & work it off." Instead, Ginney Jerry "concluded to woods it off," stealing a bit of time to rest and recuperate, which his owner considered "shirkin."[18] The repeat truant Sallie Smith remembered fondly the distance she could put between herself and the sounds of morning and the beginning of another workday. "Sometimes," she said, "I'd go so far off from the plantation I could not hear the cows low or the roosters crow."[19]

Household bondwomen's absences could have a direct impact on slaveholders that field workers' departures could not. Someone had to do their work. In some instances fellow bondwomen took up the slack, but on other occasions the woman's owner was forced to make up the difference. When Clarissa, a household slave, "took it into her head to run away," a miserable Mahala P. Eggleston Roach found herself "obliged to work some." Clarissa returned two days later, and Roach delivered what may have been the kindest punishment an enslaved person ever received: Roach "would not speak to her."[20]

On Nevitt's farm, truants ran away more often in the last months of the cotton picking season's intensive labor. The incidence of truancy (for all years together) remained relatively steady between March and October but rose in November, toward the end of the cotton picking. The number dropped again in December, perhaps in response to the holiday and frolic that Nevitt traditionally gave his enslaved laborers for Christmas. By 1 January, bondpeople at Clermont were back at work clearing the fields, making fence posts and shingles, and repairing local roads, fences, and the quarters. Again, the number of incidents of truancy rose, suggesting that absentees may have been extending their holidays.[21]

Truants who left during November and January were certainly in search of rest and amusement, but they may have also been escaping increased violence. Nevitt's demands for more labor during harvest certainly would have been underscored by the whip, no doubt spurring some to run away. The gang system used at Clermont routinized labor and imposed a relentless schedule on enslaved workers that people who worked in the task system did not experience as commonly. Both systems, however, extracted work by the lash, and running away was a frequent response to violence in both labor systems. Enslaved people in all parts of the South commonly experienced violence as a physical offense and as an affront to their human dignity. North Carolina slaveholder George D. Lewis was disdainful of the behavior of his "negro girl," but he probably accurately detected her outrage when she "took umbrage at a little flagellation and left."[22] When one enslaved Georgian "had not finished her task" one day, her driver threatened to "tie her up and flog her if she did not get it done," which sent her fleeing "into the swamp" to escape him.[23] Planters' journals and advice manuals carefully advised avoiding "*threats* of punishment," for "nothing" was believed to be "more sure to make negroes run away than a threat of punishment, especially if done in a passion." If punishment was "necessary," managers were counseled to have "it done without threatening and as soon after the offense as possible" to preempt the responses of slaves.[24] Furthermore, the consumption of alcohol was a part of harvest and holiday celebrations among black and white men and may have led to an escalation in violence by planters and overseers against bondpeople, and by bondmen against bondwomen. Drinking also might have incited more incidents of sexual abuse of women. This heightened violence would have spurred more flight around harvesttime.

Household bondwomen were subjected to the everyday violence of their owners' many moods and flashing tempers. Lorenzo L. Ivy's grandmother was owned by people who "treated her jus' lak a dog." She was a cook, and her owner "would beat her ef he didn't like" the food she had made. Ivy's grandmother "would run 'way to the woods" to escape these beatings.[25] During one ferocious episode another cook, named Bertcha, became afraid that her owner "would kill her, so she ran for the woods and hid there and stayed three weeks."[26] Former bondman Benjamin Johnson remembered how when his mistress was angry with the women who worked in her house, she would "go whuppin' on 'em." Johnson also recalled the women's responses: "sometimes de women would'nt take it an' would run away an' hide in de woods."[27]

Men, like women, ran away in anticipation of or during punishment, but there were some differences in the ways enslaved people talked about these actions. Again and again, interviews and autobiographies of former bondpeople recounted stories of women running away in response to violence, and many fewer talked of men acting in this way. "Some times dey beat 'em so bad," William Brooks said of planters' treatment of women, "dey run away an' hide in de woods." Bondwoman Julian Wright was reputed to tolerate little physical abuse. She "would work," but "when they got rough on her, she got rough on them and ran away in the woods."[28] Perhaps men actually ran away less readily than women because their conceptions of manhood mandated more stoic responses. But it is just as likely that ideals of masculine behavior muffled reports of men running away from abuse, leaving a silence that may reflect a gendered rhetoric about reactions to violence.

For their part, women may have expressed greater sensitivity to violence because they were exposed to more of it. In addition to the lash that kept them working through the day in the gang system and that held them to the completion of their task in the rice country, enslaved women were the disproportionate targets of sexual violence by planters and non-elite men. One young enslaved woman had the mixed fortune to be "real pretty"; one of her neighbors remembered her as "built-up better than anybody I ever saw." One of the woman's overseers pursued her; but her mother had taught her "not to let any of 'em go with her," and she avoided him. Still, the man "would stick close 'round her when they was workin'," trying to seduce her. He "kept followin' this child and followin' this child" until she ran away to a friend's house for "'bout three days," and from there she went to the woods, where she stayed until "she got so hungry she just had to go back." The overseer immediately "started at her again," and she could no longer postpone confronting him and turning him down "flat footed." When she did, he beat her with the "big end of his cow hide." She headed toward a nearby lake, and the neighbor who told her story believed that "if her mother hadn't run and caught her she would have walked right in it and drowned."[29]

Some enslaved men were not above exploiting the positions of relative power that they sometimes enjoyed. After the end of the Civil War, Anna Baker was able to discuss with her mother her reasons for escaping to the North. Baker's mother was pressed to this act of rupture and self-preservation "on 'count o' de Nigger overseers" who were in charge of the women "hoers." The drivers "kep' a-tryin' to mess 'roun' wid her," though she "wouldn' have nothing to do wid 'em." With a trick up her sleeve, she agreed to meet one of the men in the woods. No one stopped her when she started on her way, and when she got into the woods, she "jus' kep'-a-goin'," running away from both her owner and an enslaved man with a measure of power over her.[30]

Not only were bondwomen the victims of male violence, but they also routinely received the back of their mistress's hand. In the management of household slaves, planter women did not balk at the use of violence. Their style tended to the temperamental, as opposed to the orderly, but they, like their husbands, sons, and fathers, understood that the making of "a better servant" required "force and that of the strictest kind."[31] Slaveholding women yanked hair, pulled ears, smacked faces, burned skin, punched bodies, and stabbed at random.[32] At the end of a "lazy, cross, sleepy and altogether unprofitable day," Mahala P. Eggleston Roach took her frustration out on those who spent their days with her: "scolded the children *a little* servants more," she wrote guiltily.[33] Judith Page Aylett knew that it would take more than some scolding to stop those who had "robed the meat house" while her husband was away. She had her brother's "gun brought up in the chamber" and "intend[ed] shooting it off to impress the servants with the idea that I am very brave."[34] Benjamin Johnson's mistress certainly made an impression on the bondpeople she owned when she got "to whuppin' on" any of household bondwomen with whom she might be "mad."[35]

Household women were notoriously vulnerable to personal, moody, and sudden violence at the planter's residence. Cooks caught eating biscuits and housekeepers whose polished floors did not gleam sufficiently often were smacked and sometimes had the "blood [whipped] out of" them.[36] When one planter found that his overseer's wife had been pilfering milk and butter, it was the enslaved dairymaid he "called up" and whose "jaws" he "boxed."[37] Enslaved women were slapped around casually by their male and female owners alike. Of course, they sometimes retaliated, as Sylvia DuBois once did, striking her attacker with "a hell of a blow with my fist."[38] One young girl filled her hair with sewing pins, "points up," and the next time her owner punched the child's head, she got a fist "filled with pins."[39] All told, enslaved women were the targets of violence from all sides—from their male and female owners as well as from enslaved men. The refuge they sought in outlying areas may have promised them a bit of peace.

The plantation's push factors (overwork, violence, and illness) were only some of the reasons people ran away.[40] The rival geography's marginal spaces offered opportunities that drew runaways to them. One of the most important attractive opportunities was the chance to visit family and friends.[41] The separation of family members through sale and abroad marriages was one of slavery's gravest atrocities. Historians have shown that while separation was devastating to individuals, families, and even communities, the slave family as an institution adapted to, even as it was ravaged by, personal loss. Serial monogamy, naming children for absent family members, and the orientation toward extended family (rather than the exclusive nuclear family) were but a few of the practices that enabled the family, as a valued social institution, to survive the vicissitudes of enslavement.[42]

When the distance was not too far, separated family members sometimes reunited during nighttime visits. Frederick Douglass opened his classic 1845 autobiography with the faint memories he still had of his mother, who lived some twelve miles from him in Maryland. "I never saw my mother, to know her as such," Douglass narrated, "more than four or five times in my life; and each of these times was very short in duration, and at night." Douglass's mother ran away from her hirer as often as she could, which was not very often, to visit him "in the night, traveling the whole distance on foot, after the performance of her day's work." Douglass's account of his relationship with his mother is a mixture of bitterness about what slaveholders did to the enslaved, sorrow that he did not have more time with his mother (his father was her owner), and tenderness for what his mother struggled to provide him. "I do not recollect of ever seeing my mother by the light of day," he wrote. "She was with me in the night. She would lie down with me, and get me to sleep, but long before I waked she was gone." In this passage Douglass reflected on the effects of separation and walked a delicate line, stressing the brutalities of the system and the lingering emotional trauma of early orphanage as well as the efforts of his truant mother, who tried to maintain a connection with the son from whom she was hired away.[43]

Some women used truancy not to remedy but to protest planters' interference in their family lives. George Noble Jones's overseer, A. R. McCall, wrote to Jones to report on "the Negroes," who were in "very good helth and git on very well." All, that was, except "Mariah [who] got the Devel in her and walked of[f]." The trouble "all grew out of hur molater girl Mary," whom

McCall had recently brought into his home to "mind the flies and play with Annah," his daughter. The move had displeased Mariah enormously, and McCall tried to appease her by granting that Mary "could stay with it[s] Mother of a knight and if it wanted it cold go down to see hur of days." In addition, McCall was willing to train Mary, "if it was smart," to become a "hous servent." The overseer's wife and daughter were "willin," but Mariah was not. Perhaps Mariah wanted her daughter to spend her days with her. McCall identified Mary as a "molater," a mulatto. If Mary's father was, in fact, white, Mariah may have feared exposing her daughter to a white man, especially in an intimate space entirely under his control such as McCall's home. Mariah may have also objected to the personal subservience of domestic work, preferring that Mary work in the anonymity of the fields. For any or all of these reasons, "that knight Mariah put it in Marys head that she was not to wait on us and I had to give the chile a whipen the next morning." When Mariah got wind of that, "she came in et diner" and "cut up a swell about it." As McCall prepared to give her a "smal dresin" for losing her temper and making a scene, Mariah "walked of[f]." Mariah expressed her concerns and tried to protect her daughter with one of the few weapons available to her: truancy. But McCall saw the episode in much simpler terms: "all I wan[t] any of them to do," he lamented to his employer, is "to behave themselves and attend to the worke."[44]

Most commonly, bondmen ran away to visit their girlfriends and wives, hiding in the women's cabins or meeting them in the woods near their homes. Alice Green's father was something of a rake during his bachelor days. He told his daughter that in his youth he was in the habit of "slip[ping] off" at night, when "evvythin' got still and quiet," to "hunt him up some 'omans."[45] Henry Bibb, too, remembered fondly the days when he sowed his wild oats. "I was then a young man, full of life and vigor, and was very fond of visiting our neighbors slaves, but had not time to visit only on Sundays, when I could get a permit to go." So Bibb went "after night, when I could slip off without being seen."[46] Ellen Campbell knew a woman whose abroad husband once ran away to the woods near her home farm when he was denied permission to visit her. While he hid, she went to the woods to meet him and to give him dinner, until he was caught one night and summarily shot dead.[47]

Much of bondpeople's independent social activity depended on truancy. Christian worshipers and secular partygoers alike produced rare moments of leisure by absenting themselves to congregate in the woods, swamps, or outbuildings.[48] The mother of the Reverend W. P. Jacobs often told him about slavery in Virginia and about "how they used to slip away so they could pray together." If they were detected by the patrols, they ran for the cornfield, weaving a tricky way "down one row and jump[ing] into the next." Fields filled with the stumps of cornstalks were "better still," for "if the patterollers come in[, the stumps] were likely to" trip the horses.[49]

Enslaved healers—including midwives, root doctors, and household caregivers—found many of the plants whose leaves and roots they used to make medicine in outlying woods.[50] Enslaved people often viewed health and healing within a sacred context, and this view informed their conception of the natural environment. A creative, spiritual cosmos that included but also transcended the physical world was the setting in which bondpeople located health, illness, healing, and harming. In the worldview of slave healing practices, the woods that supplied medicinal herbs and roots were animated by spiritual and metaphysical forces. To find the remedies they sought, specialists and nonspecialists alike learned their way around woods and wetlands. By old age, it was said, many "could read the woods just like a book." As they slipped into the wilderness in search of plants, enslaved women and men crept ever deeper into a world where, in the words of historian Sharla Fett, "spiritual power intensified and the social power of slave society waned."[51]

Even as they evaded work, visited, rested, and engaged in independent activities, truants spent much of their time simply surviving. Living in woods or swamps, runaways faced extremely difficult conditions. They rummaged in the woods for berries and, as one absentee put it, "any thing we came upon."[52] Truants were often blamed by their slaveholding neighbors for the disappearance of chickens and hogs, and enslaved people knew better than to merely suspect them.[53] Charles Crawley was acquainted with truants, some of whom were long-term absentees, who lived "off of takin' things, sech as hogs, corn an' vegetables from other folks farm."[54] But not everyone was skilled at hunting, foraging, or stealing. In any case, berries, a bit of wild vegetation, and the occasional chicken made for skimpy fare. At times Sallie Smith's stomach ached so badly with hunger pangs that she "could hardly sleep."[55]

Truants were also miserable in bad weather. Smith shivered through nights so cold she "did not know what to do."[56] Some runaways built fires, but they must have been of two minds when they did so. Campfires were indispensable for keeping warm and for cooking meat. But smoke gave away a truant's location in the woods, causing many people simply to avoid the trouble that fire could make for them and to rely on makeshift shelters to stave off chilly weather.[57] In the woods, truants cleared ground and gathered tree branches together into the "brush harbors" under which they hunched, while others piled up moss and leaves into which they crawled to sleep. When bondwoman Bethany Veney once ran away, she got caught in a rainstorm. An inexperienced truant, she only managed to find some "alder bushes" under which she "crowded" her head, leaving her "shoulders and body" exposed and "dripping wet." For an entire night she "crouched in this way."[58] Needless to say, accommodations such as bushes and piled-up moss or leaves proved adequate only in the mildest weather; in wet winter months, runaways had little protection against the rain, the snow, and the cold.

Absentees with long careers occasionally built camps over the course of time. Some camps were entirely man-made, consisting of quilts or blankets hung from tree and shrub branches to form tents. Others were built around natural structures like caves and tree hollows. One slaveholder recorded the discomfort that truants would have known all too well, on the night he spent outdoors at one runaway's camp in the hope that he would catch him there. "Out all night in the rain sitting at G[inney]. Jerrys Camp," he wrote the next day in his plantation journal. "Suffered verry much from cold wet &c. part of the time in the hollow tree &c."[59] Camps such as this one appear to have been more common in the lower South than in the upper South, where recidivist or long-term truants would have been more likely to invest their energies in flight to the North.[60]

The very young, the old, and the ill were prone to succumbing to the elements. One of James Henry Hammond's truants, a forty-nine-year-old man named York, ran away for a few weeks during the summer of 1835. When he came in, he had a "cold & [was] nearly starved besides." Presumably out of consideration for his condition, Hammond had him "flogged lightly." A few days later, York "seemed nearly well." But then he "went off suddenly last night," and his cold, combined with the "light" whipping, took its toll: York died that night.[61] Pregnant women also took their chances when they ran to the woods. One woman told an acquaintance that she had "had my child here in the woods," but the child had not survived. Now, "it is dead and I buried it in a piece of my frock shirt." Absentees withstood these hardships for anywhere from a few days to a few weeks, and sojourns of several months were not unknown.[62]

THE AMBIVALENCE OF COOPERATIVE ACTION

The tenacity of women and men runaways was due in part to community efforts to assist them. Just as runaways to the North badly needed the help and complicity of other blacks to feed them and to guide them through unfamiliar land and waters, truants often needed the collaboration of the larger community; they had to rely on those they trusted and to hope for the best from strangers.[63] Women, in particular, supported runaways by extending to them the meals they prepared for their families. In so doing, even women who did not run away themselves were active participants in the alternative uses of plantation space. Men and women both created the rival geography by moving about illicitly, but women performed most of the reproductive work that enabled truants to occupy their hiding places for longer periods of time than otherwise would have been possible. When Lorenzo L. Ivy's grandmother ran away to the woods, as she did regularly to protest and prevent ill treatment, she would "stay in hidin' in de day time an' come out onlies' at night. My mama say she used to always put out food fo' her an' she would slip up nights an' git it."[64] Free black women were also known to provide assistance. Mollie Booker was "free born," and although her slaveholding neighbors tried to keep their slaves away from her and her family, local truants intermittently appeared at her door "to git somepin to eat."[65]

Field and household workers alike secretly helped absentees. Favored women, such as the bondwoman known to her owner as "aunt Fanny," were in a unique position to provide scarce items while maneuvering behind a trusted face. When someone "had the presumption to break in our meat house," the elite Aylett family initiated an investigation. Some suspected a new neighbor, while others believed that longtime runaway Jim was "at the bottom of it all." The Aylett family matriarch had always "thought well of" Fanny and placed her above suspicion. But when "Brother Henry had the servants houses searched on Friday," the source was discovered. In Fanny's house Henry found a reserve of food ("a basket of corn") as well as "a piece of bridling." It would appear that Fanny was outfitting Jim for an escape on horseback, perhaps to the North. That was not all: Jim had been "staying [in] her house for the last 12 months."[66]

Unlike Jim, most truants moved back and forth between relatively remote hiding places and the quarters, sometimes on paths with which only enslaved people were acquainted.[67] The quarters were not only a part of plantation grounds, but also an integral part of planters' geographies of containment. The quarters were where enslaved people were expected to be, at permitted times. At the same time, the quarters were an essential element in bond-people's alternative uses of space: truants' secret forays into the quarters in search of food or company brought the quarters into the rival geography. Hammond's runaways Nancy and Abram made a habit of going back and forth between the swamp and the quarters, where they would visit and be fed, but not only after dark. "Day & night," Hammond fumed, they came in from the swamp where they were "encamped" and passed their time "about the lot."[68] Similarly, Dennis, a repeat truant, told his owner from the plantation jail that "he saw & talked with several of my negroes While out."[69] Women absentees ran to and fro not only to receive sustenance but also to feed their families at night. Camilla Jackson's mother "would run away ter the woods" when her mistress hit her, "but at night she would sneak back to nurse her babies."[70] Movement between hiding places and the quarters might have been easier and more common in black-majority counties, such as those of the Black Belt and coastal South Carolina and Georgia, than in other parts of the South, where greater surveillance probably forced truants to be relatively more cautious and self-reliant.

The flow of movement between hiding places and the quarters both helped and hurt absentees. On one hand, truants needed the assistance of willing fellow bondpeople, and this support enabled them to survive and to stay out longer than if they had been left on their own. As a farmer informed traveler Frederick Law Olmsted, the runaways were "often hunted after, but it was very difficult to find them, and, if caught, they would run away again, and the other negroes would hide and assist them."[71] In a few instances, collective action even made owners adjust their responses to runaways. When Little Betts returned from one eight-day expedition into the woods with another bondwoman named Dilly, her owner opted not to "whip her lest it should prevent Dilly from coming home."[72] Lorenzo Ivy witnessed similar patterns of compromise. When the bondpeople whom Ivy knew, including his grand-mother, ran away from their owners and hid out with family, they sometimes refused to return until they had received "de word" from their owners that they would not "beat" them if they returned by the next workday.[73] A house-hold bondwoman named Bertcha ran away because her mistress lashed out at her "most every day." One day was worse than most, her daughter recalled. "She made mother strip down to her waist, and then took a carriage whup an' beat her until the blood was runnin' down her back. Mother said she was afraid she would kill her, so she ran for the woods and hid there." Enslaved people throughout the quarters had indirect access to Bertcha, because "the niggers on different plantations fed mother by carrying things to certain hidin' places and leavin' it" for her. Bertcha protected herself from possible betrayal by arranging only dropping-off points with the people who helped her, but her husband and her mother knew how to find her. It was to them that her owner, Charles Manly, appealed after she had been gone for three weeks. Bertcha's mother "got word to her" that Manly had an offer: come home now, and she could hire herself out in the neighborhood.[74] While it could not determine planters' responses, collective action strengthened tru-ancy's sustainability and, in some cases, mitigated the brutality of planters' retaliations. But bad faith and lies were more representative; usually, slave-holders did not keep their promises of no reprisals. Instead, because slaveholders typically viewed enslaved people as unworthy or incapable of honorable dealings, they did not hesitate to go back on their word. William Brooks's owner would "tell one a his slaves—tell 'em come back. He ain' gonna beat 'em any mo'." But when the person returned, "he beat 'em worse'n ever fer runnin' away. White man's mean."[75]

While movement to and from the quarters helped support truants, it also made them vulnerable to discovery by their owners. Much of the rival geography, especially the quarters and plantation outbuildings, was within planters' reach, and when runaways ventured in from the woods and swamps, they increased their risk of capture. "Caught a runaway yesterday. came to the hands," one satisfied planter wrote in his journal.[76] Similarly, at Nevitt's estate the runaway Lot was discovered receiving food "in Dilly's house," whipped, and put back to work.[77] Olmsted, too, commented on the risk of detection raised by absentees' return to the quarters. He noted that runaways "almost always kept in the neighborhood, because they did not like to go where they could not sometimes get back to see their families." As a result, "the overseer would soon get wind of where they had been; they would come round their quarters to see their families and to get food, and as soon as he knew it, he would find their tracks and put the dogs on again."[78]

To avoid being captured in the quarters, some absentees and their supporters arranged meetings in or near the places where truants concealed themselves. Cornelia Carney's mother "used to send John, my oldes' brother, out to de woods wid food" for her father when he hid from his abusive owner.[79] The overlapping of official and unofficial spaces was productive as well as risky. Two bondwomen, Lorendo Goodwin and Hattie, met at the juncture of a sugarcane field, where Goodwin worked, and a forest, where Hattie hid. One morning Hattie waited at the edge of the woods for Goodwin, who unknowingly worked her way along a row of cane toward Hattie. When Goodwin was close enough, Hattie called out to her and "asked me to give her something to eat; and I did give her all I had in my bucket."[80] In like manner, when Sallie Smith got hungry, she would "find out where the hands on the place were working, and if the overseer was away I'd get something from them." Occasionally she could count on them to bring food into the woods for her, once they knew she was there. She would go to the "edge of the woods every day" and listen for the "low piercing voice" she hoped to hear whispering " 'Sallie! Sallie!' " When she heard her name called, "I'd come running and sometimes I was nearly perished" by the time the help arrived.[81]

Women's work supporting truancy complicates the distinction between individual and collective resistance, and between the personal and the political. Absenteeism was very often a sudden, solitary reaction to a specific grievance. At the same time, individual truants partially depended on others for assistance. Many bondwomen helped runaways because they understood runaways to be protesting their conditions of labor and life. Moreover, some people assisted truants because the distinction between wrongs committed against an individual and those committed against a group were less important within communities of extended family, friends, neighbors, and occasionally even strangers of the same station. The distinction between individual and collective resistance, then, offers only an aphoristic description of truancy in practice. The reasons bondpeople ran away—violence, exhaustion, and humiliation—resonated with wrongs others had suffered or could, at any moment, be made to suffer.

Just as the difference between individual and collective resistance is misleading, so is the separation of political principal and personal sentiment. Many women helped truants—husbands, family members, friends, and acquaintances—because they loved them or because they felt loyal to them. Perhaps otherwise disinclined to assist in dangerous behavior, some women were motivated by bonds of intimacy to help people who flouted their owners' rules, withheld their labor, and broke the law. Many people in enslaved communities recognized absenteeism for what it was: social protest in which many bondpeople participated collectively for political and personal reasons.[82]

At the same time, cooperation coexisted with ambivalence, fear, and self-interest, and many refused to get involved in punishable activities. When the weather turned too cold for the "moss bed" Sallie Smith made for herself to sleep in at night, she sometimes stayed with different enslaved families. However, after being caught by the overseer in one home, Smith found it impossible to get shelter in the quarters. From that point on, she had to sleep outdoors "in chimney-corners on a plantation next to my master's."[83] But avoiding involvement did not necessarily protect a resident of the quarters from punishment. Just as absentees' movement between hiding places and quarters joined these places in a common rival geography, so the cooperation of truants and their supporters roiled the difference between resistant and compliant bondperson. It was an elision that slaveholders upheld, punishing those who helped runaways and exploiting truancy's collective nature in order to force absentees to return, and successfully undermining feelings of solidarity with the runaways that might have developed in the quarters. Both James Henry Hammond and John Blount Miller cut off the meat allowance "of all," as Miller put it, "until return," and Hammond "flogged" those who helped absentees on his farm.[84] The apparent success of these tactics indicates that there were limits to what residents would sacrifice for truants.

The limits of collective action are perhaps most evident in the outright danger to which cooperation exposed truants: it made some runaways vulnerable to opportunism. In particular, gender hierarchies among the enslaved operated to the advantage of some at the expense of others. Absentees were thoroughly acquainted with the secret mappings of their farms, could often locate other truants, and were thus in a perfect position to win favor or payment from their owners by turning in other runaways. Men appear to have been especially able to do so. At Clermont plantation, every truant who turned in another was a bondman. Women probably lacked the physical presence and the social authority to coerce a truant into returning against his or her will. These men, mainly Rubin and Jerry, were unlikely intermediaries as they themselves were regular runaways. Rubin frequently visited his wife without a pass for days and even weeks at a time, and Jerry was once shot at while being chased from the neighboring farm where his own wife lived. Yet again and again, these two men "brought home" other truants for the benefits they gained: pardons for their absences and sometimes pay. Once when Rubin returned from a one-day absence, John Nevitt turned him around and "sent him out for Maria," who had been gone a few days. By evening Rubin had returned with her. As a reward Nevitt "forgave Rubin his fault an gave Maria a severe whiping." Rubin and Jerry were hardly alone. Nevitt had exchanges with a few of his own and some neighboring bondmen who turned in truants to settle a grudge or to earn a dollar, three dollars, or brownie points.[85] The allegiances of people like Rubin and Jerry were murky and changeable, as were those of Bennet Barrow's repeatedly absentee bondman Dennis. Dennis, who a few months later was alleged to have participated in an insurrection plot, once "pretend[ed] to be run-away" in order to go "hunting for" a neighbor's "runaway."[86] Others did not waver in their loyalties. As a Union officer was told by runaway slaves during the Civil War, "There are a great many slaves who are no more to be trusted than their masters—who will be certain to betray."[87]

In a few cases, planters called on black men in leadership positions, such as drivers. James H. R. Washington, who worked as an overseer, suspected that two slaves under his supervision had run away to the nearby farm of George Paul Harrison. Washington wrote to Harrison requesting the return of the runaways, and he recommended a method for ferreting them out: "prevail upon your driver to bring them in." Whether because Washington thought the driver was feared, trusted, respected, or a combination of all three, he believed the retrieval of the absentees could "be easily done." "If his position is as you say," Washington told Harrison, "a message communicated to him, will be communicated to them." Right or wrong in his assessment of this driver, Washington offered "*Fifty Dollars* for their arrest and confinement," with "half of this sum" to go to "your boy for his fidelity."[88] Given the wretched poverty in which enslaved people lived, such a sum was likely to purchase the cooperation of many, perhaps including this driver. In addition to struggling to eat and to survive the elements, truants had to look out for slave patrols, whites in general, and other blacks, any of whom might capture them. Resistance to slavery's constraints existed side by side with conformity and opportunism.

Slaveholders, who had enormous difficulty capturing truants themselves, depended on the collaboration of slaves and assistance from slave patrols to capture runaways and bring them back to work.[89] But planters were not above personally searching for absentees, to "hunt" them, as they often put it. Annie Stephenson corrected what she viewed as a misconception about the Old South. "Dere wus a lot of talk 'bout de patterollers but marster done his own sneakin' around. He done a lot of eavesdroppin'."[90] Alone or in teams and sometimes with dogs, planters pursued truants ruthlessly. When one of the "negro Dogs" that Bennett Barrow and his neighbors regularly used to chase truants once caught a man, they stood by as the animal "nearly et his legs off—near killing him."[91] Barrow must have been especially pleased with that capture, for generally such "hunts" had "no Luck" in locating their prey. So long as they stayed within the parameters of their local knowledge—as fugitives to the North could not do—truants were surprisingly successful at evading capture. Barrow and other planters often commented in their journals on the ineffectiveness of their hunts. "Went yesterday evening to look for some runaways," Barrow once wrote. "Could'ent find them."[92] These results would not have surprised Cornelia Carney, who felt that "niggers was too smart fo' white folks to git ketched."[93] Bondpeople sometimes worked in the woods and swamps, gathering firewood or clearing land for cultivation.[94] In these ways and by running away, they became acquainted with such places better than many patrolmen and most planters. So long as truants could "git in the woods," they stood a chance of remaining in hiding, in part because they slipped around in the woods when detected.[95]

In very rare instances, women were used to capture absentees. One such case occurred when slaveholder John Blount Miller manipulated a woman he owned into retrieving her daughter, a woman who blurred the lines between being a truant and a fugitive within the South. Rachel was twenty years old when in January 1847 she first ran away from the South Carolina plantation called Cornhill. Miller did not document the source of her dissatisfaction; perhaps the young woman was becoming increasingly conscious of the meaning of her bondage, or maybe a particular incident drove her away. Whatever the source of her discontent, Rachel ran away for three to four months before returning; soon she was gone again for seven months before she was retrieved. Rachel was able to sustain these long absences because she did not camp out in the wilderness but went to a nearby town, probably Sumterville, where she "passed for free." If Rachel did go to Sumterville, she joined an enslaved community of more than 800 and a free black community of 10 people. Not uncommonly for South Carolina, blacks outnumbered whites, who totaled 500. It would not have been difficult for Sumterville's black world to absorb a runaway, and the length of Rachel's second absence suggests that she may have hoped never to return to Cornhill. If so, her plans were thwarted when her mother came to town looking for her. Sent there by Miller, Rachel's mother no doubt had her own motivations for wanting to see her daughter, who had been missing for eleven of the past eighteen months. Though Miller did not record what he told Rachel's mother to induce her to fetch her daughter, he surely must have failed to mention what he later wrote in his journal: Rachel was "sold in a just time after."[96]

Most truants were neither captured by slaveholders' hunts nor caught by patrols nor turned in by other enslaved people. Instead, they usually returned on their own because they had always intended to do so. Absenteeism was, by its nature, a short-lived event. This was especially true for women, whose ties to and roles within the family bound them more tightly to plantation life. Charlie Pye's mother ran away habitually, stayed out as long as possible, and returned only "when the strain of staying away from her family became too great."[97] Family played the inverse role in men's patterns of absence. Because they often ran away to be with their families, male truants had access to forms of support from their wives and lovers that enabled them to stay away for longer periods of time than female truants, whose escapes were relatively more solitary. At Clermont plantation, men's absences were twice as long as women's, averaging fifteen days versus women's average of six days. Three times as many men were able to sustain absences of thirty-one to forty-five days (three men compared with one woman), and four times as many men stayed out for more than forty-six days (four men and one woman).[98] Differences in gender roles and responsibilities informed women's and men's likelihood of attempting to escape to the North, and it shaped the time that women and men were each able to dedicate to truancy.

Ultimately, neither men nor women could avoid the material deprivations that would compel them to return to their quotidian lives. Food presented the greatest problem; truants' tactics for piecing together meals worked only in the short term. Though hunger often awaited them in the quarters as well, the austere rations doled out by slaveholders must have seemed appetizing after a few days or weeks in the woods. At least they were reliable, and their high fat content filled a belly. Louisa, a frequent truant, told her owner that she had only come back because she was "'most dead with hunger." Indeed, Louisa was sick with malnutrition for so long after she came back that her driver "forgot 'bout de flogging" she was supposed to receive for running away.[99] Other absentees were not nearly so strong willed as Louisa and returned well before such severe illness set in. Such was the case with Liza McCoy, who tended to "come back when I [got] hungry."[100]

Clothing posed another problem. Allowanced at most just one set of clothes for the winter and another for the summer, enslaved people routinely wore their clothes until they were in tatters. The clothing in which bondpeople ran away was generally in poor condition to begin with, and the additional wear and tear of life in the woods showed itself easily. Moreover, almost no one had extra clothing to donate, as they might, with sacrifice, spare a bit of food. One slave patrol captured a group of women and men absentees and wrote to their owner to come and get them. "As they are scarce of clothing, the sooner you get them the better," the patrolmen added.[101] When one woman returned from her trips to the woods, her owner thought she "was a most disreputable looking object," for she was covered with "mud and dust," and "her clothes hung from her like a fringe."[102]

Roswell King, the manager of Pierce Butler's Georgia plantation, pleaded with Butler for funds to clothe Butler's bondpeople. King hoped to provide a base of material "comfort" to his enslaved workers so as "to make them contended"; he also wanted to keep up appearances in the neighborhood. In 1812 King wrote to Butler, "now is the time to clothe the Negroes there is a number of them getting naked." The use of the phrase "getting naked" was no rhetorical flourish. The following year King asked Butler if he realized that "your neighboring planters give their Negroes Summer clothing every one or two years" but that Butler had given his own bondpeople summer clothing "but twice in eleven years." In 1817 King continued to beg Butler to give his bondpeople something new to wear. It is easy to understand why, in the late 1830s, women runaways from this farm sometimes returned "entirely naked."[103] Material deprivation, already severe, worsened in the rival geography.

I HAD RATHER A NEGRO DO ANY THING ELSE THAN RUNAWAY

Truants thought of absenteeism as, among other things, a way to evade work and "git a res' fum de fiel',"[104] and planters agreed, though from a different perspective. Calling absentees "shirks," "verry bad example[s]," "rascally ones," "scamp[s]," "scoundrels," and the perpetrators of "crimes," slaveholders expressed their judgment of slaves who avoided their work and "fooled the day off to no purpose."[105] But it was largely in the inchoate language of violence that they registered their objections to truancy.[106] Most truants were whipped. Alex Woods saw his overseer take absentees "into the barn and corn crib and wh[ip] 'em wid a leather strap called de cat-o-nine tails." The overseer delivered a tongue-lashing while he lacerated runaways' backs: "Are you goin' to work? Are you goin' visitin' widout a pass? Are you goin' to run away?"[107] Often such floggings were underscored with other abuses, a combination that was neither rare nor a trifle, even in the very violent Old South.[108] Absentees were forced "to work harder" than ever, put on bread-and-water diets "for long time," caned, put in stocks, shackled at their feet with a ball and chain, chained from the leg to the neck (a practice that left one person's neck "nearly a solid scab"), confined alone in outbuildings, and jailed.[109] One man had an iron cage with bells on it locked over his head for three months; another received a "decent smoking" in the smokehouse; a few were made to "ware womens cloths." Quite a few were shot at or shot.[110] One bondman who was captured while visiting his wife was tied to a tree and branded with his owner's initials "in the fleshy part of [his] loins."[111]

Some truants were sold, as were many captured fugitives. John Blount Miller and John Nevitt both sold their greatest recidivists,[112] and former bondman Charles Crawley knew a number of truants in Virginia who were "sol' by dey new marsters to go down Souf."[113] Repeat offenders were not the only ones cast into the slave market, however. Enslaved North Carolinian Hasty once made for the woods after her mistress slapped her; upon her return, Hasty learned that she had been sold.[114] Bennet Barrow, who shot at, shot, chained, whipped, clubbed, and dunked his truants in water explained why he punished absenteeism so severely: "I had rather a negro do any thing Else than runaway."[115]

The story of Julian Wright details the kind of treatment that truants feared. After an incident one day, Wright "ran away and hid for a long time." Her owner eventually chased her down "by means of bloodhounds" and found her cowering in a tree. After she was captured and returned, Wright was chained at her "leg just as though she were a dog. The band was very tight, too tight, and the chain cut a round around her ankle." The wound was ignored, and it festered during the months she spent in chains. In the meantime, she received a lashing that left her back a "mass of scars." The beating, the chains, and the infected wound left her so debilitated that it was "quite a while before she could begin work again."[116]

As Wright's story suggests, women's sex did not protect them from the full force of their owners' indignation. Women were strung up and whipped, chained and ironed, put in stocks, shot, and sold for their transgressions, just as were men.[117] When Richard Eppes caught Fanny, "a negro woman [who] had run away," he saw to it that his overseer "caned her back" with "12 lashes."[118] Another bondwoman was forced to wear "men's pants for one year"; for some of that time she also wore "deer horns on her head to punish her, with bells on them."[119] The physical and psychological trauma of a whipping could complicate a pregnancy and childbirth. One bondwoman was "whipped . . . so brutal that her back was all raw." The flogging may have induced labor, for just two hours later the woman "gave birth to a child in this lacerated condition."[120]

In many instances female gender seems to have served as a license for planters' full expression of violent rage, exposing women to cruel punishment more consistently than men. The "severest corporeal punishment of a negro" that the seasoned traveler Olmsted ever "witnessed at the South" was inflicted on Sall, a woman truant who, her overseer explained, had "slipped out of the gang when they were going to work" and had been "dodging about all day." Furious that "she meant to cheat me out of a day's work, and she has done it, too," the overseer gave no regard to her modesty and stripped Sall from head to toe. Then he laid into her. The sadistic act became a lewd spectacle before Olmsted's eyes as he watched the overseer give Sall "thirty or forty blows across the shoulders" with a rawhide and "continued to flog her . . . with as much strength as before" on "her naked loins and thighs."[121]

On John Nevitt's plantation there were disparities in the distribution of punishment that support Olmsted's impression. In the diary entries that record a punishment, women were slightly more consistently punished—by flogging, shackles, ball and chain, or jail—than men. Whereas three-quarters of male truants were reported to have been punished, 83 percent of women were; while Nevitt "forgave" a quarter of men runaways, only 16 percent of women were absolved.[122] In part the skewed distribution of punishment was due to Nevitt absolving Rubin and Jerry for running away when they turned in other truants. But other men were acquitted, so other reasons were at play as well. According to the customary norms of the rural South, there were potentially legitimate reasons for enslaved men to leave plantations, while there were almost none for women. Planter expectations regarding women's locations, then, may have been even stricter than those they had for men, and what counted as truancy in women may have been somewhat more acceptable in men. Women's alternative movement may have been more easily perceived as a trespass and more quickly and consistently punished. Another issue may have been that Nevitt viewed women as easier to punish and to use as examples. Overall, it is clear that Nevitt's bondwomen were subjected to disparate treatment based on their gender.

The cruelty of such punishments drove some women to the deepest despair. One young woman ran away twice and was twice "confined in my smokehouse for the purpose of punishing her," John R. Lyons wrote to his uncle. At the end of her second imprisonment, Lyons "went in to turn her out for work" but "found her hanging." We cannot know this woman's reasons for running away and for ending her life; perhaps they were entirely familial or intimate or perhaps they related to her chattel status, to the limitations it placed on her life, and to the consequent abuses she suffered. There is less mystery about the meaning of her death to Lyons, who let his uncle know that he was irate: "I had been offered $700.00 for her not two minutes ago, but damn her."[123]

The main reason that planters objected so strenuously to truancy was that truants withheld their labor for the duration of their absence. Slavery as a system worked most smoothly when enslaved people could be consistently compelled to do long hours of monotonous, disagreeable, and sometimes painful work. When truants absented themselves, their share of the crops went neglected, livestock was untended, and maintenance chores were not done.[124] Olmsted met one Virginia farmer who compared two violations of labor discipline—feigning illness and absenteeism—and who concluded that a "more serious loss frequently arises, when the slave, thinking he is worked too hard, or being angered by punishment or unkind treatment, 'getting the sulks,' takes to 'the swamp,' and comes back when he has a mind to."[125] Unlike those who "play[ed] possum" by pretending to be sick, those who ran away to the woods placed themselves beyond slaveholders' easy reach.[126] Truancy affected the two forms of labor organization in the Old South differently but introduced similar conflicts of interest to the spatial and temporal logic of each. For the majority of enslaved people who worked in the gang system, absenteeism punctuated their grueling, "sunup to sundown" labor, especially during harvest seasons, granting them escapes from otherwise almost unrelenting work and the violence required to make it possible. For those who worked in the task system, truancy extended the late afternoon and evening "off times" that shaped the core of slave life and culture in the South Carolina low country into days and weeks for oneself.

Absenteeism muddied the vision of spatial and temporal order toward which slaveholders strove, and its meanings went beyond the economic to hit issues of authority. Many planters viewed the "habit of going about the neighborhood" and "lurking about" as a form of "insubordination," as an act contrary to the "peace of the community," and as a "verry Bad Example." For all of these reasons, it had to "be stoped."[127] Women planters were especially likely to worry about their authority when enslaved people ran away. Ada

Bacot described in her journal the anxiety she felt on the day she discovered that "some of my young negroes have been disobeying my orders[.] they were found away from home without a pass." Though Bacot had "never had any trouble with them until now," their autonomous movement caused her to worry. "I hope that I may be able to make them understand," she fretted, "that I am mistress and will be obeyed."[128]

But in the conflict between slaveholders and bondpeople over the latter's uses of space, more was at hand than money and mastery. Truants' activities—and other uses of the rival geography—were preludes to escapes that lay a few decades ahead. During the Civil War, enslaved people ran to advancing Union lines, seeking freedom under the aegis of the federal army. Wartime migration did not erupt suddenly and without precedent. Rather, as will be explored in Chapter 5, it was the product of a history begun in slavery and in the tradition fostered in truancy of moving beyond the bounds of the plantation's legitimated spaces. During their bondage, enslaved people had established alternative ways of knowing and using southern space that violated laws and customs constricting black mobility, and that would continue into the Civil War. Truants, more than fugitives who left the South, gained and transmitted to others the infrastructure of geographical knowledge that was the foundation of wartime activity. The role that black refugees of war played in their own emancipation had been long in the making. But until the Civil War, enslaved people continued to move illicitly, often for the deceptively simple purpose of seeking amusement.

THE INTOXICATION OF
PLEASURABLE AMUSEMENT

*Secret Parties and the
Politics of the Body*

As a young woman, Nancy Williams joined other enslaved people and "court-in' couples" who would "slip away" to an "ole cabin" a few miles from the Virginia plantation where she lived. Deep in the woods, away from slave-holders' eyes, they held secret parties where they danced, performed music, drank alcohol, and courted. A religious woman in her old age, Williams admitted only reluctantly to her interviewer that she had enjoyed the secular pleasures of dressing up and going to outlaw dances. "Dem de day's when me'n de devil was runnin roun in de depths o' hell. No, don' even wanna talk 'bout it," she said. However, Williams ultimately agreed to talk about the outlaw parties she attended, reasoning that "guess I didn' know no better den" and remembering with fondness that, after all, "dem dances was somepin."

Musicians played fiddles, tambourines, banjos, and "two sets of [cow] bones" for dancers. Williams was a gifted and enthusiastic dancer; she would get "out dere in de middle o' de flo' jes' a-dancin'; me an' Jennie and de devil. Dancin' wid a glass of water on my head an' three boys a bettin' on me." Williams often won this contest by dancing the longest while balancing a glass of water on her head without spilling a drop. She "jes danced ole Jennie down." Like the other women in attendance, Williams took great pride in her outfits at these illicit parties, and she went to great trouble to make them, adorning one dress with ruffles and dyeing others yellow or red. Her yellow dress had matching yellow shoes; they were ill fitting, as many bondpeople's wooden "brogans" were, and "sho' did hurt me." But animated by her own beautiful self-presentation, "dat ain't stop me f'om dancin."[1]

By illuminating a part of everyday life that slaves kept a close secret, Nancy Williams's account of attending outlaw slave parties helps uncover one part of the story of enslaved women's lives: the role that the body played in slave-holders' endeavors to control their labor force and in black resistance to that control. Despite planters' tremendous effort, enslaved women and men routinely "slip[ped] away" to attend illicit parties where such sensual pleasures as eating, dancing, drinking, and dressing were among the main amusements.[2] Contingent upon opportunity, season, locale, the availability of resources, and the emotional climate within enslaved communities and between bond-people and their owners, slaves' illegal parties took place in the very woods and swamps with which many planters marked off illicit plantation space and declared off limits. Dense thickets of woods and murky swampland nonetheless proved irresistible to bondpeople who longed for places of independent socializing and activity.

Like another "invisible institution," slave Christianity, the secular institution was organized and inhabited in whispers and in code, in hiding and in the dark. Like the church, parties promised the rewards of congregation, a moment of release from drudgery and sorrow, and a different form of jubilation.[3] Religiosity, we must remember, was as dependent on temperament, upbringing, and life stage among the enslaved as among any people. Not all bondpeople found the hope and strength in the church that Christians did. There were those who agreed with the version of the song "Run, Nigger, Run" that critiqued enslaved clergy: "Some folks say a preacher won't steal / I caught two in my corn field."[4] The young, the cynical, the distracted, and the committed secularists all had their reasons for rejecting religious worship, and some of these worldly minded people sought release in the form of pleasurable amusement. No great divide existed between one and the other social formation, however, for the lives of many individuals coursed through both secular and sacred involvements. Nancy Williams was one among many who engaged in youthful activities of which they later disapproved.

Together enslaved women and men ran to abandoned outbuildings, woods, or swamps where they enjoyed music, dancing, the company of others, and a shared secret. Enslaved partygoers had a common commitment to delight in their bodies, to display their physical skill, to master their bodies through competition with others, and to express their creativity. They also had in common the capability of exorcizing discontents violently on one another. More than men, women indulged in fancy dress, to the extent that they could manage it, and men, more than women, delighted in drinking alcohol. That they engaged in these bodily delights as slaves gives their activities a significance beyond the personal gratification that they, as individuals, experienced. Slaves' dishonor was in large measure "embodied."[5] Inhabitants of a premodern society, bondpeople were made to suffer domination largely through the body in the form of captivity, commodification, exploitation, and physical punishment.[6] As late nineteenth-century activist Ida B. Wells said, slaveholders attempted to "dwarf the soul and preserve the body."[7] However, brutality did not constitute the whole of slaves' bodily experience. For those who encounter oppression through the body, the body becomes an important site not only of suffering but also (and therefore) of enjoyment and resistance.[8] Studying the body through a framework of containment and transgression grants us access to new perspectives on resistance and the workings of gender difference within enslaved plantation communities.

THREE BODIES

The body, French historian Dorinda Outram has written, is at once the most personal, intimate thing that people possess and the most public. The body, then, can provide and has provided a "basic political resource" in struggles between dominant and subordinate classes. Second-wave feminists said that the personal is political, but earlier, C. L. R. James had already argued that the twentieth century's working people "are rebelling everyday in ways of their own invention" in order to "regain control over their own conditions of life and their relations with one another." James found that often "their struggles are on a small personal scale." Enslaved people's everyday battles for "regaining" a measure of "control" took place on very "personal" terrain: their bodies.[9] Thinking about enslaved bodies in space allows us to see them materially, to watch as the prime implement of labor in the Old South moved in ways inconsistent with the rigors of agricultural production. Attention to the body also facilitates thinking about issues beyond the material, such as the roles of movement and pleasure in the culture of opposition developed by enslaved people. A somatic approach, such as the one employed here, risks objectifying people, but my purpose is the opposite: to demonstrate how enslaved people claimed, animated, politicized, personalized, and enjoyed their bodies—flesh that was regarded by much of American society as no more than biddable property.

Most of all, attention to uses and experiences of the body is mandatory for those interested in the lives of women in slavery, for it was women's actual and imagined reproductive labor and their unique forms of bodily suffering (notably sexual exploitation) that most distinguished their lives from men's. Historians of enslaved women have demonstrated the falseness of the dichotomy between the personal and the social to a large degree by exploring how the body, so personal, was also a political entity, a site of both domination and resistance.[10] Women employed their bodies in a wide variety of ways, from seizing control over the representation of their physical selves in narrative and photographic forms (both of which were in enormous demand among antebellum northerners) to abortion.[11]

Perceptions of the proper uses of the black body, especially the female body, were central, materially and symbolically, to the formation of slaveholding mastery. As the English became entrenched in the slave trade in the second half of the seventeenth century, their preexisting perceptions of Africans concretized into constructions of blackness that justified the trade. In addition to Africans' "heathenism," the English used representations of bodily difference to rationalize the economically expedient turn to bound black labor. Jennifer L. Morgan has demonstrated that these constructions relied in large part on representations of African women's bodies as inherently laboring ones. Englishmen came to see African women as drudges through sixteenth- and seventeenth-century male travelers' representations of African women's rugged reproductive and laboring bodies that stood in stark distinction to the idealized idle and dependent Englishwoman. Male travelers to Africa in the earliest years of contact remarked on what they saw as African women's sexual deviance: they lived in "common" (polygamously) with men and they bared much of their bodies, most remarkably their breasts, with "no shame." Englishmen represented African women's breasts ("dugs") as large and droopy, "like the udder of a goate," as one traveler put it. Animal-like, African women's exposed "dugs" struck male travelers as evidence of Africa's savagery and inferiority. African women's reproductive bodies demonstrated to European eyes their physical strength: they gave birth "withoute payne," suggesting that "the women here [Guinea] are of a cruder nature and stronger posture than the Females in our Lands in Europe." Confirming this conclusion was the fact that African women commonly worked in agriculture. Unencumbered by the delicacy that prevented the ideal Englishwoman from arduous labor, African women, then, were fit—*naturally* fit—for demanding agricultural and reproductive labor on the plantations of the Americas. Over the seventeenth century, representations of African women's rugged reproductive capacity proved the inherent laboring nature of African women and, by extension, African men and helped to justify the slave trade by naturalizing it.[12]

Englishmen encoded their ideas of racial difference based on constructions of African women's laboring bodies into law in England's colony in Virginia in 1643. In that year free African women were declared tithables (their labor could be taxed), along with all free white men and male heads of households, Kathleen M. Brown has shown. Because white women were viewed as dependents, as "good wives" who performed household, not agricultural, labor, they remained untaxed. The very different treatment of African and English women lay in diverse conceptions of their capacity to work in the fields and articulated distinct projections of the roles each would play in the life of the colony. Two years later, African men also became tithables and thus fell within the legal construction of African bodies as inherently laboring ones. Buttressed by constructions of Africans as heathens and savages, which themselves relied heavily on representations of African women's sexual and reproductive bodies, English lawmakers could, by 1670, force those servants who had arrived in Virginia "by shipping" (Africans) to serve lifelong terms of servitude, while those who had "come by land" (Indians) served limited terms. This law combined with the earlier law of 1667 banning the manumission of converted Christians to crystallize the racial form of the emergent slave economy.[13] In the context of slavery, issues of representation of the black body, especially the female black body, and material expropriation could not be separated.

By the antebellum period, planters had so thoroughly assimilated ideas that reduced enslaved people to their bodies that they often referred to them by their parts: "hands" was a common term, and "heads" was not unfamiliar. At other moments women slaves, those natural workers, were as one with their farming tools and called, simply, "hoes."[14] Planters, and white southern men generally, had also learned of black women's tough, sexual nature and preyed on them shamelessly. Among some enslaved people the white men who seduced or raped bondwomen earned the name "Carpet Gitters"[15] and were understood to be a flourishing population. "Did de dirty suckers associate wid slave wimmen?" the Reverend Ishrael Massie exclaimed to his interviewer in the 1930s. "I call 'em suckers—feel like saying something else but I'll 'spec ya, honey. Lord, chile, day wuz common."[16] "Dat happ'ned a lots in dem days," and liaisons were scarcely considered extraordinary. Nonetheless, they were the subject of comment and (disparate) judgment by both black and white.[17] Bondpeople and many planter women often shared a critical view of white sexual predators as "suckers" and "vile wretches."[18] But white women also tended to agree with white men that black women possessed a certain "*wickedness*" and were, essentially, "prostitutes."[19] Slaveholding woman Rachel O'Connor thought her overseer a despicable "villain" when he was found "together" with the bondwoman Eliza. Eliza had been a "good girl before that villain came here," although that did her no good when O'Connor "whipped her myself, and cut her curls off." Months later the association between Eliza and the overseer continued, as did O'Connor's abuses. February and March found Eliza's neck in a "rather tight" iron. Eliza not only endured her owner's judgment. Of greater anguish, no doubt, was the possible end of her engagement to a bondman who O'Connor now did not "expect . . . will take her."[20] Rape of enslaved women broke bondmen's hearts, too. And a few enslaved men broke hearts when they, also, assaulted women.[21]

Antebellum planters, as we have seen, were very interested in the control of black movement. They were also keen to master their slaves' senses of pleasure. Seeking to contain black bodies even further than laws, curfews, bells, horns, and patrols already did, some planters used plantation frolics as a paternalist mechanism of social control. Plantation parties, which carefully doled out joy on Saturday nights and holidays, were intended to seem benevolent and to inspire respect, gratitude, deference, and importantly, obedience. As North Carolinian Midge Burnett noted sardonically, his owner held plantation frolics on holidays, gave bondpeople Christmas trees in December, and organized an Easter egg hunt in the spring—all " 'case Marse William intended ter make us a civilized bunch of blacks."[22] The person who "acted rude" instead of grateful and deferential might find him- or herself punished, perhaps even put "in Jail."[23] Those who attended without passes were certainly reprimanded; when one planter caught two of a neighbor's bondmen with "no pass[es]" at a Christmas frolic for his slaves, he ran them off and "broke my sword Cane over one of their skulls."[24] It was one planter's policy to provide "a dance house for the young, and those who wish to dance" or pray. He made "it a rule to be present myself occasionally at both" types of events. He did these things because he believed "negroes will be better disposed this way than any other."[25]

Most of all, these frolics were supposed to control black pleasure by allowing it periodic, approved expression. Paternalist slaveholders accomplished this goal by attending and surveilling the parties. Indeed, the most important component of paternalistic plantation parties was the legitimating presence of the master. It was common for whites to attend these frolics and to "set around and watch" while bondpeople would "dance and sing."[26] Though sanctioning black pleasure, the slaveholder's gaze oversaw and contained that pleasure, ensuring that it would not become dangerous. For example, to ensure that the alcohol, music, dancing, "sundrie articles," and "treats" he provided his bondpeople at holiday time served the dual purpose of simultaneously giving limited expression to and containing their bodily pleasure, John Nevitt made sure to "s[i]t up untill 2 oclock in the morning to keep order with them."[27] Both former slave Henry Bibb and former slaveholder R. Criswell remembered slaveholders' supervision of plantation frolics, and both illustrated the constrictive effects of that gaze in their memoirs of antebellum plantation life.

The Sabbath among Slaves, from Bibb, *Narrative*. This illustration shows plantation festivities as Henry Bibb, a man who had been enslaved, remembered them. Enslaved people dance, play music, lounge, tussle, and drink while four elite whites on the left watch, amused. The plantation patriarch, to the right of center, distributes alcohol to a respectful bondman who has removed his hat and gratefully bows slightly. Note the very strong presence of a "fence" on the right, here represented as a wall. The wall and the four white onlookers contain and control this scene of black pleasure. (The Library Company of Philadelphia)

Alcohol proved an important lubricant of production at plantation affairs. Neal Upson watched singing adults set a rhythm for their work of shucking a season's corn harvest. Incorporated into their timekeeping was a "little brown jug" of liquor that was "passed 'round." The jug gave the workers just enough drink to warm their muscles and their spirits to the enterprise at hand: "when it [the jug] had gone de rounds a time or two, it was a sight to see how fast dem Niggers could keep time to dat singin'. Dey could do all sorts of double time den when dey swigged enough liquor." Similarly, Bill Heard's owner provided "plenty of corn liquor" to his bondpeople at cornshuckings in order to speed up the work. "You know day stuff is sho to make a Nigger hustle," Heard remembered. "Evvy time a red ear of corn was found dat meant a extra swig of liquor for de Nigger dat found it."[28] Even as planters attempted to master slaves' bodily movement and pleasure in these ways, however, some enslaved people were not satisfied with official parties. They sought out secret and secular gatherings of their own making.

Enslaved people, then, possessed at least three bodies. The first served as a site of domination; it was the body acted upon by slaveholders. Early con-

The Festival, from Criswell, *"Uncle Tom's Cabin."* This illustrated memory from a former slaveholder's autobiography depicts the centrality of white surveillance at plantation parties. (The Library Company of Philadelphia)

structions of African and black women's bodies and sexuality played a central role in rationalizing the African slave trade and gave license to sexual violence against enslaved women. Colonial and antebellum slaveholders believed that strict control of the black body, in particular its movement in space and time, was key to their enslavement of black people. By the late antebellum years, planters were working energetically to master such black bodily minutiae as nourishment, ingestion of alcohol, and even dress, all as part of their paternalist management strategies. In the Old South the slave body, most intensely women's, served as the "bio-text" on which slaveholders inscribed their authority and, indeed, their very mastery.[29]

The second body was the subjective experience of this process. It was the body as vehicle of feelings of terror, humiliation, and pain. The senses of this second body were "associated with poverty, suffering, and shame," with "dark fears and darker realities."[30] In planters' controlled and controlling landscapes, vulnerable to sale, sexual and nonsexual violence, disease, and exploitative labor, enslaved bodies were, in the words of colonial theorist Frantz Fanon, "surrounded by an atmosphere of certain uncertainty."[31] They were, then, the source of frequent anxiety and misery.

Within and around plantations, however, enslaved people's bodies were a hotly contested terrain of struggle. Again and again, slaves sought out illicit, secular gatherings of their own creation. They disregarded curfews and pass laws to escape to secret parties where sensual pleasures such as drinking, eating, dancing, and dressing up were the main amusements. This was the slave's third body: a thing to be claimed and enjoyed, a site of pleasure and resistance. For enslaved women, whose bodies were so central to the history of black enslavement, the third body was significant in two ways. First, women's third body was a source of pleasure, pride, and self-expression. The enormous amount of energy, time, and care that some bondwomen put into such luxuries as making and wearing fancy dress and attending illicit parties indicates how important these activities were to them. Pleasure was its own reward for those experiencing it, and it must be a part of our understanding of the lives of people in the past, even—especially—people who had precious little of it. Slaves' third body was also a political entity: it was an important symbolic and material resource in the plantation South and a fiercely contested terrain between owner and owned. Just as exploitation, containment, and punishment of the body were politically loaded acts, so, too, was slaves' enjoyment of their bodies. Far from accommodating bondage or acting as a safety valve within it, everyday somatic politics functioned in opposition to slavery's symbolic systems and economic imperatives. The nineteenth-century plantation system was a symbol for larger social relations, though, and the importance of rules of containment went beyond plantation efficiency and issues of production. The need for rules struck at the core of what it meant to be a master in the antebellum years. For slaves were more to their owners than just property, and more than just workers; they were the building blocks of planters' way of life, social mobility, and self-conceptions.[32]

THE KNOWING ONES

Bondwomen and -men who worked in the gang system, the predominant form of labor organization in the Old South, toiled hard all day almost every day of the year, with breaks only on Sundays and some holidays. "Dey wucks us from daylight till dark, an' sometimes we jist gits one meal a day," Charlie Crump said describing his slavery experience. Bondpeople in South Carolina and parts of Georgia who worked in the task system did not necessarily have to wait for the evening to end their toil, but they, like bondpeople employed in gang labor, were prohibited from leaving their home farms without a pass. Even bad weather meant only a change in routine, respite from field labor but not from plantation maintenance chores. As they worked, bondpeople, in the words of one folk song sung by women textile workers in Virginia, kept their "eyes on the sun," watching it cross the sky as the day wore long. Because "trouble don't las' always," they anticipated the end of the workday and on occasion planned illicit parties in the woods.[33]

Speaking for slaves everywhere, Charlie Crump recounted that "we ain't 'lowed ter go nowhar at night." "Dat is," he added, "if dey knowed it." In violation of the rule against leaving at night, Crump and many of the young people he knew who had worked "from daylight till dark" sometimes ventured out at night, the dark sheltering their movements. "Night is their day," one planter complained about slaves' nighttime activities.[34] Risking punishment, blacks "from all ober de neighborhood [would] gang up an' have fun anyhow." Similarly, Midge Burnett and his friends knew that "de patterollers 'ud watch all de paths leadin' frum de plantation" to prevent bondpeople from running away. What the patrollers did not know, however, was that "dar wus a number of little paths what run through de woods dat nobody ain't watched case dey ain't knowed dat de paths wus dar."[35] Many partygoers traveled to their covert events along just such paths. Some audacious men went on horseback, seeing the world from planters' viewpoint, about a yard higher than slaves' foot-borne perspective.[36]

"Yes, mam, they had dances all right," Georgian Jefferson Franklin Henry remembered. "That's how they got mixed up with paterollers. Negroes would go off to dances and stay out all night."[37] The secrecy of illicit dances demanded a high level of planning, so they were often prepared well in advance. Austin Steward and his neighbors and friends in rural Virginia were well aware of the laws and rules that prohibited enslaved people from leaving "the plantation to which they belong, without a written pass." Nonetheless, they regularly left their plantations to visit family and, sometimes, to gather for festivities. One spring the enslaved people on a nearby estate held an Easter frolic with the permission of their owner. But word of this legitimate "grand dance" quickly spread to "a large number of slaves on other plantations" who were determined to attend the event whether or not they could obtain official passes.[38] The dance now straddled legal and illegal spheres.

Meanwhile, the hosts began preparations. Theft was the main way of obtaining the goods they needed. "They *took* without saying, 'By your leave, Sir'" the food and drink they wanted, Steward wrote, "reasoning among themselves, as slaves often do, that it cannot be *stealing*, because 'it belongs to massa, and so do *we*, and we only use one part of his property to benefit another.'" The women took the ingredients and moved their owners' culinary property "from one location to another"—a relocation that also gave new values to the frolic and the food. With the ingredients in hand, women hid themselves in "valleys," swamps, and other "by-places" in order to cook

A Live Oak Avenue, from *Harper's New Monthly Magazine*, November 1859. Avenues around the plantation, the concourses of slaveholding leisure and business, branched off into smaller paths known only to enslaved people. Bondpeople used these paths to reach the secret spaces in the woods where they held outlaw slave parties. (The Library Company of Philadelphia)

in secret. "Night after night" women prepared dishes into the late hours. Then, "in the morning," they headed back to their cabins, carefully "destroying everything likely to detect them" on their way. At the same time, the "knowing ones" continued to plan the celebration, encouraging one another's high spirits "with many a wink and a nod."[39]

Finally the appointed night arrived. A little after 10:00 P.M. the music began when an "old fiddler" struck up "some favorite tune," and people danced until midnight, when it was time to feast. The food was "well cooked" and the wine was "excellent." But Steward recalled more than the events; he went to the trouble of recording the affect of the moment. Steward had written earlier that planters believed that enslaved people hobbled through life "with no hope of release this side of the grave, and as far as the cruel oppressor is concerned, shut out from hope beyond it." Yet despite—and, in part, because of—their abject poverty and the humiliations and cruelties of bondage, here at the party "every dusky face was lighted up, and every eye sparkled with joy. However ill fed they might have been, here, for once, there was plenty. Suffering and toil was forgotten, and they all seemed with one accord to give themselves up to the intoxication of pleasurable amusement." In the context of enslavement, such exhilarating pleasure gotten by illicit use of the body must be understood as important and meaningful enjoyment, as personal expression, and as oppositional engagement of the body.[40]

But there were limits to slaves' amusements. Late in the night the fiddler suddenly stopped playing and adopted "a listening attitude." Everyone became quiet, "listening for the cause of alarm." The dreaded call came when their lookout shouted, "Patrol!" and perhaps ran away from the party, a common technique to throw off patrols. If the lookout did so, he was unsuccessful. The slave patrol, whose job it was to ensure that enslaved people (in Steward's words) "know their place" and stay in it, found the party and broke it up. Many people had run away immediately after the call came, but others, including Steward, had only managed to hide and now overheard the patrolmen talking.[41]

Two of the patrolmen debated the wisdom of a few white men attempting to disband a meeting of so many bondpeople. One hesitated to push the matter, arguing that they might "resist." After all, "they have been indulging their appetites, and we cannot tell what they may attempt to do." His colleague mocked his apprehension and wondered if he was really "so chicken-hearted as to suppose that those d——d cowardly niggers are going to get up an insurrection." The first patrolman defensively clarified that he only worried that "they may forget themselves at this late hour." In these woods was a black majority made up of slaves who already had proven their lack of deference to slaveholders' authority and their willingness to break rules. While unprepared and perhaps unwilling to "get up an insurrection," they might be capable of "forgetting themselves" by challenging white authority to an incalculable extent. Indeed, in a sense they already had forgotten themselves, having abandoned "their place" in the plantation spatial and temporal order—and the "self" they had to be there.[42]

The party that Austin Steward remembered illustrates what was generally true: that the most important part of preparing a night meeting was evading slave patrols. In addition to doing their best to keep their own movements stealthy, bondpeople carefully monitored patrol activities. Appropriating, and in the process inverting, the dominant ideal of plantation surveillance, household, skilled, and personal bondpeople monitored their surveillants and sometimes learned of a patrol's plan to be in the area. These bondpeople would pass the word along in the code "dey bugs in the wheat," meaning the scheduled party had been found out. Sometimes the party was canceled; when it was not, some bondpeople would avoid the party completely, while others would attend anyway, alert and ready to leap out of windows and sprint out of sight when the patrol arrived. Revelers also protected their space by constructing borders of their own: they stretched ropes and vines across paths approaching their location to trip patrolmen and their horses, they posted lookouts at key locations along the periphery, and they stationed people "on the roads" to "create a disturbance to attract the patrollers' attention."[43] Watching a patroller fall off his tripping horse added to the night's entertainment and was "a favorite sport of slaves."[44]

Young people gathered in unoccupied cabins in the woods or simply in the open air. Occasionally, on very large plantations where barns or churches could be quite a distance from the slaveholding house, they would meet in such outbuildings or even in the quarters.[45] Typically, elderly and very young people did not attend. But there were exceptions, such as one rascally group of children who "slip[ped] off" to the place where a dance was being held and got "in de corner or up in de loft of de house an' sp[ied] on" the revelers. When the partygoers, among whom were probably many older siblings and cousins, caught the youngsters, they "thrashed us out," one former peeper recalled.[46]

Planters' habit of giving passes to men more than to women meant that women were much less likely than men to have them when attending parties. When permitted plantation frolics were expanded by local slaves, men might obtain a pass to attend, while the women who came from the neighborhood would have had to sneak away. Even wholly secret gatherings were shaped by planters' patterns of pass distribution and by enslaved men's relative mobility. A bondman named Ike returned one day late from an errand he was running for his owner because he had stopped to visit "de gals" at a neighboring plantation. The group "got up a dance," and the plantation men brought out their whiskey. Ike then "drunk too much er liquor" and needed to sober up before heading home the following day.[47] Ike and the women he called on assumed it was up to him to visit, and it was his mobility that gave the occasion for celebration. On the other hand, women who slipped away to dances were much less likely to have passes and were, therefore, more likely to be punished if caught by patrols. Patrols were a distinct threat to enslaved women, for in addition to punishing women for breaking the law, patrolmen

A Negro Funeral, from *Harper's New Monthly Magazine*, November 1859. It was in the remote spaces in the woods bordering plantations that enslaved people gathered for funerals, religious services, and secret, secular parties. (The Library Company of Philadelphia)

were known to abuse women. Samuel Hall could recall how patrols "would come to our place of enjoyment and drive and whip the husbands away from the wives and use those same women for their own pleasure."[48] When they attended covert festivities, women more frequently did so without any form of permission, and they undertook enormous risks.

Men musicians performed for their friends and neighbors, playing fiddles, banjos, and tambourines. They also made their own instruments, such as the popular "quill" devised in places where sugar was grown. Five to ten cane stems were cut to different lengths, a hole was drilled in the top of each, and all were bound together to make a homemade harmonica. Musicians im-

The Country Church, from *Harper's New Monthly Magazine*, November 1859. Deep in some woods were abandoned or unoccupied church buildings, old barns, and other outbuildings, like this one. Enslaved people occasionally used these structures to hold outlaw parties. (The Library Company of Philadelphia)

provised melody-making instruments from reeds and handsaws and created percussion with spoons, bones, pans, and buckets to play "Turkey in the Straw" and other popular tunes.[49] When no musicians were available, and even when they were, outlaw partygoers made music with their voices, singing and dancing to lyrics sure to amuse. According to Dosia Harris, one went "somepin lak dis:"

> Oh! Miss Liza, Miss Liza Jane!
> Axed Miss Liza to marry me
> Guess what she said?
> She wouldn't marry me,
> If de last Nigger was dead.[50]

Dancers also sang, perhaps gloatingly, of their subterfuge:

> Buffalo gals, can't you come out tonight,
> Come out tonight, an' dance by the light of the moon?[51]

As morning approached, those who had caroused the night away warned one another of the approach of day and the danger of violating that temporal boundary (which located them properly at work): "Run nigger run, patty-rollers ketch you / Run nigger run, it's breakin' days."[52]

A variant elaborated:

> Run nigger run, de patterrollers ketch you—
> Run nigger run, fer hits almos' day,
> De nigger run; de nigger flew; de nigger los'
>   his big ole shoe.[53]

Dance tunes contained political meanings as well as entertainment value. The self-deprecating song about a rejected lover is one example: the object of affection is called by a title, "Miss," a sign of respect that whites denied bondpeople. Many of these songs were sung at plantation frolics under slaveholders' supervision, and no doubt planters and their friends found them entertaining. Indeed, most aspects of illegal parties paralleled the goings-on at plantation frolics; many of the songs, the tunes, the dances, and other activities were identical. But not all were; some songs were surely not sung in the presence of owners. Mississippian Mollie Williams danced to and sang the following song, which is inflected by the spirit of resistance nurtured at outlaw parties:

> Run tell Coleman,
> Run tell everbody
> Dat de niggers is arisin'![54]

Together, women and men performed a variety of period dances. Many formerly enslaved people described the dances of their youth as proper and respectable, as not "all hugged up." Consistent with African kinesic morality, slave dancers commonly rejected embracing as immodest and even "indecent."[55] When she was young, Liza Mention said, "dances in dem days warn't dese here huggin' kind of dances lak dey has now" but were, instead, proper dances, like "de cardrille (quadrille), de Virginia reel, and de 16-hand Cortillion."[56] To the tunes produced by fiddles, voices, banjos, and flutes, they danced respectably (without "man an woman squeezed up close to one another"), performing such dances as "pigeon wing" (flapping the arms like a bird and wiggling the legs while "holdin' yo' neck stiff like a bird do"); "gwine to de east, an' gwine to de west" (leaning in to kiss one's dance partner on each cheek but "widout wrappin' no arms roun' like de young folks today"); "callin' de figgers" (following the fiddler's challenging calls); and "hack-back" (in which couples stood facing each other and "trotted back and forth"). Other dances included "set de flo'" (partners began by bowing to each other at the waist, hands on the waist, then the dancers tap-danced, patting the floor firmly "jus' like dey puttin' it in place"); "dancin' on the spot" (the same as "set de flo'" except dancers had to remain within the circumference of a circle drawn in the ground); "wringin' and twistin'" (the early version of the "twist"); the "buzzard lope"; "snakehips"; and the "breakdown."[57] Enslaved dancers also "watched white folks' parties where the guests danced a minuet and then paraded in a grand march." Then they imitated white dancers, but with a twist: "We'd do it too, *but we used to mock 'em*, every step."[58]

Competition was a common form of amusement at outlaw dances, one that sometimes forged camaraderie among equals. To win a dance competition, one had to expertly execute complex dance moves while maintaining an outward demeanor of "control and coolness," dance historian Katrina Hazzard-Gordon has written. For example, Nancy Williams competed with another woman, Jennie, to see who could perform a dance the most deftly and with the most mastery of her body. To make the challenge even greater, the women danced with glasses of water on their heads; the winner was she who maintained her cool and made the execution of the dance look easy. Dance competition allowed some women to demonstrate the strength and agility of their bodies, as compared with men's, whose physical power was usually recognized as greater. Jane Smith Hill Harmon "allus could dance" and enjoyed, even as an old woman, "cut[ting] fancy steps now sometimes when I feels good." Her talent was awe inspiring when she was young, and she regularly competed with men. "One night when I wuz young, I danced down seben big strong mens, dey thought dey wuz sumpin'! Hun, I danced eb'ry one down!"[59] Dance competition could provide women moments of relief from black gender hierarchies as well as from slaveholding control.

The uglier side of competition, violence, must have been an issue at outlawed gatherings, although extremely little documentation describes it. Still, violence existed in other parts of slave life. Enslaved families, like free ones, were home to resentments, betrayals, anger, and other disappointments of family life. Physical and verbal abuse between spouses, especially by men against women, was a part of life in the quarters. Hoping to prevent his wife from attending a holiday celebration their owner was giving them, one bondman "gave his wife Hetty a light cut or two & then locked her up to prevent her going to the Frollick." As owners sometimes did, theirs intervened, "turning her loose & fastning him."[60] James Cornelius, who had been enslaved in Mississippi, openly told of the time he hit his wife. During their marriage ceremony, Cornelius had interrupted the preacher to make his wife promise never to accuse him of lying. She promised, and Cornelius reciprocated and pronounced the exchange a "bargain an' den de preacher went on wid de weddin'." Years later his wife was suspicious about his whereabouts one evening, and when his excuse failed to convince her, she told him, "that's a lie." Cornelius responded in the manner he viewed as appropriate: "right den I raised my han' an' let her have it right by de side of de head, an' she niver called me a liar ag'in. No ma'm, dat is somethin' I won't stand for." While rates of domestic violence may have changed in the transition from slavery to freedom, such incidents as these were certainly not new. Moreover, Cornelius learned from multiple sources that it was his manly prerogative to violently enforce the rules of his marriage, and a major influence on his conception of domestic life must have been his own (enslaved) family. Domestic violence was a source of both comedy and moral judgment in the folk song "Old Dan Tucker," in which Tucker, a "mighty mean" man who "beat his wife wid a fryin' pan," ends up falling down drunk onto the "red hot" coals of an (earthly) fire.[61]

Violence was also a common part of drinking culture among both whites and blacks, and it certainly was a side effect of a drinking problem. In particular, men's drinking must have created some difficulties for bondwomen. In one extreme case a bondman named Isaac, who was "often intoxicated," got into the "habit of visiting" an enslaved woman named Charlotte around the kitchen where she worked. His attention seems to have been unwelcome, as at one point, perhaps in retaliation for her rejection of him, Isaac "threatened to murder" her. Mrs. Taylor Clay, who owned Charlotte, called in the county authorities, who then ordered the sheriff to arrest Isaac. Though officials were aware only of the "constant fear and dread" that Clay felt, we may be sure that Charlotte was more than equally terrified by Isaac's threats.[62] It is difficult to imagine that violence, an element of life in the quarters, did not occur among men and between men and women at outlawed parties.

But violence was not solely a male form of expression or conflict resolution. Women, too, communicated frustration and anger physically. A woman named Jane had a "terrible row" with a household slave named Lucy during which she delivered a "blow from a chair." Needless to say, that blow "cut a great gash in Lucy's face" and "hurt her severely." Whatever the root of the conflict between Jane and Lucy, the end result was a real "scene of horror": the "quarreling and screaming, the blood streaming down Lucy's face, and

Jane's fiery looks and speeches" all testify to some enslaved women's capacity for gruesome fighting.[63] Sometimes outlaw slave parties gave space for the continuation of rivalries or the end of festering arguments between women who were not always, or even often, motivated by feelings of honorable competition between equals. During one affair two women, Rita and Retta, misunderstood "Aunt" Vira's laughter as directed at them; they punished the offender by poisoning her and her infant.[64]

A DRESS FOR THE 'OMAN

While women and men danced together, they also had slightly different ideas about other enjoyable activities. More than men, women had clothing on their minds when they headed, under cover of night, for secret frolics.[65] For their part, men were much more inclined to drink alcohol. It was not commonplace for bondpeople to have many sets of fancy attire, or even multiple sets of ordinary work clothing. But some enslaved people, especially women, worked hard to piece together one special outfit that could be worn on Sundays and special occasions, such as church meetings, weddings, funerals, plantation frolics, or secret parties. The scarcity of fancy clothing underscores the importance and the value that women seem to have given it, for it is important to analyze "clothing behavior" as well as clothing itself.[66] Bondwomen pushed themselves to stay up late when they were tired and to direct some of their extremely limited resources toward dress and style.

When at work, when their bodies were in the service of their owners, bondpeople looked, according to one observer, "very ragged and slovenly." Planters dressed slaves in clothing of the poorest quality made of fabric reserved for those of their station. In the summer, enslaved people wore tow, a material made from rough, unprocessed flax, or uncolored white or gray cotton. Many women's dresses were straight and shapeless, stintingly cut, sometimes directly on the body, to avoid wasting fabric. Charity McCallister's clothes were "poor. One-piece dress made o' carpet stuff, part of de time." Others' were cut fuller and tapered at the waist, and most dresses were long. Fannie Dunn disagreed with her mother's assessment of conditions under slavery in North Carolina on the basis of the clothes she was forced to wear: "My mother said dat we all fared good, but course we wore handmade clothes an' wooden bottomed shoes."[67] Slaves' crude clothing, along with their gestures, posture, and language, let the world know what their place in society was.

Some planters, as part of their system of rule, annually or biannually distributed clothes with dramatic flair in order to represent themselves as the benevolent source of care and sustenance and thereby instill loyalty in their bondpeople. Many other plantations were characterized more by slaveholding neglect and avarice than by paternalistic management systems; on such farms, slave owners gave little thought to enslaved people's physical conditions. Year after year, for example, plantation manager Roswell King implored his employer, Pierce Butler, who lived in Philadelphia, to provide his bondpeople with clothing. King subscribed to the paternalist school's combination of cruel violence, stern order, and benevolent encouragement of disciplined behavior, but he could not find an ally in Butler. "Do you recollect," King wrote Butler on one occasion, "that you have not given your Negroes Summer clothing but twice in fifteen years past?" It was only due to the work Butler's bondpeople did "for themselves" on "what is called their own time" that they were able to "git a little Summer clothing, a piece of meat, a pound of sugar or Coffee &c."[68] Old, torn, shredded, and dirty clothing resulted in more than saved costs for slave owners; it had social effects. Poor-quality attire reflected and reified slaves' status and played a role in their subjugation. Former bondwoman Harriet Jacobs wrote bitterly in her narrative of life as a bondwoman that the "linsey-woolsey dress given me every winter" by her mistress was "one of the badges of slavery."[69]

Another badge of slavery was the androgynous appearance imposed on some bondwomen by work and dress. While many women performed gender-specific work in the fields as well as in black and white households, many other bondwomen slaved away at grueling chores that seemed little different from men's work. With a mixture of pride and bitterness, Anne Clark recalled that during her life in bondage she had "ploughed, hoed, split rails. I done the hardest work a man ever did." "Women worked in de field same as de men. Some of dem plowed jes' like de men and boys," George Fleming recalled. Fleming claimed that the women he knew even resembled men in the fields; he "couldn't tell 'em apart in de field, as dey wore pantelets or breeches."[70]

Conversely, when bondpeople, especially women, outfitted themselves for their own occasions, they went to a great deal of trouble to procure or make clothes of quality and, importantly, style. For church some preferred simple white clothing, while others enjoyed something fancier. Certainly secular meetings encouraged attention to ornament. Some women exchanged homespun goods, produce from their gardens, and pelts with white itinerant traders for good-quality or decorative cloth, beads, and buttons. While enslaved South Carolinians had an especially independent economy, some slaves throughout the South engaged in selling or trading that enabled them to obtain goods such as cloth, clothing, and dye.[71] Enslaved women located near ports or major waterways were able to trade with black boat workers, who carried on a lively exchange with the plantation bond-people they encountered in their travels. Even inland, women traded the produce of their gardens, their hens' eggs, the berries they picked, and their handiwork such as baskets and animal skins for items like calico, decorative cloth, kerchiefs, or ornamental objects such as buttons. In distinction to their "ragged and slovenly" appearance at work, some of the enslaved Virginia women that traveler Frederick Law Olmsted encountered were able to "look very smart" on their own time, dressed in a few items that they had "pur-chased . . . for themselves." Women also occasionally earned fancy clothing as a reward for exceptional work. Some planters were aware of bondpeople's preferred treats and rewarded men and women with different prizes at harvest celebrations: "a quart of whiskey for de man what picked de most and a dress for de 'oman what was ahead."[72]

Most women, however, procured fancy apparel—when they could at all—simply by eking out time at night to make it. They grew and processed the cotton, cultivated and gathered the roots and berries for the dye, wove the cloth, and sewed textiles into garments. Women, whose bodies were subject to sexual exploitation, dangerous and potentially heartbreaking reproductive labor, and physically demanding agricultural labor, worked hard to bring personal expression and delight into their lives. Women wove and dyed color, patterns, and designs into their clothing. "Aunt" Adeline was, like her mother had been, an accomplished dyer. On one occasion she wore a dress that she would never forget "as long as I live. It was a hickory stripe dress they made for me, with brass buttons at the wrist bands." She was "so proud of that dress"; her identity refashioned by it, she "felt so dressed up in it, I just strutted!" Tree barks, bamboo, and poison ivy were used to make dyes of yellow, red, brown, and black.[73] Women in Georgia and South Caro-lina raised indigo for dye, and women outside those areas sometimes bought indigo dye.[74] Women set the colors fast in their cloth with saline solu-tions, vinegar and water, or "chamber lye" (urine). They hung the fabric on clotheslines to dry and then sewed it into garments.[75] None of this was easy work, and the time and resources for it were not easily found. "Patterns wus a GREAT trubble," Clara Allen remembered.

In addition to the symbolic value dress held for plantation blacks and whites, clothing held more tangible meanings as well. The production, dis-tribution, and uses of King Cotton—and cotton products such as apparel—were very material issues in the slave South. Textile production complicated the plantation's temporal order along gender lines. The nighttime was less neatly "off" time for bondwomen than it was for men. While both women and men could quit working for their owners at sunset, many women began their second shift of labor, their nightly toil for their families. At night and sometimes on Saturdays or Sundays, after agricultural work was done, women had another set of labor to do for their own families. Henry James Trentham saw women plowing during the day, working hard to "carry dat row an' keep up wid de men," quit at sunset, "an den do dere cookin' at night."[76] To be sure, men also worked for their families' benefit after work in the field or around the plantation was done; they hunted, fished, gardened, and taught their children these skills in the "off" hours. Nonetheless, women generally performed more work during their second shift. Most bondwomen returned to their quarters at sundown to cook supper, hoping to make enough for the next day's lunch; to clean their cabins; to produce household goods, such as soap and candles; to work in their gardens; and also to wash and mend their own and their family's clothing. In their off time and during the winters, women were also responsible for the production of some or all of the textiles that plantation residents needed, including apparel for the slaves and cloth for jackets, blankets, linens.[77]

Elite planters enjoyed store-bought goods, and only on the South's largest plantations was textile production concentrated in the hands of women specialists such as weavers, seamstresses, and knitters.[78] A prosperous farm might boast a spinning room in which women carded cotton and wool, spun fibers into thread, dyed the thread, and then wove it into fabric and woolens for plantation use.[79] Though such labor was sedentary and considered "women's work" (light and unskilled), it was physically taxing. The work required extremely long hours of constant repetitive motion well beyond the setting of the sun. Weaving engaged the whole body, compelling arms and hands, which carried the shuttle between the warp threads, to coordinate with the efforts of legs and feet, which worked the pedals in rhythm with the movement of the shuttle. Anna Mitchell's mother told her about the grueling nature of a seamstress's work: she labored "all night an' half de day ter make clothes for de slaves."[80] The volume of production could be dizzying. In one day Elizabeth Coles delivered to Nancy, one of her spinners, 14 pounds of cotton and 28 pounds of wool to be spun into thread and yarn. Coles then presented "Old Buffy" with 30 pounds of wool and 110 pounds of cotton to spin. Another bondwoman, "Saly," would knit their yarn into clothing. This volume left its mark on women's bodies; as one woman knitter aged, her finger gnarled into a "twisted an' stiff" appendage—the embodiment of a life spent at work, "holdin' her knittin' needles."[81]

But on most plantations, many women, not only specialists, were involved in this work, and they produced at least some goods for their owners' as well as slaves' use. Especially during the winters, women were responsible for some to all of the production of textiles for plantation residents, black and white.[82] On most plantations the winter season greeted women with production quotas demanding that they "card, reel and spin" one or two "cuts" (about ninety-one inches of thread) per night.[83] Assisted perhaps by a fatigued child who could hold a candle to provide light or card rolls of cotton or wool before adult women spun it,[84] bondwomen then had to weave the thread into cloth and sew the cloth into clothing, or knit the yarn into usable goods. In Bill Collins's experience, "older slave women" spun the material that was made into "pants and shirts" for plantation blacks. "They did most of this at night" as well as during the winter months. Some of them had to work in the "fields all day and spin at night."[85] Bondwomen resented the extra labor. Georgianna Foster's mother used to complain that "women had to work all day in de fields an' come home an' do de house work at night while de white folks hardly done a han's turn of work." Frequently, bondwomen did not experience plantation time in the same ways men did, in large part because of the second shift of reproductive labor they performed.[86]

Enslaved women's second shift of labor, however, presented the opportunity for self-expression. Just as bondwomen made creative work of quilt making, they spent some of their evenings turning the plain, uncolored tow, denim, hemp, burlap, and cotton cloth they had woven into fancy, decorative cloth. Robert Shepherd remembered his mother's handiwork: "Everything was stripedy 'cause Mammy liked to make it fancy." Catherine Slim's mother, a talented weaver, wove stripes of red, white, and blue as well as flowers into the cloth that she then sewed into dresses for her daughter. Women dyed the coarse material allotted them colors they liked. Nancy Williams's dedication to style was unusual, but it remains instructive. "Clo'es chile? I had plenty clo'es dem days," she claimed. "How I get 'em? Jes' change dey colors. Took my white dress out to de polk berry bush an' a-dyed it red, den dyed my shoes red. Took ole barn paint an' paint some mo' shoes yaller to match my yaller dress."[87]

Once they had the fabric, enslaved women went to great effort to make themselves something more than the cheap, straight-cut dresses they were allowanced. When possible, women cut their dresses generously so they could sweep their skirts dramatically and elegantly. Some women accentuated the fullness of their skirts by starching them crisp. Annie Wallace remembered that when her mother went "out at night to a party some of the colored folks was havin'" she would starch her skirts with "hominy water. . . . They were starched so stiff that every time you stopped they would pop real loud." Wallace's mother instructed her children to listen carefully for her return, in case the party was broken up by the arrival of Virginia's rural patrols. "When we heard them petticoats apoppin' as she run down the path, we'd open the door wide and she would get away from the patterroll."[88]

Other women "thought those hoops were just the thing for style" and hooped their skirts with grapevines and "limbs from trees." Though Salena Taswell's owner "would not let the servants wear hoops," Taswell and the other household bondwomen often sneaked to "get the old ones that they threw away." Secretly they "would go around with them on when they were gone and couldn't see us." Hoopskirts came into fashion during the 1850s and stayed in style through the mid-nineteenth century, coinciding with the cult of domesticity. Among the elite women who wore them, hoopskirts symbolized "Victorian ideals of domesticity and . . . of a separate woman's sphere," Drew Gilpin Faust has suggested. The style flaunted high levels of consumption and idleness (the wide skirts made physical labor tricky), and consistent with Victorian ideals of respectable womanhood, the hoopskirt hid the lower body. No doubt bondwomen's frocks were smaller than their owners', whose skirts could measure up to five feet in diameter. Nonetheless, Ebeneezer Brown told his interviewer, hoopskirts were "the fad in those days" among black as well as white women, one that enabled bondwomen to appropriate a symbol of leisure and femininity (and freedom) and denaturalized their slave status. "In dem days de wimen wore hoops. . . . De white folks dun it an' so did the slave wimen," Brown said.[89] Enslaved women liked the luxury of abundance, the elegant feel of "wide hoop-skirts, fluffy sleeves and high collars."[90] As much as women's bodies were sources of suffering and sites of planter domination, women also worked hard to make their bodies spaces of personal expression and pleasure. If, as it has been said, dress reflects something about the perceptions people have of their place in the world, then it would appear that many bondwomen did not concur with the Old South's view of them as joyless drudges.[91]

If it is also true that "relations become embodied in things," then women's outfits hinted at a distinctive understanding of social relations.[92] Women's style allowed them to take pleasure in their bodies, to deny that they were only (or mainly) worth the prices their owners placed on them. But not all enslaved people agreed that such self-regard was justified. When a young slave girl named Amelia walked out of her house on her way to church in the hoopskirt she adored, to her mortification the other children "laugh[ed] at me" and accused her of "playin' lady," of affecting a status to which she had no right. She was so hurt by their mockery that she ran back into the house, took off the offending skirt, "and hide it in the wood."[93] Violation of the Old South's racial etiquette was not uniformly appreciated by all bondpeople, old or young.

Yet black women's style did not simply mimic slaveholding women's fashions. Enslaved women's use of accessories most accentuated their originality. Topping off many women's outfits were their headwraps, a unique expressive form in nineteenth-century America, or hair done just so. Some women wore their favorite headwraps to outlaw parties, and many others removed the scarf to display the hairstyle under it: cornrows, plaits, straightened hair, or tidy Afros. Women straightened or relaxed their curls by "wrapping" sections of their hair in string, twine, or bits of cloth and covering it during the week with a scarf to hide the wrappings and to keep their hair clean and protect it from the sun's harsh rays. On special occasions, such as church or a dance, they removed the scarf and the strings to reveal hair that was straightened or in looser curls.[94]

Beyond the headwrap, other accessories were more difficult to obtain but nonetheless not skimped on. Some women made straw hats from "wheat straw which was dried out." They made buttons and ornaments for their clothing out of "cows and rams horns" and from "li'll round pieces of gourds" covered with cloth.[95] Inspired women used buttons, shells, and animal horns to decorate their clothing. And earrings could be made from something as simple and plentiful as straw.[96] They made necklaces from dried, painted cranberries and perfumed themselves by wearing rose and honeysuckle flowers.[97] When Frances Kemble moved to a Georgia plantation after her marriage to a wealthy planter, she was struck by the women's style, which combined elements that seemed discordant to Kemble. She described what she saw in prim, racialist detail: "Their Sabbath toilet really presents the most ludicrous combination of incongruities that you can conceive—frills, flounces, ribbons; combs stuck in their wooly heads . . . , finery, every color of the rainbow . . . chinzes with sprawling patterns . . . ; beads, bugles, flaring sashes, and above all, little fanciful aprons, which finish these incongruous toilets with a sort of airy grace, which I assure you is perfectly indescribable."[98] The clash of colors and textures and the mixture of formal and informal elements (finery, chintzes, and ribbons worn with aprons) that flabbergasted Kemble and a great many other whites delighted enslaved women. At least since the eighteenth century, with roots in African visual arts, black style had distinctively stressed the dynamic interplay of color and texture over the harmonies of similar elements, and surprise, movement, and argument over predictable patterns and order.[99]

Shoes posed a special problem. Many bondpeople wore no shoes at all during the warm months and received wooden "brogans" against the cold only once a year. On some farms women received footwear even more infrequently. Perhaps because their agricultural labor was denigrated as "women's work" and therefore considered easier, some women received no shoes at all. Skilled men and drivers might sometimes receive their owners' castoff work-boots, but women had much less access to such practical footwear. W. L. Bost was appalled at the hardships women faced, especially their inadequate dress in cold weather: "They never had enough clothes on to keep a cat warm. The women never wore anything but a thin dress and a petticoat and one under-wear. I've seen the ice balls hangin' on the bottom of their dresses as they ran along, jes like sheep in a pasture 'fore they are sheared. They never wore shoes."[100] Henry James Trentham was also sympathetic to the hard-ships women slaves faced. "Some of de women plowed barefooted most all de time."[101]

Women's creation and appropriation of cloth and clothing helped them to express their personalities and their senses of style, but their attire also raised material issues. In their uses of dress, women claimed the product of their labor: they took the cotton that they raised and harvested and used it for their own purposes. "How I get 'em?" Nancy Williams was pleased with her inter-viewer's question and eager to tell of her ingenuity. In addition to dyeing her rations of plain cloth, Williams stole what she needed. Williams pilfered paint to make yellow shoes to go with the yellow dress she wore to an illicit dance held in a cabin in the woods. "Had done stole de paint and paint de shoes color de dress."[102]

Similarly, Mary Wyatt's Virginia owner had a dress that Wyatt adored. "Lawdy, I used to take dat dress when she warn't nowhere roun' an' hole it up against me an' 'magine myself wearin' it." One Christmas season Wyatt de-cided to wear the dress to a plantation frolic. "De debbil got in me good. Got dat gown out de house 'neath my petticoat tied round me an' wore it to de dance." Donning the fancy dress of her mistress, Wyatt shed the most out-ward markers of her slave status and adopted instead a symbol of freedom. Like other women who reappropriated their owners' clothing for outlawed or for plantation parties, when Mary Wyatt stole her owner's frock, she committed not only a symbolic transgression of place, by "'magin[ing]" herself in the dress, which was made of a design and material reserved for the free white women who could afford it, but an act of material consequence. She reclaimed the product of her own labor. She had picked the cotton, and women like her had processed it and made it into a dress; the institution of slavery made the dress her owner's, but Mary Wyatt made it hers. In Wyatt's case, the act of reappropriation was limited temporally. She returned the dress, putting it "back in place de nex' day." The terror that gripped her while she stole and wore the dress reveals the fearsomeness of her owners, and it also reveals the strength of her commitment to wearing it. Bondwomen took tremendous risks in procuring and wearing fancy apparel to plantation frolics and outlawed slave parties, and the extent of the danger to which they exposed themselves is also a measure of the significance of activities and interests that might otherwise appear to be trivial.[103]

By dressing up to go to outlaw parties, bondwomen heightened the risk they undertook, because their conspicuousness exposed all of them (especially household bondwomen) to detection. The degree of danger involved in dressing up and running away for an evening and women's willingness to take it suggest just how urgently they needed to extricate themselves from their proper places. Frances Miller, a slaveholding woman, encountered such determination as she endeavored to impose a "system of management" within her Virginia household. She rose at 4:30 every morning, in advance of her bondpeople, to wake them and prod them to work, not shying from physical violence when their "insubordination" proved too much for her. Miller dedicated herself, in what she described as a "herculean" manner, to "always righting things up." Her bondpeople, with the exception of the two men Miller used to discipline the others, refused to submit to her desire for mastery. Thanks to the "open rebellion, impudence and unfaithfulness of domestics," things were "never righted" in her household.[104]

Among the most egregious acts of "unfaithfulness" and "insubordination" that Miller witnessed in her household was the determination of one bondwoman, Rose, to sneak away at night to a party. On her way to bed one night, Miller encountered Rose on her way out of the house, "dressed up as I supposed for a night's jaunt." Caught, Rose thought quickly and, thrusting the candle she held to light her passage toward Miller, asked Miller to carry it back for her. Miller had been hardened by Rose's long history of disobedience and was not distracted from the issue at hand. She sarcastically "asked her why she did not do it herself," and Rose claimed that "she was going to wash." Rose's explanation for still being up and heading out when, according to the late hour, she ought to have been in bed in her room was not convincing. Miller could tell by the way Rose was "dressed so spry" that she was not going to wash and so "didn't believe her." Instead, she reminded Rose of her curfew and of where she ought to be, observing the hour and telling her "it was bedtime and she must go directly upstairs." Rose "refused" and remained determined to go out to "wash." Rose's plans were thwarted only when Miller "shut the door and locked it." With no key, Rose could not get out. Angered that she would now miss the party, Rose insulted Miller, telling her "that I was the most contrary old thing that she ever saw."[105]

As punishment for attempting to disobey the house rules, as well as for her effrontery, Miller told Rose that she was going to flog her, prompting Rose to assert that she "would not submit to any such thing and that she would go to the woods first." Rose's threats were not idle, as she rarely submitted to whippings without a huge struggle involving two enslaved men and a great deal of time. On this occasion, however, perhaps because she was so disappointed about being caught and prevented from going out, Rose did not carry out her threat and instead "yielded with less difficulty than usual" to the bondman William's "switches." Miller succeeded in stopping Rose from leaving the household, but the incident left her "sorely grieved—sorely." She was frustrated "that the necessity had existed" to whip Rose because Rose had not simply obeyed. Rose's transgression of place mandated, to Miller's mind, the deployment of violence, violence that contradicted Miller's ideal of a mastery so effective as not to warrant its explicit use in the first place.[106]

THE GOOD DRINK

The antebellum years saw a general decline in rates of alcohol consumption from the national binge of the Revolutionary era. Like the free people around them, enslaved people probably drank less than they had in the early eighteenth century, when spirits were considered good for health, strength, and relaxation, and less, too, than in the second half of the eighteenth century, when liquors were produced more cheaply and were therefore consumed in greater quantities.[107] Of course, this is not to say that bondpeople were unable to procure alcohol, for to the great consternation of their owners, they did manage to trade for it illegally with cooperative white shopkeepers and poor whites (including white prostitutes) in the rural areas and with the free blacks who owned the occasional cookshop, grocery, or grogshop in towns and cities.[108] The sellers of such items were among the few whites to be included in the transportation of goods around the rival geography.

While women typically enjoyed dress more than drink, some did partake of whiskeys or brandies when they could get them. When Caroline Hunter and her husband Elbert Hunter found a bottle of whiskey by chance, it was Caroline who suggested drinking it, and Caroline who held her alcohol better. Elbert became "wobbly in the knees" and soon passed out.[109] Lucy Mc-Cullough also liked to drink—enough that when she was charged with bringing a "quart er brandy" to a group of men working outdoors one winter, she warmed herself along the way by "sippin' dat brandy." By the time she found the men, she was "crazy drunk en tryin' ter sing"; the men were furious with her and roughed her up for consuming the brandy that would have mellowed the bitter chill.[110]

Likewise, bondwomen were also involved in procuring alcohol for those who drank it.[111] Household bondwomen were aptly positioned to act as pivots between planters' households and wider networks of enslaved people. James Henry Hammond discovered what he called a "system of roguery," a coordinated and "long" effort involving Urana, "our house woman," who "gave the key" to Hammond's "wine cellar" to Frank, another household "servant." Frank and a bondman named Abram "dug under" the house and ferreted out "wines & other spirits, corn, glass, meats &c." Urana further assisted them by doing "her conjurations" and " 'root work,' " which together "screened" the men from detection. Hammond "punished all that have had any thing to do with the matter" or with the other "depredations" that he had recently "brought to light."[112] Similarly, during one of their owner's trips away from home, household bondwomen Jane and Lavenia "broke into" the storeroom for some of "the good drink"; they "helped themselves verry Liberally to everything" and shared the spoils with their friends. When their owner returned and learned of their offense, he "Whiped" them "worse than I ever Whiped any one before."[113]

On some plantations the production of ciders and brandies was women's work. At the end of the rice harvest, Charles Ball reported, while most women and men cleared the rice lands, a group of twenty or thirty people, "principally women and children," were put to work for two weeks "in making cider of apples which grew . . . in an orchard on part of the estate." The cider was "converted into brandy, at a still in the corner of the orchard."[114] Sylvia DuBois knew the nooks of her owner's home well—including the whereabouts of "one keg of brandy that I knew was made very good, for I helped make it." DuBois made the most of her insider knowledge on the night of a housewarming party her owners held. At the arranged time, DuBois and a friend met and went to the storeroom where the apple and peach brandy was kept to "see if it had kept well." The pair had forgotten to bring cups, and they drank from an "earthen pot" they found in the storage room, a choice that encouraged them to drink "all we could" and then, not wanting to throw the remains in the bowl away ("that looked too wasteful"), to drink still more. By night's end, more of DuBois's friends had to find her and help "put her to bed."[115] Household bondwomen and women who made liquors would have been instrumental in procuring alcohol for consumption at slaves' illicit parties.

Enslaved women and men who sneaked off to parties to stay up late amusing themselves and perhaps fighting returned exhausted from their exertions, and morning-after tardiness and fatigue in the field were not uncommon. Even churchgoers knew the feeling. Religious congregants sometimes stayed up late worshiping and would be "sho tired" the next day. Charlie Tye Smith recalled how, no matter how late they had been up the night before, bond-people "had better turn out at four o'clock when ole Marse blowed the horn!" They dragged themselves through the motions of their chores all morning and at lunchtime collapsed in the field, too tired to eat. Those who had not attended the meeting looked upon a field "strowed with Niggers asleep in the cotton rows" until the midday break ended and they all resumed work.[116]

Instead of resting in preparation for the next day's labor, women stayed up late preparing their fancy dress for parties, they danced the night away, and some drank alcohol with the men.[117] Some planters suspected that enslaved people kept some of their energy back during the day in anticipation of better uses at night. Frederick Law Olmsted agreed with those suspicions, noting that bondpeople sometimes seemed "to go through the motions of labour without putting their strength into them. They keep their power in reserve for their own use at night, perhaps."[118] Jefferson Franklin Henry remembered how other bondpeople, but not he, "would go off to dances and stay out all night; it would be wuk time when they got back." These revelers valiantly "tried to keep right on gwine," but they were worn out; "the Good Lord soon cut 'em down." These mornings-after did not inhibit future parties, how-ever, nor did the Christian objections of other slaves make an impact: "You couldn't talk to folks that tried to git by with things lak that," Henry regretted. "They warn't gwine to do no diffunt, nohow."[119] People like that made one think of the song "Poor Sinner":

> Head got wet with midnight dew,
>> What you goin' to do when your lamp burns down?
> Morning star was witness, too,
>> What you goin' to do when your lamp burns down?[120]

A SERPENT GNAWING

"Upon ringing my bell" to summon his slaves one evening, Richard Eppes discovered that his "servants" were "all absent." This was not the first time. "The absence of the negroes at night from their houses has become intoler-able and finding that talking and threatening had no effect I was resolved to put a stop to it by administering in full effect our plantation laws." Whether for religious or secular meetings, or for separate informal reasons, the de-partures of Eppes's slaves were not viewed by him as just another part of plantation life. They had reached an "intolerable" level and now prompted the full implementation of Eppes's enforcement measures. How slaveholders regarded the nighttime activities of their bondpeople matters a great deal, for their responses reveal some of the significance of these activities in their own time.

An extraordinary document survives that articulates not the "success" of slave resistance using the body but, given the extent to which the body was a point of conflict between slaves and their owners, what meanings the latter group gave to that conflict. In the mid-1840s slaveholders in the Edgefield and Barnwell Districts of South Carolina formed the Savannah River Anti–Slave Traffick Association in an attempt to stop disorderly house owners' practice of selling alcohol to bondpeople. The group's published regulations expressed anxiety about slave drinking and the theft and black-marketing bondpeople engaged in to obtain liquor from obliging non-elite whites. One result, the Savannah River neighbors jointly thought, was "very considerable losses." Bondwomen and -men—like association member James Henry Hammond's own Urana—appropriated property from their owners by breaking into "dwelling houses, barns, stables, smoke houses, &c" and by using "false keys which abound among our negroes" or by "pick[ing locks] with instruments at which they have become very skilful" at crafting and using. Moreover, the neighbors complained that their crops were susceptible to theft: "Not content with plundering from Barns, our standing crops are beginning to suffer depredation." Because of these various activities, local slaveholders thought they had noticed their profits decline. "Once when a Farmer has expected to sell largely, he finds himself compelled to use the most stringent economy to make his provisions meet his own wants, and sometimes has actually to buy."[121]

Slaves' trading, stealing, and drinking were not the only "evils" worrying these South Carolina planters. Equally vexatious was the practice of "prowling" off to "night meetings." Because of the "too great negligence of slave owners in maintaining wholesome discipline" every night, or so it seemed, bondpeople could be found sneaking "abroad to night meetings." The association claimed that "hundreds of negroes it may be said without exaggeration are every night, and at all hours of the night, prowling about the country," stealing, trading, drinking, and meeting, almost certainly for secular affairs.[122] The association weighed heavily the financial loss incurred when enslaved people were too hungover and too tired to work efficiently: "The negroes themselves are seriously impaired in physical qualities." The association's regulations further detailed that "their nightly expeditions are followed by days of languor." Seeing their "owners, and especially their overseers, as unjust and unfeeling oppressors," slaves, it seemed to these South Carolinians, responded with insubordination and work characterized by "sullenness [and] discontent."[123]

The Savannah River neighbors were mobilized to action by what they saw as a second pernicious effect of black nightly "prowling." In addition to the damage nightly pleasures had on productivity, the South Carolina neighbors complained of the corrosion of slaveholding mastery. Black "minds are fatally corrupted" by these nighttime activities, these planters believed. In the revisionist history that the association wrote, bondpeople were "beginning to" dissent from the paternalist contract that supposedly governed their estates. "Formerly Slaves were essentially members of the family to which they belonged, and a reciprocal interest and attachment existing between them, their relations were simple, agreeable, easily maintained, and mutually beneficial." It seemed that the freedom bondpeople tasted at night compromised their willingness to be deferential and obedient during the day. The association complained of the "difficulty in managing" slaves, since night activity appeared to encourage many bondpeople to see their "Masters" as their "natural enemies." This egalitarian perspective—hardly unique among slaves in the Americas—facilitated more disorderly behavior, and the members of the Savannah River organization were forced to admit to one another that they were having trouble "preserving proper subordination of our slaves."[124]

The apocalyptic end was clear to the Savannah River residents: in alarmist tones, they predicted the end of slavery as they knew it if such unruliness continued. Reappropriating the "fruits of their own labors," working only with "sullenness [and] discontent," and skeptical of the authority of their owners, bondpeople in their neighborhood were creating "such a state of things [that] must speedily put an end to agriculture or to negro slavery." Engaging in these small, outlawed activities, the association argued, the "negro ceases to be a moral being, holding a position in the framework of society, and becomes a serpent gnawing at its vitals or a demon ready with knife and torch to demolish its foundations."[125]

Drinking and dancing at night rather than resting for the next day's labor could not and did not bring down the house of slavery. Nonetheless, the histrionics of the Savannah River Anti–Slave Traffick Association are more than amusing; they are revealing. Their claim that when engaged in these activities, enslaved people ceased to hold a "position in the framework of society" is key to understanding their disquiet. When engaged in these activities, enslaved people ceased, their owners thought, to hold a proper "position in the framework of society" because they disregarded slaveholders' control over their bodies. Stealing time and space for themselves and for members of their communities, those who attended secular parties acted on the assumption that their bodies were more than inherently and solely implements of agricultural production. While many planters desired and struggled for a smooth-running, paternalistic machine, some bondpeople created, among other things, a gendered culture of pleasure that "gnawed" at the fundamentals—the "vitals"—of slaveholding schemes for domination of the black body, a body that slaveholders had (ideally) located in a particular "position in the framework of society."

In a context where control and degradation of the enslaved person's body were essential to the creation and maintenance of slave-owning mastery—symbolically, socially, and materially—bondwomen's and -men's nighttime pleasures insulted slaveholders' feelings of authority. Mastery demanded respect for spatial and temporal boundaries, but bondpeople sometimes transgressed these borders and made spaces for themselves. While slaveholders' drive for production required rested slave bodies, bondpeople periodically reserved their energies for the night and exhausted themselves at play. Perhaps most important of all, enslaved women and men struggled against planters' inclination to confine them, in order to create the space and time to celebrate and enjoy their bodies as important personal and political entities in the plantation South.

AMALGAMATION PRINTS
STUCK UP IN HER CABIN

Print Culture, the Home, and the Roots of Resistance

Looking back on his childhood home, former bondman Thomas Jones saw a twoness in it. His parents "tried to make it a happy place for their dear children"; they worked "late into the night many and many a time to get a little simple furniture for their home and the home of their children." They "spent many hours of willing toil to stop up the chinks between the logs of their poor hut, that they and their children might be protected from the storm and the cold." Jones could "testify" to the "deep and fond affection which the slave cherishes in his heart for his home and its dear ones." While they tried to make a life for their family in their quarter, Jones's parents could not escape the unhappiness they expected would enter it. They took it as their parental responsibility to "tal[k] about our coming misery" and to warn their children of the "inevitable suffering [that was] in store" for them by speaking "of our being torn from them and sold off to the dreaded slave trader." As they taught their children the needed lessons, they "wept aloud" in the home they cherished, site of their present joy and likely future sorrow when one or more of their six children might be sold.[1]

Slave cabins were extensions of two worlds. They encompassed the public life of the plantation, reproducing and confining the workers who would turn out into the fields, the yards, the kitchens, and the smoking and curing and ginning houses of antebellum farms and onto the auction blocks of the slave markets. The quarters were also private places, home to slaves' family and community lives and essential elements in the rival geography. Thus far, we have explored the movement of bodies in various changing spaces; now let us turn to the movement of objects in a physically stable place. Slave cabins were simultaneously public and private: they were public spaces of labor reproduction and private spaces of community formation and family life. White plantation residents similarly lived publicly and privately at once, and their households, as well, were places of both work and sustenance, of production and reproduction. But only the enslaved embodied that "double character" in their persons; they were always at once people and commodities, "person[s] with a price," as one historian has aptly put it.[2] Slave cabins manifested a similar twoness: the quarters were spaces of labor reproduction and key instruments in the larger social agenda of containing and exploiting enslaved people. They were also, uneasily, enslaved people's homes. Just as the chattel principle described paradoxical, and not opposed, facts of life in the old South, slave cabins encompassed slavery's cruelties and the internal life of the home; they were both object and subject.

Historians have discussed and debated life in the quarters, examining the forms and functions of slave families, childhood, education, and the architecture of the structures themselves.[3] We know a great deal about slave rebellions, plots, flight to the North, and other forms of slave resistance. Less is known, however, about the connections between the two—about the inception and ongoing development of and changes in slaves' culture of opposition. Individual slaves' political consciousness was never inborn but always learned; it was acquired in places of work, such as the field, and places of anguish, such as under the lash—and it was developed in the home. The secret life of slave cabins offers glimpses of the practices and ideologies that lay behind the development of visible slave resistance.

But an investigation of life in the quarters must be about more than reworking the public/private connection, and it must dig deeper than the claiming and redefining of space. It must include an analysis of the passions with which enslaved people invested their homes, and the larger significance of those passions. In particular, what did women, who performed so much necessary reproductive domestic labor, make of their quarters? How did they make and remake their minds and spirits and those of their families? How was community belonging produced? Even as slave "communities" were fractured by rifts of status, gender, and personal conflict, bondpeople living in the rural South also typically understood themselves as a common people, a contradictory, unequal "we."

Moreover, after the emergence of a radical abolitionist movement in the early 1830s, slaveholders' (ideally) sealed estates were increasingly punctured by the words and voices of organized opposition. In this way, "high" politics helped to intensify the significance of slaves' rival geography. Increasingly over the antebellum period, enslaved people came into indirect, sporadic contact with the northern abolitionist movement and were occasionally able to consume its messages. Connection with abolitionists' propaganda acted just as planters had feared: awareness of antislavery sentiment in the North raised expectations that freedom was close at hand. Hardly mere sentimentalism, such high hopes often precipitated the organizing of revolts throughout the Americas.[5] In the cases presented here, these hopeful feelings were expressed by some women quite plainly on the walls of their homes.

This chapter analyzes evidence from two instances in which bondwomen procured, preserved, and displayed abolitionist propaganda in their homes. In these cases, the women made little effort to conceal the texts they had obtained; their audacity is key to the survival of documentary evidence about acts that in other instances were much more carefully concealed. These fragments hint at what may have been larger patterns of slave uses of abolitionist materials. Documentation is sparse, but documentation does not indicate significance; indeed, many social truths are unspoken and therefore undocumented. Certainly, in a pre-psychoanalytic world, the deepest anxieties were not often openly discussed as such. Even moments of profound social crisis can present source problems, as research into slave rebellions illustrates.[6] Though written records do not measure the pertinence of past events and often miss the unspoken, they are the medium through which the voices of the past come; they are historians' primary tool, and we must recognize their limitations. But even as we work with our written evidence—whether it remains in shards or in linear feet—we can also employ the imagination, closely reading our documents in their context and speculating about their meanings.

Reading the evidence in context presents circumstantial evidence that the episodes discussed here reflect wider practices and are not simply exemplary stories. Abolitionists disseminated their messages with enough vigor to infuriate planters, who worried about the dangers presented by such materials getting into the wrong (their slaves') hands. From the North, abolitionists tried to break the seal that isolated enslaved people from the world and, increasingly, the South from the North. Within the South planters tried to mitigate the success and the consequences of antislavery agitation. All around bondpeople were parties interested and invested in their access to antislavery materials. Are we to believe that despite abolitionist aggression and slaveholders' distress, there were as few leaks in the seal as the archival record would suggest? Or, as seems more likely, was the procurement of these materials both rare *and* kept deeply underground? This chapter elaborates how the use of abolitionist print materials by two women invested their homes with antislavery political meaning, created usable texts out of the materials made by abolitionists, undermined their isolation, and connected enslaved viewers with larger, national, movements for emancipation. Most of all, the stories explored here offer slaves' and slaveholders' imaginations as a point of historical investigation.

In 1842 an enslaved woman named California was living in Waverly, Mississippi, with her husband, Isaac, and some of their children when the man who hired them, George H. Young, and his wife decided to move their household. Young managed the land and slaves of James McDowell, a Virginian who had briefly tried the life of a Mississippi planter before returning home to pursue a career in state and national politics.[7] Despite Young's inclination to rid himself of California and her family, about whom he complained regularly, California and Isaac went with him to his new residence. The reason, according to Young, was simple: "California made quite a to do to follow my wife here. & here she and Isaac are."[8] California's reasons for wanting to continue to work for the Youngs, for whom she washed laundry, must have been as straightforward as her method for making it happen.[9] Whereas going on the hiring market would surely have separated California and Isaac, with the Youngs they continued to live within "2 + miles" of their children George, Henry, and Susan, while the youngest, Jim, was "in sight."[10] In ensuing years some of these working-age children would return to Young's farm, and California would have at least one more child, a daughter, who would live with California and Isaac. California's "to do" successfully preserved her family's integrity against the kind of devastating separation that so many other bondpeople experienced.

But it was not only California's "to do" that convinced Young to keep her with him. The business of hiring out slaves was onerous, and the work in this case was not made any easier by the personalities involved. In 1843 Young described Isaac as "faithful & steady" in his post at "a cart" with which he "hawls wood," although he "rarely attempt[ed] anything more laborious."[11] Young believed that it was simpler for him to hire "Isaac & his family" himself rather than farm them out on the hiring market, for he did not think they "would do well to be hired out at random." When he referred to Isaac's "family," Young meant his wife, California. "I know his *family* would not [do well to be hired out at random]. His Wife is not of a temper to get along with most Mississippians."[12] Just a few months earlier, Young had let McDowell know that California had worn his wife's nerves to tatters and that his wife had "vowed she would be provoked with her no longer." The Youngs decided to allow California to "attemp[t] to make her own support," probably as a laundress.[13] Young initially had doubts about California's ability to succeed, but a few years later he continued to describe her as someone who "does for herself gets meal without stint from my mill—has plenty of poultry." By then Isaac, too, was hiring himself out to the nearby ferry and "brings me the money weekly."[14] Allowing California and Isaac to hire out their own time seems to have resolved the tensions of 1843, when Young had written that California "has in her head that she is, or ought to be free" and suggested to McDowell that "when this is the case, I think they either ought to be made so, or disabused of the error." But Young was not prepared to strike California "a lick," and "Isaac never needs it."[15] Neither, it appears, was Young willing to suffer the repercussions of hiring out such a troublesome bondwoman, for complaints from her hirer, disputes over the value of her labor, and perhaps even insinuations about Young's competency as a manager would certainly have ensued.

The resolution of tensions was temporary, for McDowell's bondpeople had long been complaining about the unsettled nature of their arrangements, and they would continue to do so. Owned by a distant slaveholder and hired out annually, they were never sure where they would be living from year to year. "At all times & under all circumstances" the slaves' grievances were "numerous enough," but by late 1845 "the objections to hiring are increasing with them" even more. In particular, Young noted that two of California and Isaac's children, George and Susan, soon would "be marrying & making their dispositions more painful & embarrassing." Another one of their children, Henry, already "has a wife & must be hired nearby else running away & ill usage are the consequence."[16] When McDowell's term as governor finished in 1846, Young urged him to take advantage of his new "foot loose" status and choose whether he would return to Mississippi to buy "Land & settl[e] these & the rest of your negroes here. . . . Yea or nay It is time to decide & act." With unusual directness, Young pressured McDowell to "settle them or sell them & I know the negroes say amen."[17]

The problems that hiring raised were many: it destabilized community and family life for enslaved people, who protested regularly, and placement was sometimes difficult because demand for hired slaves was uneven from year to year and because it was a "great difficulty" to find "suitable" employers.[18] In the summer of 1847 Young penned a striking letter. Reprising an old theme, he recounted his "hope [that] you will not let another year pass away without making some new provisions for your negroes." But now Young mentioned an entirely new problem. More and more, Young was finding it tricky to manage "anothers negroes as well as my own." Discipline was uneven, and the consequences were notable: "Your California especially has an idea that she is free. Goes & comes & does as she pleases, infuses a good deal of these feelings & notions in her childrens heads, has Amalgamation prints stuck up in her cabin. Which I constantly fear will be observed by the Patrol & unpleasant difficulties ensue. & the example of all this is against my own slaves."[19]

This extraordinary letter reveals that California had obtained what Young derisively called "Amalgamation prints," abolitionist printed matter of some sort, which she had "stuck up in her cabin." The phrase "Amalgamation prints" refers to proslavery representations of abolitionists as race-mixers. Though, like most enslaved families, California's would have been nonliterate, Young's letter reveals that he was worried about what she and her family, as well as others, would gain from these prints. This letter also reiterates what Young had mentioned before: that California "has an idea that she is free," an idea that took the form of going and coming and doing "as she pleases," including obtaining outlawed antislavery literature. California's Amalgamation prints were but one example of her larger sense of entitlement to liberty, one instance of her exceptional independence. They also appear to have inspired similar "notions" in the minds of those around her. California's sense of her right to freedom was one that she "infuse[d]" into her "childrens heads" and that served as a bad "example" to Young's "own slaves." The abolitionist prints in California's cabin were both the product of and instruments in the reproduction of unrest in the quarters at Young's farm and in the wider network of hired people of which McDowell's bondpeople were a part. California's story raises a number of questions; foremost among them is What made her remarkable activities possible?

First, there were California's inclinations and her ability. California was skilled as a laundress and was allowed to hire out her own time. Hiring granted her mobility and money that few enslaved people had; only other skilled slaves—healers, personal slaves, and tradesmen—would have enjoyed anything like the relative freedom of movement and the access to cash or trade goods that California must have had. Likewise, Isaac hired himself out to a local ferry. Surely Isaac would have come into contact with the cosmopolitan black watermen who traversed the country, north and south, carrying with them the news, information, ideas, and sometimes texts that circulated through the Atlantic maritime world. These men connected agricultural slaves to the larger, more informed world beyond plantation borders.[20] Isaac may even have pointed those who needed the services of a laundress in California's direction; in exchange for this work, California would have received cash or goods of all kinds, including, apparently, abolitionist printed matter. California's and Isaac's occupations were key to her procuring such forbidden materials.

Then, too, there was Young's complicity. Highly unusual was Young's claim that he "constantly fear[ed]" the prints would "be observed by the Patrol & unpleasant difficulties ensue." Why did he not order California to remove the prints? Why did he not remove them himself? Young knew that these were obvious solutions and that McDowell would have asked these same questions. "You will say, why don't you remedy all this?" Young wrote. "My reply is I never punish my own if I can avoid it—& others not at all."[21] But there appears to be more to the story than the maintenance of Young's self-image as a benevolent man and his inherently compromised position as a hirer. Young's wife probably exerted some pressure on him not to whip enslaved people. Not only was she the person to whom California turned when the latter needed help keeping her family together in 1842, but Mrs. Young also felt "sympathy" for the bondman Moses when his wife was sold—his third wife to be sold away from him. Moses had developed a habit of "too great use of Liquor" and was devastated when he heard that yet another loved one had been sold. Mrs. Young "promised" Moses that she would, "& actually did," buy his wife back from the "Trader" who had purchased her, probably after Moses appealed to her for help.[22] Clearly, in Mrs. Young the enslaved people owned, hired, and hired out by Young had an uncommon potential advocate.

In addition to the opportunities of their particular situation, though, the broader context also facilitated California's activities. To fully understand California's actions—thinking of herself as "free," possessing and promoting abolitionist print material, and "infusing" her children's minds with these same "feelings and notions"—we must consider the broader context in which she operated, for it was a context in which issues of geography and print culture were momentous.

THE POLITICS OF IMAGES AND SPACE

California acted during an important moment in the history of the book and print culture and of American opposition to bondage. The antebellum period was revolutionary for the printers and publishers of books and other texts. Beginning in the second quarter of the nineteenth century, developments in technology and changes in the content of printed matter democratized the publishing industry, bringing in many more readers than the gentlemen and clergy who had previously made up the majority of the reading public. At the close of the eighteenth century, the invention in France of the papermaking machine, in combination with the 1833 introduction of the steam-powered press to the United States, accelerated the production of printed matter, lowered the costs of many types of publications, and helped to feed a growing demand for reading material. The result, in the words of historian Isabelle Lehuu, was an era of "print exuberance": cheap books, journals, magazines, news sheets, and fliers proliferated like never before.[23]

The mass production of inexpensive reading material made it possible for large numbers of people to buy published items, at least occasionally. But technological developments and lowered costs alone did not create demand; demand was increased and then fed by changes in the content of published matter. Inspired by the mass potential of reading, some publishers sought to appeal to popular audiences. The development of the Penny Press illustrates the antebellum popularization of reading and its link to technology. Major newspaper dailies were charging six cents per issue when the *New York Sun* began publishing in 1833 and initiated a major change in newspaper publishing by charging only one penny. The *Sun* appealed to a wider audience because of its low price and its new and different content. The *Sun* and the "penny papers" that followed it in Boston, Philadelphia, Baltimore, New York, and Virginia introduced such features as local news, crime and courtroom reports, and human interest stories. These features appealed to a wider audience than did the sober financial reports, international news, and political punditry of the major dailies. In combination with the lower prices, the innovative and scandalous content helped to popularize the newspaper. Indeed, one historian has argued that it "helped make newspaper readers."[24]

Similar innovations were developing in other areas of publishing. Magazine publishers in the 1830s began targeting women as a specialized audience and introduced women's magazines to the American public. These publications included literature, fashion, and practical information on domestic management; colored images illustrated the fictional stories and the fashion articles. These new colored images were so popular among middle-class southern and northern women readers that they often tore them out and decorated rooms of their homes with them. Nineteenth-century women's magazines were designed for viewers as much as for readers.[25]

American abolitionists had not waited for these developments to use images in their propaganda; their work had long been visual in nature. American abolitionists produced newspapers and books in quantity as early as 1816, and they, like their English predecessors, used images to help depict their objections to human bondage. In order to expose the brutality of bondage, eighteenth-century British abolitionists had used both images and rhetoric heavily in their campaigns. These eighteenth-century activists created the political vocabulary that nineteenth-century abolitionists would also use. English abolitionists introduced three major icons into the struggle for emancipation: the wildly popular cameo of a kneeling slave beseeching the reader, "Am I Not a Man and a Brother?"; the image of a cross section of a slave trading ship showing the "tight packing" of African human cargo; and the representation of violence, including whippings, auctions, runaway hunts, and the separation of families.[26]

Nineteenth-century American abolitionists recycled these icons, but with a difference. In the antebellum years abolitionists were able to "amplify," as Phillip Lapsansky has argued, the accessibility of these images and, therefore, their impact. Following the example of the penny papers and popular magazines, abolitionists exploited the newly popularized medium of print culture to mass-produce cheap editions of political pamphlets, tracts, and books. In the two years after the introduction of the steam-powered press in 1833, the production rates of Philadelphia's printing houses increased more than ten times. By 1835 these presses were issuing 55,000 impressions an hour. In preparation for one particular direct action, the infamous "Postal Campaign" of 1835, the American Anti-Slavery Society (AASS) printed more than a million publications. This figure was nine times the publishing rate of the previous year, "at only about five times the expense," the AASS noted with satisfaction. In addition to publishing reading material, radicals imprinted antislavery imagery on a variety of items: stationery, song sheets, candy wrappers, pin cushions, envelope stickers, draw-string bags, medallions—and prints. The use of illustrations allowed abolitionists to reach a wider audience. Images could be viewed by all, even those who could not read. Like antebellum women's magazines, abolitionist publications had viewers as well as readers in mind. Since abolitionists used intense representations of violence, their images often provoked a visceral and sympathetic response.[27]

Nineteenth-century abolitionists further amplified the emotional power of eighteenth-century images by adding sensationalist accounts to their narrative and visual work, just as the penny papers were doing in the field of journalism. They augmented earlier representations of violence, explicitly portraying cruelty to bondpeople in gory detail and dramatic style. When Theodore Weld and Angelina Grimké researched their book *American Slavery As It Is: Testimony of a Thousand Witnesses*, they sent out a call for contributions, especially the most gruesome. They sought reports on "PUNISH-MENTS—please describe in detail the different modes, postures, instruments and forms of torture. . . . Facts and testimonies are troops, weapons and victory, all in one." The tactic seems to have worked well. Their book became and remained the best-selling antislavery text from its publication in 1839 until Harriet Beecher Stowe published *Uncle Tom's Cabin* in 1852. In the 1840s black abolitionists added their voices to the movement as many formerly enslaved people began publishing autobiographies of their lives in bondage. Some of these authors and narrators published with abolitionist presses, agreeing with (or acceding to) the movement's focus on bodily violence as a tactic for gaining attention and sympathy. With titles like *Life and Narrative of William J. Anderson, Twenty-Four Years a Slave; Sold Eight Times! In Jail Sixty Times! Whipped Three Hundred Times!* autobiographers such as William J. Anderson promised sensational accounts of life as a slave.[28]

As early as 1831 abolitionists sent some of their publications southward, hoping to convert southerners. But not until 1835, when abolitionists began the Postal Campaign, did abolitionist activism include the aggressive dissemination of antislavery tracts throughout the South as well as the North.[29] In 1835 the AASS announced a new program of activism and organizing that would include among its goals "[to] circulate unsparingly and extensively Anti-Slavery tracts and periodicals." For this purpose the society intended to "enlist the pulpit and the press in the cause of the suffering and the dumb." The AASS and other abolitionist societies coordinated a torrent of antislavery propaganda into the South, of which the AASS's 1 million publications were but one part. The societies sent their newspapers to slaveholders through the mail, and they also dispatched agents throughout the countryside to distribute their materials. In Enfield, North Carolina, abolitionist newspapers were found scattered along a road, apparently dropped there by a traveler in a carriage.[30] The Postal Campaign was highly successful: cities, towns, and rural areas all over the South witnessed the appearance of exactly the types of publications that slaveholders liked least. Abolitionists' energetic strategies violated southern space and, potentially, individual plantations.

The work of organized abolitionism might not have made the impact in the South that it did in the 1830s were it not for an earlier success. In 1829 David Walker wrote his *Appeal to the Colored Citizens of the World, But in Particular, and Very Expressly, to Those of the United States of America.* Walker's *Appeal* was an impassioned call to slaves to emancipate themselves from mental slavery to their "natural enemies," to act like "MEN" who had "souls in our bodies," and to follow the example of enslaved Haitians and avenge their women, their families, and themselves by rising up against the planter class. "The whites want slaves, and want us for their slaves, but some of them will curse the day they ever saw us," Walker warned.[31]

As his title openly states, Walker intended for "colored" Americans, free and slave, to hear his message. He recruited black sailors from the port near his used-clothing shop in Boston to spread the word—and the work. The black sailors he enlisted and the postal service he used to mail the *Appeal* to blacks and whites in the South proved to be effective channels. In December 1829 the *Appeal* surfaced in Savannah, followed by seizures in Atlanta, Richmond, Wilmington, and New Orleans. In New Bern, North Carolina, a jailer's wife eavesdropped on a conversation between enslaved runaways who discussed a conspiracy widespread throughout the towns, swamps, and pine barrens of eastern North Carolina. From the hub of the plot in Wilmington, a "fellow named Derry" "brought some of those pamphlets" to New Bern and perhaps also to Elizabeth City to the north. By and large, though, Walker knew that most enslaved people would be unable to read his words. Rather than turn to visual aids, Walker counted on a tradition: oral culture. As historian Jeffrey W. Bolster has argued, Walker "realized that the clandestine and far-flung distribution of radical ideas among the black population could best occur by word of mouth."[32]

The fear and rage that Walker had ignited among slaveholders burned all the hotter after organized abolitionism assaulted the South with its visual message. All over the South, knowing that enslaved people could "read" images that expressed a measure of northern solidarity with their plight, slaveholders responded. Planters had long attempted to isolate bondpeople, in part by preventing them from gaining literacy skills, but they grew particularly anxious after David Walker's *Appeal* reached southern ports in 1829 and 1830, after Nat Turner's bloody insurrection in 1831, and with the increasing dissemination of black- and white-authored abolitionist literature. "The vile Pamphlets, Prints &c distributed by the Abolitionists and their agents all through the southern states," one planter in Georgia wrote to his brother in late 1835, "have had a tendency to do much mischief already in one or Two counties in this state."[33] In response to the actual and potential "mischief" that these materials might incite, planters censored the movement of antislavery materials into the South, reinforcing (they hoped) their power over local geographies.

Laws and customs controlling black movement within and out of the South were well in place by the nineteenth century. So, too, were laws and customs prohibiting whites from teaching blacks to read or write, a practice that one former bondperson thought helped planters "to bind them tighter."[34] Southern lawmakers paid ever-more-strict attention to the movement of printed texts into the South. In 1835 Virginia passed a law that banned the spoken or written repudiation of the right to hold slave property, which required postmasters to notify the justice of the peace when they received antislavery newspapers or books. The postmaster was ordered to burn the texts in the presence of the justice of the peace. In 1837 Missouri also outlawed the expression in speech, print, or writing of opinions likely to incite enslaved people or free blacks to insurrection.[35]

This trend was also prevalent in Mississippi, where California lived. In fact, Mississippi was among the first to detect and respond to the second wave of the abolitionist movement. In 1830 Mississippi passed a law making it illegal for whites and blacks to "print, write, circulate, or put forth . . . any book, paper, magazine, pamphlet, handbill or circular" that contained "any sentiment, doctrine, advice or inuendoes calculated to produce a disorderly, dangerous or rebellious disaffection among the colored population of this state, or in anywise to endanger the peace of society, by exciting riots and rebellion among said population." Whites who were found guilty of this offense would receive a fine of up to $1,000 and a minimum three-month prison term, with a twelve-month maximum. Blacks, however, whether free or enslaved, who were found guilty "shall suffer death." Another section of the same 1830 law prohibited printers from employing blacks, free and slave, in a printing office in any capacity, especially in any work related to "the setting of types." Any printer who violated this law forfeited $10 per black employee or hire.[36] By 1840 Mississippi had clarified that objectionable material included "any composition, in manuscript or print, or any pictorial representation calculated to produce disaffection among the slave population hereof."[37] So by 1840 Mississippi had clearly outlawed words and pictures that critiqued slavery and had established the price for violating these laws: a hefty fine for whites and death for blacks. California risked capital punishment for her criminal actions.

Elsewhere in the South, contamination became a thematic concern. In 1829, the year of Walker's *Appeal*, the Georgia legislature strengthened its "quarantine" laws that guarded the waterways into the state, this time identifying a social, not a biological, threat.[38] Before Walker's *Appeal* had appeared in Savannah and Atlanta, the legislature had never restricted black sailors' access to the state. Indeed, an 1818 law regulating free black mobility specifically exempted black sailors. But things changed after Walker's *Appeal* surfaced in Savannah.[39] Titled (in part) "An Act . . . to amend the several laws now in force in this State regulating quarantine in the several seaports of this State, and prevent the circulation of written or printed papers within this State, calculated to excite disaffection among the colored people of this State, and to prevent said people from being taught to read or write," this law viewed black sailors as potential contagions, as people who could make contact with Georgia's enslaved population and infect them with "disaffection." The legislature enacted means "to prevent such persons of color from coming into this State, or from communicating with the colored people of this State."

The law separated black from black, explicitly barring black sailors from "communicating with the colored people of this State" and from setting foot "on shore" during the "quarantine" that ships with black sailors were to "ride" for their first forty days in port. Black Georgians, in turn, were not to board such vessels "for any purpose whatsoever."[40]

In a spirit similar to Georgia's quarantine code, South Carolina strengthened its censorship laws in 1835. No one was permitted to bring into the state an enslaved person who had been north of the Potomac River, to the West Indies, to Mexico, or to Washington, D.C., for fear that they had been contaminated by contact with antislavery politics.[41] Throughout the late 1830s and early 1840s, municipal and state legislators in North Carolina, Florida, Alabama, and Louisiana passed laws similar in spirit to South Carolina's quarantine law.[42]

Walker's nationalist vision of black pride and self-assertion had drawn lines of identification around blacks as a common people, linking them across plantation, sectional, and even national lines. A similar connection—"communication" and exchange between black sailors (free, cosmopolitan, and perhaps the carriers of abolitionist ideas and papers) and ideally isolated slaves—was the crux of the matter. Georgia's 1829 law banned such communication in the strongest terms possible. Anyone, especially any "slave, negro, mustizoe, or free person of color" who "shall circulate, bring, or cause to be circulated or brought into this State . . . any written or printed pamphlet, paper, or circular, for the purpose of exciting to insurrection, conspiracy, or resistance among the slaves" would be "punished with death." As if to deepen the legal isolation of bondpeople, the legislature also reinforced a 1770 ban on teaching enslaved people to "read or write either written or printed characters."[43] In 1841 the legislature strengthened the 1829 law, suggesting that white shopkeepers were not as cooperative as elites would have liked. Lawmakers had to spell out a prohibition on "any shop keeper" selling, bartering, giving, "or in anywise furnish[ing]" slaves or any "free person of color" "any printed or written book, pamphlet, or other written or printed publication, writing paper, ink, or other articles of stationary."[44] Together, Georgia's laws of 1829 and 1841 indicate some of the efforts (if not their actual enforcement) made by elites to separate and isolate bondpeople from these items. They also reveal an important source of abolitionist material among southern slaves: black watermen.

It was with good reason that slaveholders fulminated against black sailors, for a minority of them were, in fact, active abolitionists who transported antislavery messages into the South and smuggled runaways out. Black New Yorker William P. Powell, founder of the Manhattan Anti-Slavery Society, ran a boardinghouse for black mariners that he used as a platform for pious and dramatic sermons. "Slavery is the creature of sin, and not of Law!" he preached to his lodgers. It was a "violation of God's holy law, thou shalt not Steal." Powell arranged the export of antislavery books from England and into the United States by the hands of various skippers he knew "will be glad to serve me."[45] A Wilmington, North Carolina, newspaper editor astutely opined that black sailors "are of course" abolitionists and "have the best opportunity to inculcate the slaves with their notions."[46] Suspicion of black mariners was matched only by that of free blacks, who, it was suspected, acted "as carriers out of the plans suggested by the abolitionists for . . . creating inquietude among" the enslaved.[47]

One northern observer became convinced that the "servitude of the slaves is far more rigorous now" than it had been before abolitionist "interference." As slaveholders increasingly feared the "danger of revolt and insurrection" presented by abolitionist propaganda, they increased the "severity of the enactments for controlling them [enslaved people] and the diligence with which the laws have been executed."[48] Vigilance committees formed in southern locales took up the work of enforcing the laws, watching suspicious characters such as riverworkers, gamblers, black men's white lovers, peddlers, and clergy who ministered to bondpeople for any signs that they might promote abolitionism or black literacy. Nonsouthern visitors came in for new levels of scrutiny. "They are upon a strict lookout," Anna (Howe) Whitteker, a northerner working on a Virginia plantation as a private tutor, wrote to her sister. "They are organizing and sending out patrollers, to watch the slaves, and all strangers who come among them (especially Yankees) pass their strict scrutiny." Abolitionist agitation had "produced a most violent excitement" among the southerners Whitteker knew. "The Southern people are naturally violent & passionate, and this touches them to the very quick, it has aroused their indignation to the very utmost." When the "indignation" of Whitteker's elite friends was supported by "any evidence" that the "strangers" who were being watched had, in fact, "conversed with slaves, or have circulated papers," censorship was strict and discipline swift. "No less than 250 or 300 lashes satisfies them." Whitteker must have scandalized her sister with such a report and with her conclusion that "so great is their vengeance the poor culprit is glad to escape with that." Strangers in the South, more than before abolitionist activism infuriated planters, were vulnerable to the region's culture of violence.[49]

Explosive, too, were responses to the texts themselves when they were uncovered. One infamous example was a riot that took place in Charleston during the summer of 1835. In July the steamship *Columbia* entered Charleston harbor with the abolitionist newspapers the *Anti-Slavery Record*, the *Emancipator*, and the *Slave's Friend* in its cargo. The editor of a local newspaper heard about the shipment and wrote a provocative article in which he encouraged city residents to act. Charlestonians met the challenge. They held a mass meeting on the evening of 29 July that turned into a mob; the rabble spilled into the streets, broke into the post office, seized the newspapers, and agreed to meet again for a second night of destruction. The next evening the city's leading citizens joined the mob for a spectacular bonfire that put Charleston in the news across the country.[50]

On one level, planters' anxiety about the introduction of abolitionist materials into the South appears to be incompatible with the legal and customary prohibitions on slave reading and writing. If the enslaved could not read the words that preached antislavery, what difference could it make if they had access to them? But the visual nature of much abolitionist propaganda overrode slaves' illiteracy, made it accessible to them, and struck slaveholders as one of the most dangerous aspects of antislavery's work. Angelina Grimké, the daughter of an elite South Carolina family who left with her sister Sarah to join the abolitionist movement, heard some objections to abolitionists' use of images, probably from her familial and social ties in the slaveholding South. "Great fault has been found with the prints which have been employed to expose slavery at the North," she wrote in an essay titled "Appeal to the Christian Women of the South," published in 1836 on the heels of the Postal Campaign. Grimké defended abolitionists' use of graphic imagery, particularly their explicit representations of violence, by pointing out its necessity and its effectiveness. "My friends, how could" awareness have been raised "so effectually in any other way? Until the pictures of the slave's sufferings were drawn and held up to the public gaze, no Northerner had any idea of the cruelty of the system." Travel and contact had not educated the northern public, for southerners in the North seemed like genteel people. Northerners "never suspected that many of the *gentlemen* and *ladies* who came from the South to spend the summer months in travelling among them, were petty tyrants at home." And, Grimké continued, when northerners went South, they might encounter the realities of bondage but were "too *ashamed of slavery* even to speak of it" after they returned home. "They saw no use in uncovering the loathsome body to popular sight." More than mere information was needed: slavery's inhumanities, its "loathsome body," had to be brought from the catacombs of shame to the light of political organization and activism for "popular sight." "To such hidden mourners the formation of Anti-Slavery Societies was as life from the dead."[51]

The use of images was important to the work of "uncovering the loathsome body" of slavery. The use of images, Grimké wrote, had been an effective tactic in other political campaigns, and it was working for American abolitionists. "Prints were made use of to effect the abolition of the Inquisition in Spain, and Clarkson employed them when he was laboring to break up the Slave trade, and English Abolitionists used them just as we are now doing." Though some abolitionists, like Grimké, hoped to convert a few white southerners to their cause, they were unwilling to give up this tactic in order to do so. Protest as slaveholders might against graphic visuals, abolitionists simply could not afford to abandon them: "They are powerful appeals and have invariably done the work they were designed to do, and we cannot consent to abandon the use of these until the *realities* no longer exist." This was just what many slaveholders feared.[52]

Thus by the mid-1830s, slaveholders were reviving old and inventing new legal, customary, and mobocratic methods for sealing off their human property from the world changing around them, to prevent the world from having access to them. To a large degree they were successful: extremely few bondpeople learned to read or write, extremely few escaped slavery through flight to the North, and nearly all toiled for the benefit of their owners. Yet George H. Young's letters suggest that the story is more complicated than that, and that there were leaks in the seal. Even as pro- and antislavery advocates fought over control of and access to southern geographies, enslaved women and men themselves struggled against containment and isolation. When they were able to, bondpeople made contact with the world around them, beyond plantation borders. A vibrant, if rare, part of the rival geography was the occasional use of antislavery print culture, made accessible by technological developments that enabled mass production of cheap reading matter, and by abolitionists' decision to use images—a decision that was calculated to reach a large audience. But abolitionists rarely saw slaves themselves as their target audience; rather, abolitionists sought to educate northern sympathizers, to nurture indigenous southern antislavery sentiment, and perhaps even to convert a few slaveholders. If bondpeople wanted access to the northern antislavery world, it was up to them to make it happen. And so they did: enslaved communities maintained underground communication networks, sometimes called a "grapevine telegraph" by black and white alike, which sustained relationships between family and friends.[53] The grapevine telegraph—made up of personal servants, plantation men performing transportation work, black river-workers, and temporary port crews—connected bondpeople on different plantations, and it connected black plantation communities to black urban populations in the South and in the North.[54] This group of mobile bondpeople, which consisted mostly of men but included some women as well, carried messages, news, rumors, and goods for trade or sale wherever they went. Such was the stuff of contamination, some planters thought. At the end of a trip to Washington, D.C., Sarah Bruce Seddon concluded that her enslaved maids were "so contaminated by abolitionists that one is afraid to carry them home." It was 1850, and Seddon knew that "soon it will be impossible to bring a slave here."[55]

Through this underground network, mobile and immobile enslaved people exchanged information and goods; in some instances they were able to move the most subversive kinds of materials: abolitionist texts. Black and white activists produced antislavery materials in unprecedented numbers and in distinctly visual style. Enslaved people exploited the developments of the moment; they obtained, distributed, and used antislavery material. When they did so, they did more than simply consume the prints; they actively interpreted them.

CALIFORNIA'S DREAMING, II

We cannot know with any precision what the prints that California had in her home looked like. We do know, however, what antislavery images were typical in the 1830s and 1840s. Characteristic icons in second-wave abolitionism included the kneeling slave, the cross section of a slave ship, and most of all, representations of violence against enslaved people, especially exotic punishments and slave auctions separating mothers from their children. It is unlikely that any print California possessed showed a liberatory image of black people. To the contrary, the abolitionist prints California owned probably represented enslaved people in degraded, abused, and exploited terms. If, as George Young suspected, the prints were an important part of California's imaginary landscape in which she "thinks she is free" and encouraged her children to dream the same dream, then it was not because the images *themselves* inspired such ideas. Rather, the enslaved viewers of the abolitionist prints had to interpret them as signs of something else; in the images viewers caught a glimpse of the struggle for emancipation being waged in the North. The viewers of California's prints probably did not value them for what they actually depicted, but for what they stood for.

Seeing what they were not supposed to see, the viewers of California's prints were able to imagine forbidden things, such as a community beyond their own committed to the possibility of emancipation and freedom. The "readers" in California's family joined a larger community of readers of antislavery literature. Nell Irvin Painter has persuasively argued that when northern abolitionists purchased commodities such as books, pamphlets,

Am I Not a Woman and a Sister? from the *Liberator*, 7 March 1832. This image of the beseeching enslaved woman offered a female version of its predecessor, *Am I Not a Man and a Brother?* The second-wave abolitionist movement combined the energies of black women, black men, white women, and white men—unlike Revolutionary era organizations that were exclusively for white men. But like earlier abolitionists, nineteenth-century antislavery activists exploited the image of the suffering slave. (The Library Company of Philadelphia)

and sugar bowls emblazoned with abolitionist icons (items that she calls "virtuous objects"), their consumption of this particular "world of goods" became something more than economic support for the cause; it "attested to the vigor of their convictions."[56] There is no way to discern in the extant record how California obtained her prints, though it seems likely that she bought or traded for them with her laundry earnings. We can be sure that she did not purchase them as a consumer in a capitalist economy. Nonetheless, like northern consumers of "virtuous objects," California and her family signaled their identification with a movement, and with a readership, outside the bounds of the plantation and opposed to the existence of human property. One form of community belonging was produced in California's cabin.

Mother Separated from Her Children, from A. M. French, *Slavery in South Carolina and the Ex-Slaves* (New York: Winchell M. French, 1862). Enslaved women and children on the auction block being torn from one another were a standard in antislavery imagery.

By their readership of antislavery texts, the enslaved imagined themselves into the national, interracial abolitionist movement. California's conscious embrace of antislavery propaganda rendered her home a part—the most egregious part—of larger abolitionist incursions onto slavery's ground.[57]

Young's letters attest to concrete as well as ideological effects of California's actions. Having roiled the boundary separating the literate and the nonliterate, and the enslaved from the free, readers of California's abolitionist prints felt encouraged to imagine freedom, to long for it, and even to strive for and act upon it. Young complained bitterly that California "has an idea that she is free" and that she "goes & comes & does as she pleases." Not only did California act as if she were "free" by moving and doing as she chose, but she also instilled the same values in her children. According to Young, she "infuses a good deal of these feelings & notions in her childrens heads, has Amalgamation prints stuck up in her cabin." Young saw a connection between California's ideas, her actions, and those of her children.

If we cannot know exactly what images California and Young were looking at, we can nonetheless know what Young saw, for he tells us: "Amalgamation prints." Young perceived abolitionists in the same way that many other proslavery thinkers did: as fools and race traitors whose calls for emancipation were the equivalent of advocating miscegenation. In abolitionism, slavery's apologists saw the specter of political rights for blacks, which would lead to social integration. In turn, rights and integration would result inevitably in race mixing; this was the teleology according to which abolitionists became amalgamationists. For example, in 1839 the proslavery northerner Francis Philpot published *Facts for White Americans, with a plain hint for dupes, and a bone to pick for white nigger demagogues and amalgamation abolitionists, including the parentage, brief career, and execution, of amalgamation abolitionism.* Throughout the pamphlet Philpot referred to abolitionists as "amalgamationists," and to abolitionism as "amalgamation abolition." In Philpot's view abolitionists sought not just emancipation but also social and political equality between blacks and whites. "They tell us," Philpot wrote, "that in elevating the negro to a standard with the white man in every situation in life, it will *benefit* the country, and *save* the republic, &c. &c.!!!—I feel fainty. What a conglomeratible idea!" To a mind like Philpot's, "elevating the negro" would erase the hierarchical relationship between black and white, would democratize their relations, and worst of all, would encourage social and sexual intermixture. The movement that pretended to the noble cause of serving justice and saving the republic was, in fact, no more than a pack of "white niggers," an illegitimate and evil spawn: "a BASTARD CHILD OF THE D——L."[58]

Slavery's apologists commonly used derisive images to mock and belittle the convictions that sprang from the "distempered brain[s]" of antislavery activists.[59] In an 1850 cartoon drawn by "Zip Coon" called *Abolition Hall*, abolitionists appear to be driven by little more than libidinous excitement for the Negro. The cartoon mocks the intentions of an 1838 convention of women abolitionists. The women kiss and caress black men in the streets of Philadelphia in front of the convention hall. An earlier 1839 print, *Practical Amalgamation*, depicts a lovely and dainty white woman who sits on the lap of a guitar-playing black man and kisses his elongated face on the unseemly, large lips. By their side, a round-shouldered, bare-headed white man bends his lanky legs to kneel and kiss the hand of a rotund and overheated black woman. The whites here do more than mix with blacks; they give themselves up to them, revealing themselves (the white man especially) to be weak and contemptible. Even the black and white dogs on the left side of the print seem to know better: they sit beside each other, but the black dog appears to growl at the white dog, who responds with dignified aloofness. These images reveal the worst that abolition meant to slaveholders—amalgamation of the black and white races—and they help us to imagine what George H. Young saw when he looked at California's abolitionist prints and called them Amalgamation prints. Young saw in them the threat of social equality and its organic result: sexual and familial intimacy. Yet chances are that nothing in

Abolition Hall, drawn on stone by Zip Coon, ca. 1850. This racist cartoon depicts an antislavery meeting, but instead of conducting political business, the conference attendants flirt and cuddle interracially. (The Library Company of Philadelphia)

the prints themselves implied this message; Young, like California, interpreted the prints and saw in them what his interest and his heart told him to see.

Young worried about California's prints, her behavior, and that of her children, but he knew he should worry more. He was aware of another party who would be much more disturbed by the contents of California's home than he was: the local slave patrol. Because Young hired and did not own California and Isaac, because his wife probably placed some moral pressure on him to be a kind master, and no doubt because of his own personality, Young did not create the kind of orderly discipline for which many other planters labored. It was in part to compensate for just such uneven diligence among owners that slave patrols had been devised. Young knew that neighborhood patrollers would not permit California to have the prints. More than that, he "fear[ed]" the "unpleasant difficulties" that would "ensue" should the patrol "observ[e]" California's prints. Surely the patrol would punish California and perhaps Isaac as well. Or perhaps they would insist that Young do so, placing Young in the uncomfortable position of choosing between his neighbors' demands and his wife's wishes. Then, too, the discov-

Practical Amalgamation, by Edward Williams Clay (New York: published and sold by John Childs, ca. 1839). This print also mocks the motives of abolitionists, representing them as more interested in interracial necking than in genuine engagement with the founding principles of the nation. (The Library Company of Philadelphia)

ery of California's prints would prompt much talk in the neighborhood about Young's indulgent nature as well as questions about his ability to manage slaves. Most of all, the discovery of California's acquisition would suggest to locals that even as slave patrols policed race and place in rural areas, they were also evaded, and much escaped their notice. The neighborhood would have glimpsed the networks of exchange and subterfuge that existed to facilitate the procuring of the most objectionable materials and that slaves, most of the time, concealed so effectively.

TURN ABOUT WAS FAIR PLAY

During the Civil War, with emancipation seemingly just around the bend, the rival geography slowly came into the open. Bondpeople put less and less effort into hiding their views and behaviors, even such illicit activity as possessing antislavery materials. Mattie Jackson had been enslaved during her childhood as the daughter of a rural Missouri cook. William Lewis, their owner, was a tobacco farmer and the owner of a tobacco factory in St. Louis.

When the Civil War began, Lewis and his wife were "astonished" at the numbers of soldiers the Union was able to present on the battlefield and were troubled by their implication that the war would not result in a quick and easy Confederate victory. As the Lewises discussed their creeping doubts, Mrs. Lewis "cast her eye around to us for fear we might hear her" and glean the fact of Confederate vulnerability. "Her suspicion was correct," Mattie Jackson wrote in her autobiography. "Not a word passed that escaped our listening ears."[60] Like California, Mrs. Jackson profited from her position as a skilled worker to gain access to information and learning unavailable to most bondpeople.

They listened carefully, and Jackson and her mother employed other skills as well. They had learned how to read well "enough to make out the newspapers," and the pair benefited from the moment's new opportunities. The presence of Union soldiers in parts of the South introduced an unpredictable factor into the struggle between containment and movement. Many northern soldiers cared little or not at all for enslaved people, others hated the rebels enough to take pleasure in aiding their enemy, and still others were or were becoming opponents of slavery. Union soldiers who fell into any of these categories could have been among those who "took much delight in tossing a [news]paper over the fence to us." Jackson's mother scooped up the newspaper and stayed up at night to read it aloud to her daughter, keeping them both "posted about the war." Whether Jackson's mother shared what she knew with other enslaved people in the household is unknown. Certainly, Jackson's access to updates on the war's progress and to the Union's perspective on the meaning of war and its causes "aggravated my mistress very much." Mrs. Lewis once made a "bitter complaint" about the "sad affair" that was the Union's capture of rebel soldiers, and her well-read slave rejoined with what would become the victor's account of the war. She "reminded her of taking Fort Sumpter . . . and serving them the same and that turn about was fair play." The rebuttal sent Mrs. Lewis flying from the room "with the speed of a deer, . . . replying as she went that the Niggers and Yankees were seeking to take the country."[61] So they were.

Perhaps they already were taking it. For a reason unspecified in Jackson's narrative, Mr. Lewis one day "searched my mother's room" in the Lewis house. When he did, he "found a picture of President Lincoln, cut from a newspaper, hanging in her room." Mr. Lewis asked Mrs. Jackson "what she was doing with old Lincoln's picture," and she told him "it was there because she liked it." In her room in her owner's home Mrs. Jackson had posted a picture of Abraham Lincoln, whose election had inflamed the South to secession and who represented to both black and white southerners the promise and the threat of emancipation. Though Lewis had to enter the room to find the picture, Mrs. Jackson does not appear to have made any effort to conceal it. She had not buried it in a drawer or under a mattress; the picture was simply "hanging in her room." This discovery outraged Lewis more than finding out that Mrs. Jackson could read newspapers; only on this occasion does Jackson report that her mother was disciplined. Lewis "knocked her down three times, and sent her to the trader's yard for a month as punishment."[62]

During the fall of 1862, after the announcement of the Emancipation Proclamation freeing bondpeople in the Confederate states, "it was not much of an object to purchase slaves." Even Missourians who worried about the ultimate fate of slavery in the Confederate states "would, for a trifle purchase a whole family of four or five persons" with the intention of sending them to unionist Kentucky, where slavery was temporarily protected. Mattie Jackson and her mother were sold that fall in a spree of buying and selling that appeared to some Missourians to be a last-ditch effort by planters to cut their losses. Mattie Jackson believed that her owner had deeper reasons than most for selling. He "would rather have disposed of us for nothing than have seen us free," she wrote. "He hated my mother in consequence of her desire for freedom, and her endeavors to teach her children the right way as far as her ability would allow." He also "had a charge against her for reading the papers and understanding political affairs." Lewis could not "bear the idea of her being free. He thought it too hard, as she had raised so many tempests for him, to see her free and under her own control."[63]

Before too long, Lewis would see Mattie Jackson, her mother, and all his slaves under their "own control." Mrs. Jackson's actions in the early 1860s and California's in the 1840s were early harbingers of the saturnalic claims on southern space to come during and immediately after the Civil War. Using printed matter produced and disseminated by northern abolitionists and further spread by an underground slave network, these noteworthy enslaved women promoted antislavery, a principle widely accepted among bondpeople, in an unusual way. They used their homes—a slave cabin and a room in a slaveholding house—as places where they could encourage opposition to slavery and teach their children that others, outside the South, agreed. Slaves' culture of opposition, so well documented by historians of American slavery, was at least sometimes nurtured at home under the careful attention of enslaved women. Some skilled women were able to procure materials with which to contest slavery's legitimacy, making their homes key locations in the rival geography. It was in this rival geography that before and during the crisis of war, whole other worlds, free worlds, were imagined and, ultimately, made.

TO GET CLOSER
TO FREEDOM

Gender, Movement, and
Freedom during the Civil War

If slavery meant confinement, freedom seemed like liberation from that imprisonment. "I felt like a bird out of a cage," said Houston H. Holloway, who had been sold three times before he reached the age of twenty at the end of the war. "Amen. Amen. Amen. I could hardly ask to feel any better than I did that day."[1] When J. Vance Lewis's parents learned about emancipation, they first thanked God and then tried to explain to their young son what was happening. "Son, we have been slaves all of our lives," Lewis's mother told him. But now "Mr. Abe Lincoln done set us free, and say we can go anywhere we please in this country without getting a pass" from their owner, "like we used to have to do."[2] The old spatial and temporal tethers were undone with emancipation, and freedpeople were glad for their newfound ability to travel openly "around at night . . . jest ez late ez you please" without heeding "no marster" who might instruct "to be back when de clock strikes nine."[3] Many freedpeople quickly took advantage of their new liberty and "started on the move."[4] They left the plantations where they and their families had labored for generations in favor of southern towns or nearby farms; a few went west. As freedpeople moved, the metaphorical and the prosaic came together in their imaginings of freedom. "They seemed to want to get closer to freedom, so they'd know what it was—like it was a place or a city," one freedman said.[5]

Though freedom had no specific location within or outside the postwar South and resided at no certain destination, it nonetheless had a spatial nature grounded in one of the same principles that had guided slaves' antebellum rival geography: motion.[6] For the first time, claiming land formally became a possibility, one exploited by coastal South Carolinians who briefly took possession of abandoned lands during and immediately after the Civil

War.[7] Elsewhere in the South, alongside the dream of owning land was the ambition to move. Movement was at the core of what historian Leon Litwack has called the "feel of freedom." The Reverend Richard Edwards described the urgency of moving to the feel of freedom when he addressed newly freed people in 1865. He told them that "so long ez de shadder ob de great house falls acrost you, you ain't gwine ter feel lak no free man, an' you ain't gwine ter feel lak no free 'oman. You mus' all move." Edwards did not advocate movement for movement's sake but for the sake of engaging in new social relations and donning new self-regard. "You mus' move clar away from de ole places what you knows, ter de new places what you don't know, whey you kin raise up yore head douten no fear o' Marse Dis ur Marse Tudder."[8]

Postwar movement to freedom, as if it were a place, reflected a migration that had begun during the Civil War. Indeed, that the war ended in a general emancipation was, in large measure, the result of wartime flight by thousands of enslaved people who sought freedom at Union camps. Military advances by the Union army into Confederate territory first in coastal Virginia, North Carolina, and South Carolina and then in the Mississippi Valley were designed to encircle and isolate the Confederacy. But the introduction of Union camps onto rebel terrain prompted an unexpected series of events. When the northern army set up camps or claimed forts and fortresses, the word spread quickly, and bondpeople from near and far came seeking refuge and, they hoped, emancipation. The fugitives, who quickly came to be called "contrabands," received diverse treatment from the Yankees, including being returned to their owners. Objections from Union officers to providing the enemy with labor, humanitarian concerns, and especially the growing numbers of the runaways themselves placed pressure on the army to make a uniform policy. Abraham Lincoln followed the example of many of his officers in the field and decided to admit blacks into the army, but first he had to emancipate them. For a number of reasons ranging from the pragmatic need for soldiers to boosting domestic morale to maintaining international diplomacy, Lincoln announced the Emancipation Proclamation in September 1862, effective January 1863. One effect of the proclamation, in addition to its manumission of bondpeople in the Confederate states, was to allow the federals to arm runaways and muster them into the army, along with free blacks in the North. Military expediency demanded the use of "the power which slaves put into the hands of the South," as W. E. B. DuBois put it. DuBois detailed the effect of the migrations on the morality of the war: "with perplexed and laggard steps, the United States Government followed the footsteps of the black slave" toward freedom.[9]

The announcement of the Emancipation Proclamation further encouraged bondpeople to leave their owners and, in the words of historian Laura Edwards, "opened a second front" on southern plantations, "in the very heart of the Confederacy."[10] Even more than before the proclamation, enslaved people labored slowly or not at all, openly disrespected and disobeyed their owners, and worst of all, escaped to the Union army. Union officer C. B. Wilder marveled at the quickened pace of movement after the announcement of the proclamation. A "great many courageous fellows," he said, had "come from long distances in rebeldom," because they "knew all about the Proclammation and they started on the belief in it."[11] Belief in emancipation and the hope of attaining it motivated many enslaved women and men to head for the places where they thought they would find it. Enslaved people thus "raised the black flag"; they fought for an end to their enslavement from within the Confederacy's home front by leaving it behind them.[12]

Derisively called by planters "the negro movement," a "stampede," and a "great stampede,"[13] wartime migrations had not erupted suddenly and without precedent. Rather, the role that slaves played in their emancipation was the product of both northern military victories and a history begun in slavery, in the antebellum tradition of moving beyond the plantation's legitimated spaces. Wartime and postwar movement was, in the phrasing of political scientist James C. Scott, a "political breakthrough," an open and mass enactment of previously covert practices. No new and sudden development, wartime flight had been long in the making. Antebellum everyday forms of resistance were the furtive prehistory that made the visible, and historically charismatic, wartime movement possible. The crisis of war and its consequent destabilization of planter power created a moment when the "frontier" between enslaved people's hidden and public lives was crossed. Revolutionary moments, historian Ira Berlin has pointed out, offer subordinate groups opportunities that are usually reserved for ruling classes: to express and act on "the assumptions that guide their world as it is and as they wish it to be."[14] During the war, enslaved people—most of all those closest to Union lines—built on an infrastructure of knowledge and practice developed in the prewar years. Now they began to speak their minds and act on their inclinations more freely than ever before, and gender continued to influence movement and forms of expression.

GAINING ON THE PROMISED LAND

The conditions of war presented bondpeople with opportunities to move in new ways. The absence of planter men and the proximity of Union soldiers opened the possibility of escape and diminished the need for secrecy. As a group of young Confederates socialized on the porch one evening, "a run-away Negro passed just in front of the house." The "boys" in the group "rushed out after him, but he soon outdistanced them. . . . The runaways are numerous and bold."[15] Similarly, the enslaved people on another plantation were encouraged by the protection offered by the Union army. "Down the road" went the "Bluecoats" with "all the slaves . . . , journeying, as they thought, to the promised land." A witness carefully noted that "some of them fared better than the others," referring to those who rode out on stolen carts, horses, or mules rather than walking. The plantation seamstress rode her owner's "beautiful white pony, sitting [on] the red plush saddle of her mistress." The "Hughes's family carriage" was employed along with "other vehicles" to carry off soldiers and "negroes."[16] Planter Catherine Barbara Broun witnessed a similar sight "from the window where I am sitting" watching a "road full of Yanks" ride by, taking bacon "from every one" who had any. Broun also saw her "servant girl Sallie passing with her bundle and child running off." Broun "started to go after her but some Yankees rode up and I was afraid to venture."[17] Secrecy was of decreasing concern in some quarters.

A newfound extroversion, even exuberance, was in the air, especially after the enactment of the Emancipation Proclamation. The large ensemble of northern Virginia slaves shown in the dramatic illustration accompanying a French newspaper article "criss-crossed" the land on their way to federal camps. The group made no effort to conceal their movements; "traveling under the protection of the proclamation," they were "gaining on the promised land." Waving the Emancipation Proclamation in the air, carrying what they owned in small bags and large packs, wearing everything from rags to fitted dresses, jackets, and top hats, these women and men courageously marched in mass formation toward Yankee lines. Their faces bespeak the complex of emotions that this revolutionary moment brought: exultation, apprehension, curiosity, weariness, and youthful certainty. By featuring the Emancipation Proclamation prominently in the picture, the illustrator high-lighted its power to embolden and shelter enslaved people in their journeys to Union lines. The jubilation of this exodus was replicated in other places, even within the Union. In St. Louis the news of the Emancipation Proclamation landed among the (officially unfreed) slaves of loyal slaveholders "like a torrent of oil onto a burning city"—with the consequent "reprisals" from planters.[18] By the end of the war, 19,000 bondpeople were said to have fol-lowed Sherman to Savannah.[19]

Bondwomen seemed to want to give their exhilaration the shape of their own form, and they became notorious among slaveholders for their taste in

Illustration from "Les esclaves et la proclamation du président Lincoln" [The slaves and President Lincoln's proclamation], *Le Monde Illustré*, 21 March 1863. In Virginia and elsewhere in the South, news of the Emancipation Proclamation was interpreted by many enslaved people as their long-awaited deliverance from slavery. Believers and nonbelievers alike joined an exodus of thousands to Union lines. The public, even spectacular quality of many wartime escapes often depended on habits and knowledge formed before the war.

fine clothing. "The Negro women marched off in their mistresses' dresses," one slaveholding woman wrote in astonishment.[20] When her bondpeople left just days after the Emancipation Proclamation went into effect, another planter woman found that "at least a hundred dollars worth of my clothing was stolen."[21] Women secured the clothing out of need and accessorized with glee; pragmatic concerns were not necessarily separable from merriment. In addition to dresses, other, less practical items were often reported missing. On one plantation, departing bondwomen took a great deal of sensible "clothing, . . . underclothes and dresses" but also "all my fine and pretty things, laces, etc."[22] "Ribbons and trinkets" were among the "collection of stolen finery" another group of women made off with.[23] The "pink ribbons" and "dozen bows" bondwoman Peggy tied into her children's hair exhibited "the pride of their freedom."[24] It was not hard for the enslaved to enjoy the shift in fortunes that the war seemed to bring. One Confederate soldier returned from military service to find a group of bondwomen wearing their owner's clothing, playing the piano, and singing, mockingly "playing the mistress and her guests."[25]

The joyful feeling of freedom that was embodied in women's claims on their owners' symbolic dress seeped as well into their movements. Among the women and children corralled by Union soldiers onto one plantation were women who "were dressed up in their mistresses' clothes, and were dancing and scampering all over the place."[26] Another group of "Negro women" held by Union soldiers were observed by a southern Unionist to be "Strutting about doing Nothing and are quite a nusance."[27] Josephine N. Pugh "looked vainly in familiar faces for the old expression," finding instead "hard" looks that brought "unbidden" tears to her eyes.[28] Reflecting on the sight of the "saucy negro women" who had "over-run" Richmond's Capitol Square at the end of the war, Emma Mordecai lamented that "the eye is offended by all it sees," and the ear, she added, "by all it hears."[29]

The sounds that slaveholders like Mordecai now heard included not only the Yankee bands whose triumphant blares made Mordecai's "heart sicken" at the war's end, but also the tongue-lashings and rudeness of enslaved people who openly verbalized their contempt for their former owners.[30] As one group of bondpeople left for Union lines, they cursed their mistress to her face. The first to leave used "the most abusive language to Mrs. Hardison." Those remaining "declar[ed] they are free and will leave as soon as they get ready." In the meantime, they continued to use "very abusive language." Eventually, all of the Hardisons' bondpeople did leave, and as the last departed, they "vow[ed] vengeance against Mr. Hardison." The Hardisons' neighbor watched the events with dismay. "This country is in a deplorable state," she wrote in her diary. It was "possessed by demons, black and white."[31] One young planter eavesdropped on his slaves one night before removing them into the Confederate interior and was appalled to hear two enslaved women "abus[e] the whole family in round terms." "They were abusing Mamma, calling her 'that Woman,' and talking exultantly of capering around in her clothes and taking her place as mistress and heaping scorn on her." The young planter who heard the exchange "says that he never heard a lady get such a tongue-lashing."[32] When the enslaved Samuel Hall, who had made it to Union lines, returned to his former home to get his family, he also took the opportunity to say a few "things to his old master." Showing "the scar on his neck" where his owner had once cut him almost fatally, Hall "delivered himself of a few thoughts that were not calculated to ease Wallace's peace of mind."[33] In many quarters the Old South's racial etiquette was crumbling.

Antebellum patterns of gender difference deepened during the exodus from plantations to Union army camps, behind whose lines bondwomen and -men similarly hoped to find freedom. In the prewar years some enslaved men had gained official and unofficial knowledge of local geographies. A few had learned how to navigate waterways or had become acquainted with the routes between their home plantations and other farms, woods, ports, and towns.[34] Some of the many men who had never had the privilege of journeying outside their home plantations before the war now learned from those who had. One elderly bondman, "Uncle Phil," entertained the questions of younger men who wanted to find the nearby Union lines but did not know the way. Perhaps feeling too old for the voyage or for the uncertainties of freedom, Uncle Phil did not want to make the trip himself. Still, he gave the younger men "the direction they must take when they wish to run off to join the Yankees."[35] A young enslaved man named Allen was helped by an older man when they escaped—a case of a young innocent being "fooled off" by an "old fool," as far as their mistress was concerned.[36] Union officer C. B. Wilder asked the men who arrived in his camp and left again in order to retrieve their families if they were "not afraid to risk it." They told him, "no I know the Way." Wilder explained that "colored men will help colored men and they will work along the by paths and get through."[37]

It was not unusual for men to leave federal camps in order to go home for their families and neighbors. Such men were able to do what antebellum fugitives had often dreamed of: retrieve their loved ones and free them. The first men to leave their plantations or neighborhoods familiarized themselves with effective routes to the camps, assessed conditions in them, and investigated rumors, such as that northern soldiers sold runaways to Cuba or placed the contrabands in the "front [lines] of Battle."[38] A fraction of those who made it to the camps returned to their homes, reported on what they had found, and encouraged others to make the trip. One planter woman complained to her husband that "the men that went off to see how they liked" the Union camps "are coming back pretending that they are tired of the yankees & before you know it they are gone again & more with them." When her father's "*men* gave a favorable account of the yankees" she was certain that they would "take off their *families* & *others*" and go back to the federals.[39] Soon after their flight to the Yankees, a few of Colin Clarke's bondmen returned, but Clarke suspected that one of the men had only returned to "carry off *his wife*" and that others would follow. "I am satisfied my dear Max that I shall *not have a servant* left in a fortnight."[40] When Union soldiers made inroads into Kate Stone's neighborhood, the first to leave were six men, belonging to her friends the Hardisons, who took their children and a few items of clothing. One month later one of them came back and led a "party of Yankees and armed Negroes" to the Hardisons' plantation. The group took "every negro on the place" to the Union lines.[41] Countless men did their best to bring their families out of slavery into freedom, but many could not overcome the various obstacles—Confederate pickets, distance, and planter retaliation—that stood in their way. Of those who left Wilder's camp, "several have brought back their families," but many others were "never heard from" again.[42]

For abroad couples, the endeavor to get to the federal army as a family entailed additional collaboration and work in order to compensate for women's lesser mobility. On his way westward through Gloucester County to the city of Richmond on an errand for his owner, bondman Billy picked up a runaway who was going to meet his wife. The couple intended to go together to the camps the Union had established in the area. The runaway "got out just above" a crossroads by the woods somewhere in Gloucester County. As he descended the cart, the stranger told Billy that "he had a wife in Mathews who was to meet him there." Mathews County was the first county east of Gloucester, so the runaway's wife would have had to travel westward through parts of Mathews and Gloucester Counties to find her husband at the specified "X roads." The runaway traveled openly with Billy, giving the appearance of two bondmen on their way to Richmond for work. The pair even passed rebel pickets, provoking Billy's owner to chastise his Confederate son: "What sort of pickets can you have?"[43] By contrast, the runaway's wife no doubt traveled through the byways as much as possible, remaining hidden to evade the impediments that a slave of her sex would have encountered if detected on the road. Another abroad husband, Peter, and his wife decided to head for the northern army. Because Peter knew his way around fairly well from his visits before the war, it was he who "went to Dr Byrd's, carried off his wife" as well as "15 others."[44]

To leave or not was a decision that many couples made together, and that process was laced with the power dynamics inherent in any personal relationship. From the outside, it often appeared that men led the way in their relationships. "If Henry Turner went, Rosina would go," Colin Clarke calculated. If Billy did not return, then his wife, Sally, "will leave us" as well. "Even Fanny would go, if old Isaac wished it."[45] In other cases, the women held sway. Clarke was sure that "if their wives take offence" to something Clarke did, "or for any cause should propose to go," then "Sterling & Charles will go."[46]

When men did not do as their wives wanted, freedom's charms could prove the strongest. After her husband elected to stay where he was, the bond-woman "Carolina left him."[47]

With the choice between freedom or slavery at stake, women could not afford to wait for their male relatives or friends to help them, for men were increasingly hard to find. In addition to men's wartime escapes to Union lines, the antebellum separations of abroad marriages, and the sale of men into the slave trade feeding labor to the Old Southwest's cotton lands, new pressures further bled men from slave communities. Many bondwomen lost their husbands, fathers, sons, and brothers to the Confederate interior, where planters took their slaves, especially their bondmen, in the hope of preserving their human property from seizure by the Yankees. Many other bondmen were impressed for labor by both the Confederate and Union armies, and some men were taken with their rebel owners to serve them on the bat-tlefield.[48] For all of these reasons, young bondmen were disappearing from plantations during the war.

Consequently, despite women's relative spatial illiteracy, cooperation among themselves became a vital part of their escape strategies. In an impor-tant shift from antebellum patterns, women represented large proportions of runaways.[49] One census of runaways admitted into Union-occupied territory shows that almost half were women, reflecting a great rise from women's antebellum rates of fugitive and truant flight.[50] Bondwomen Maria and Mary left their mistress "perplexed" when she discovered they were planning to go "off with their children to the Yankees."[51] Other women took their chances and acted alone. "To the surprise of all," a bondwoman called "Old Hannah" packed up her things and "off she went."[52] Aware of the gender norms that limited her movement, an unnamed woman felt that she would be somewhat less suspicious as she traversed an immense distance to federal soil if she dis-guised her gender. The woman "came through 200 miles in Men's clothes."[53] Whether they traveled alone, with other women, or in mixed-sex groups, women runaways stood less chance of making their getaway successfully. The only fugitives that Colin Clarke knew of being captured, among the hundreds who escaped from him and his neighbors, were "three negro women of Mr Selden's who ran off last night & were caught."[54] When another group of runaways wound up in a shoot-out with a Confederate trying to stop them, the only ones seized were a woman "with three girls."[55]

Bondwomen could not predict the reception they would receive among the Yankees. Many women were accepted within Union lines and awaited their freedom as contraband or worked as cooks, nurses, and laundresses for the Union.[56] But the military wage scale paid women less than men, increasing their dependency and restricting their mobility. Countless others were seen as mere burdens and were refused admission into the camps. Many of these women "supported themselves . . . by washing and ironing, cooking and making pies, cakes &c. for the troops."[57] Whether or not they found work at the camps, runaway women frequently encountered official neglect, received "rude shelter" or none at all, and generally suffered "from overcrowding, privation, neglect, and sickness," as one northern female volunteer remembered.[58] Many bondwomen were even given back to their owners. Kate Stone and her slaveholding neighbors received a request from "the Yankees" who had recently installed themselves in the area to "come and take their negro women and children as they are now starving."[59] In other places Union men did not initiate such captures but responded to planters' demands for bondwomen. One planter named Nicholas Bray "obtained an order" from the federal army to which a number of his bondpeople had run to "carry off his slave woman." Bray located the woman he sought, "dragged her forth" from the building where she "was staying," and "drove away with her to the plantation." Bray, "elated at his success," returned for her sister, a seventeen-year-old "of unusual attractions" for whom Bray had recently been offered $1,500. The young woman had been "almost frantic" about the kidnapping of her sister and was terrified when she heard that Bray was coming back. While he "drove up and without ceremony began a search of the premises," she "flew with lightning speed" and "concealed herself in an out-building." When Bray failed to find "the object of his search," he drove off, perhaps to try again later. Kidnappings such as these terrorized all runaways, not only women; "a perfect panic prevails among them" that they would be reclaimed by planters, a Union observer wrote.[60]

While the introduction of northern soldiers presented certain opportunities to enslaved people, it also presented the dangers that invading armies frequently pose to women. The Union men who advanced into Margaret Tilloston (Kemble) Nourse's neighborhood went into one enslaved woman's house "and destroyed what little" of her property that "remained" and then assaulted her. They "stripped" her "to see if she had any money concealed about her." The next day they returned and "carried off all her clothes," a tactic that must have been designed simply to humiliate her; what use did soldiers have for a slave woman's clothing? "The soldiers seem very wroth against the colored people now," Nourse commented. Women on the home front bore the brunt of it when the antagonism became personal. These same soldiers "treated" another bondwoman "so rudely that she ran off," which only prompted the soldiers to "chas[e] her."[61] Elsewhere rumor had it that "over 90 mulattoes have been born near Fortress Monroe" within the first year of occupation. "O they are having jolly times I hope," one local Confederate woman wrote.[62]

KEEPING SLAVES IN

The closer enslaved people got to freedom, the further removed some of their owners felt from their own liberty. The freedom of all southern whites had long rested on the enslavement of Africans and Creole blacks. In the second half of the seventeenth century, the southern colonies' increasing importation of African slaves liberated working and poor whites from indentured servitude. By the early eighteenth century, bound English labor had given way to black slavery. Planters, aspiring planters, and even small farmers bought slaves, who worked for them producing profits. Slaveholders saw themselves as independent men. Their farms supported them; they had no masters, no lords, and no employers to whom they had to answer or on whom they had to depend. Especially after the American Revolution, this "independence" based on landholding (and therefore on the dispossession of Indian people) and dependent on slavery was the very lifeblood of American freedom. Equally important were the status and honor that accrued to the owners of slaves. Planters presided over households of dependents, and they enjoyed varying degrees of idleness. By buying and owning human beings, they filled their plantation households with dependents from whom they hoped to receive deference and obedience. The ownership of slaves brought these men comfort and social mobility; it bought their wives feminine leisure and thus made the men good husbands; and the quality of planters' mastery—manly or passionate, disciplined or indulgent—constituted part of their reputations among their peers as honorable or dishonorable men. In short, much of planters' selves was centered in their ownership of slaves.[63]

For many Confederates, the Civil War was a battle to preserve these privileges and their way of life, what planter Colin Clarke called "*our way of Comfort*." When enslaved people ran away from "service," they withdrew more than their labor. They shook the very foundation on which their owners' conceptions of themselves and their freedom lay. "I believe *every negro* will leave the county in a *short time*," Clarke scrawled in a letter. "They are leaving daily," he continued, "*every negro* down to babies. . . . What a situation!" Clarke promised to write again, "as soon as I feel like a *freeman* . . . but whilst I feel the fetters of slavery galling my wrists, I feel ashamed to write to the free

& unshackled."[64] Their liberty built on the unfreedom of others, planters like Clarke felt it slip away from them as bondpeople left in a movement that seemed to shake the earth.

During the antebellum years, it had been essential for bondpeople to move and act under the cover of dark. During the war the "old habit" of counting on the night to shelter illicit movement "prevail[ed]," one Union official observed, noting his impression that "more people passed" on a road in his district "in one night than in three days."[65] But clandestine escapes were more than a "habit"; they were, as before the war, a matter of necessity. During the Civil War, slaveholders strove to prevent bondpeople from running away to the northern army, devising new techniques and renewing older ones to reinforce their long-standing geographies of containment. Continuity as well as change characterized planters' wartime responses to black movement.

Confederate pickets were a new element of slave control. Partially established to look out for enemy soldiers and for deserters, pickets near Union strongholds also prevented runaway slaves from reaching their destinations. Some contemporaries thought the latter purpose was their primary one. "The pickets are stationed with a view to keeping slaves in rather than others out," one Union officer thought. From what he observed, this officer concluded, as have many historians, that slaveholders' primary orientation was to their own domestic worlds. "They are disposed more with reference to internal than external approaches."[66] Even as pickets worked alongside slave patrols and replaced them where patrols could no longer be manned, new patrols and vigilance committees continued to be organized, reflecting the persistence and expansion of such traditional techniques as curfews, confinement, and policing. Hoping to defend his "entire social system," another planter intended to "*seal* by the most rigid police all ingress and egress" into and from his farm.[67] Early in the war, a group of North Carolina "Citizens made up a fund & purchased a pack of Hounds at heavy cost to accompany" the county's newly formed "Patrol guard." The citizens were convinced that the patrol and its hounds would be "of *great* service in preventing escapes of Slaves" as well as "preventing desertions &c." by exhausted or disgruntled Confederate soldiers.[68] The most assiduous slaveholders met and pledged to one another to "still keep a sharp look out every night" and to "cooperate" with one another "in every movement."[69] While pickets and patrols redoubled formal efforts to contain bondpeople, city and state officials canceled exemptions from patrol duty, repealed bondmen's passes to visit their families, and voided hiring arrangements that placed some enslaved people in the cities.[70]

In tandem with these organized mechanisms, planters, at least as much as they had in the antebellum years, took matters into their own hands on an informal basis. Susie Burns's owner always could "drink somep'n terrible," but his problem accelerated "in de war days when he thought de slaves was gonna leave him." With that thought on his mind, the man "used to set in his big chair on de porch wid a jug of whiskey by his side drinkin' an' watchin' de quarters to see that didn't none of his slaves start slippin' away."[71] Slaveholders "caged up" and "locked . . . up" bondpeople at night and on Sundays.[72] One planter woman who aimed to put her "servants" "in the fields," begged her son to have "them locked up every night & every Sunday and make them see that they are not free and that they must work."[73] Other planters engaged in "all sorts of terrorism and desperate things . . . to intimidate the negroes, and make them say they don't want to go."[74] Guns and dogs were two familiar instruments of terror. Bondpeople who had escaped their plantations, evaded pickets, and dodged patrols might find themselves hiding in the woods from their owners who stood ready to shoot them. Successful runaways told one northern officer "that their masters had been firing at them and driving them back in the woods to prevent their communicating with the United States forces." The officer could tell from slaveholders' "manner that they would commit any act of retaliation that opportunity offered."[75] Newer to the war-time situation were the bondmen who managed to procure rifles and other weapons to protect themselves. When these men encountered armed Confederates, the shoot-outs that ensued seemed inevitable.[76] Runaways braved the dead bodies of those who had been "shot down" and remained "lying unburied in the woods." More than before the war, captured runaways were executed. One Mississippi planter publicly hanged one of a group of four runaways that he caught. A South Carolinian made an example of three runaways he captured, noting that neighboring "blacks were encouraged to be present" when he hanged them. He expected that "the effect" would "not soon be forgotten."[77] As one French newspaper reported, "stringency, reprisals, the principle of an eye for an eye" were the "order of the day."[78]

Slaveholders and their allies were not the only ones interested in confining enslaved people; many Union officers shared some values with the planters, among them the importance of containing and controlling the human contraband of war. During his tour of duty in occupied Louisiana, Thomas P. Knox detected some consistencies between the orders issued by General Nathaniel P. Banks and slave management manuals. In a book chapter he called "Rules and regulations Under the Old and New Systems," Knox explored the common ground. Under the "old management," bondpeople were prohibited from moving around without permission, and plantation managers were encouraged to take "frequent strolls about the premises, including of course the quarter and stock yards, during the evening, and at least twice a week during the night," according to one advice manual that Knox read. Knox compared such principles with General Banks's regulations, which included the reinstitution of pass laws and required yearlong contracts.[79]

Abolitionists howled with outrage at Banks's orders. Frederick Douglass denounced them as making a "mockery and a delusion" of the Emancipation Proclamation, while a black New Orleans newspaper charged that "any white man . . . subjected to such restrictive and humiliating prohibitions, would certainly call himself a slave." Black abolitionist and ex-slave William Wells Brown agreed, protesting Banks's "system of treatment of the colored people" that revived "the old slave-law, requiring colored persons to be provided with passes to enable them to be out from their homes" in the evenings. Wells Brown identified Banks's system as "nothing less than slavery under another name," one that now criminalized the unmonitored movement of all black southerners regardless of status or skill. "The laborer, slave and free; the mechanical waiter, slave and free" alike were policed and imprisoned.[80] The freed Louisianians to whom the orders applied were also disturbed by the regulations and by their implications for the limits of emancipation. "There were many who could not understand why, if they were free, they should be restricted from going where they pleased at all times," Knox wrote. He "explained that it was necessary, for the successful management of the plantation, that I should always be able to rely upon them. I asked them to imagine my predicament if they should lose half their time, or go away altogether, in the busiest part of the season." Reportedly, the freedpeople at once "saw the point" and conceded the "necessity of subordination." More likely, what these freedpeople "saw" was a foreboding of the ambivalence of emancipation.[81]

The demands of their own military combined with the incursions of the federals to make it more difficult than ever for slaveholders to maintain their grip on their slaves. The Old South's geographies of containment were gradually unraveling. Yet this unraveling was, indeed, gradual; while planter efforts at confinement failed more than ever before to keep "slaves in," they also worked in many respects. Because many enslaved people could not or would not go to the Union lines, they remained on the plantation home front for the duration of the war. Yet even there, uses of southern terrain proved relevant to the war's outcome.

ON THE HOME FRONT

Slave labor was critical to the Confederacy's home front war effort. If planters had been preoccupied with the politics of expansion and secession before the war, they were now consumed with more pragmatic issues: food, crops, and the suppression of slave rebellion and flight. They gave more attention to the practical survival of the plantation system for which they were fighting than to the abstract principles justifying and explaining it.[82] The "question of food" was "today the most important question before us."[83] Enslaved people, though, proved uncooperative.

"Demoralized" was the word that planters used to describe enslaved people who no longer adhered to the racial etiquette, including the great majority of bondpeople who did not run away to the Union army but instead remained behind.[84] Many of those who stayed, as slaveholders were unhappy to discover, were not necessarily "more faithful than many that went off but staid out of policy to see how the thing would turn out."[85] Because of the loss of men from plantation communities, this group consisted disproportionately of women. One bondwoman, "Aunt Lucy," who had been "head of them all," ran away to the woods one morning "but was back by dinner." Her owner did not bother to have her punished, as she would ordinarily have done, for the situation was hopeless: "all of them are demoralized." The "house servants" in general were "infected" by the "excitement in the air."[86] When they did not leave, bondpeople, especially women resentful about the loss of so many of their men, slowed down the pace of their work or refused to work at all.[87] A slaveholder named Valentine "was in very low spirits indeed" when he visited his neighbor to commiserate about their slaves. "His Negroes will not even pretend to work and are very impudent and he thinks they will go off in a body the next time the Yankees come on his place."[88] Throughout the South, "complaints keep coming from the plantations around saying that their negroes refuse to work," Union soldier Henry L. Wood wrote to an officer. "When practicable I sent some one to see them, and instruct them to work." When it was "not practicable," he "instructed the owner to put the refractory negroes into the stocks for a short time."[89]

It was mostly planter women who needed the assistance of men such as Wood. The demands of war created an upheaval in sex ratios among plantation whites. Beginning in 1862, Confederate conscription laws drafted white men into service in the military. Although a number of exemption laws were passed over the course of the war, three-quarters of the South's white men of military age would eventually do their duty in the army. Most planters, their sons, overseers, and their sons went off to fight, leaving farms with few or no white men on them. The responsibility of running wartime plantations fell to slaveholding women, many of whom had little experience managing slaves outside their homes. While planter women were no strangers to the use of violence, their style differed from that of male slave managers. Feminine violence was, typically, impulsive and passionate. Elite women slapped and hit their slaves in the face, pulled their hair, burned them with hot water and candle wax, stabbed them with knives and hairpins, and ordered others to whip them—all on the spur of the moment when they lost their tempers. Some planter women even believed that moody violence was an effective display of authority. One slaveholding women explained to her son that slapping her household slave women was "a good way to show them that we aren't afraid of them. We shall always be their masters."[90] Such behavior was the antithesis of the orderly lashings that male managers idealized. True manly mastery exhibited control, not passion; honor was not satisfied by the meting out of vindictive beatings to social inferiors. As one advice manual warned, cruel and emotional whippings were "absolutely mean and un-manly"; the manual's readers were advised to "keep cool."[91] Although it was more than commonplace for them to fall short of their temperate ideals, elite planter men nonetheless liked to supervise whippings that were executed by overseers or drivers, keeping their distance and maintaining their sense of de-tached superiority. By the same token, lacking the experience with the disci-plined, "cool" violence required to make others obey consistently, planter women had a difficult time enforcing rules and maintaining order on the Confederacy's home front. Slave discipline, and the lack thereof, became a considerable part of home front battles.[92]

Wartime movement of blacks was enabled, then, not only by the proximity of Union soldiers but also by the distance of Confederate men, who when present as owners, overseers, and slave patrollers, used the tremendous force at their disposal to win a measure of obedience from enslaved people. The absence of white men resulted in an overall decline in the coercion that otherwise held bondpeople in place. Runaways told one Union official that they managed to escape because "there was nobody on the plantations but women and they were not afraid of them."[93] When it was possible, planter women enlisted the aid of male relatives and neighbors. "I don't fear yankees now but *darkies*," one woman wrote to her husband. "I have someone to watch if they are going to run off [who] will try to stop them."[94] But the assistance on which planter women could call was often inconsistent, defi-cient, or nonexistent, and many floundered when their slaves were surly and dismissive, when they worked lackadaisically, and when they ran away. One of Emma Mordecai's bondmen took to "spending his days away from here," probably with his abroad wife, while one of her household bondwomen acted "like a mule." As for the rest, they were "all doing as they please." The reason for the openly unruly behavior, Mordecai herself knew, was that "no one" was "asserting any authority over them."[95] Likewise, the decision of two bondwomen to "go off with their children to the Yankees" was the result, their mistress believed, of their "taking advantage of Hal's absence."[96] As observant as ever, Kate Stone raised an eyebrow to her mother's plan to "have the men taken to the back country" in the hope of preventing them from running away to or being captured by the advancing northern army. Stone wrote skeptically in her diary that she doubted her mother "can get them to go."[97] Needless to say, not all slaveholding women were at a loss about how to manage their bondpeople. Sam McCullum's mistress "had to do de bes' she could" because she "didn' have nobody to he'p her." Her best seems to have been fairly formidable. "When she hear'd de Niggers talkin' 'bout bein' free, she wore 'em out wid a cowhide."[98]

As emancipation inched onto the Union's agenda and as the Union advanced into the Confederacy, freedom came closer, even for those who did not go to Yankee lines. More than ever, black southerners could "say they are free at home without following the yankees," as one plantation mistress bitterly recorded.[99] For planter women, household slaves, many of whom were women, presented the greatest problems. They could be more "lazy and disobedient" than field workers at times, while in other instances their behavior simply mattered more to slaveholding women.[100] In both cases, household bondwomen, though a minority of laborers in the Old South, played a considerable part in dampening Confederate women's support for the war.

Elite slaveholding women, like men, had committed to the Confederate cause out of a devotion to their traditional life of privilege, comfort, dominance, and relative idleness. But when slave communities slipped away, so did the basis for that way of life. The departures of household women left "the ladies" to do household labor like "cooking, washing, etc." Initially, planter women could find humor in their inexperienced efforts at work. When neighbors of Kate Stone's "got up one morning," they "found every Negro gone, about seventy-five, only three little girls left." They did the only thing they could do: "The ladies actually had to get up and get breakfast. They said it was funny to see their first attempt at milking."[101] People out of place are often funny, and elite women were nothing if not ill at ease with domestic chores. After her maid ("my dunce of a Rosalie") left, another planter woman knew that her son "would laugh to see me doing the housework and setting the table." She did her best to maintain perspective, but she could not deny that she was "not yet accustomed to" the work, which "exhausted" her. The drain on the body made her worry: "sometimes in the evening I think that I have the fever," she wrote with a hint of self-mockery.[102]

In time, the work lost its comedy, in part because it became less a temporary solution to wartime need and more a permanent readjustment of labor relations. Forcibly transferred from the supervisory role of plantation mistress to the position of directly performing household labor, slaveholding women underwent a key shift in both labor relations and self-conception. Kate Stone had a "strong presentment that we shall yet lose all that we have and be compelled to labor with out hands for our daily bread."[103] The double entendre is important. Elite women's household slaves had, in fact, acted like their hands, performing the tasks that they wished done and acting on their cares. With the loss of their slaves, elite women would learn to labor without hands, as if some part of their selves had been lost—perhaps the selves whose freedom and femininity had been fabricated in the projection of agency onto the bodies of their slaves.

Elite women were more than "surprised" and disappointed by the departures of their household bondwomen;[104] many could only understand the escapes of domestics in intimate terms, as personal betrayals. Planter women expected the old paternalist contract that they had imagined into existence between themselves and their slaves to hold true during the war. But the behavior of the enslaved slowly disabused elite women of their illusions of loyalty and mutuality. "Two house servants" named Nancy and Mary Ann "left" their mistress one morning. "Now Mrs D. has to do the house cleaning and nearly all the house work." The neighbor who witnessed the abandonment wondered at the women's lack of sympathy for their mistress. "It seems that if the rest who are here if they had any feeling they would feel sorry for Mrs D and remain faithfull."[105] The lack of "feeling" touched women like Belle Edmondson, who spent much of the war sewing with her "faithful slave" and "only companion," Laura. But when Laura ran away with two neighboring bondwomen, the escape so rattled Edmondson and the other women's owners that they searched desperately for them in the woods. The scene of "excitement and confusion" was one that Edmondson hoped she would "never witness again."[106] These trials wore on the elite women who had invested great emotion in their slaves; the bitterness of betrayal soon set in, and after a couple of traumatic years of war and home front hardships, many planter women decided that they were "out of patience with them as a race."[107] "We are all tired of them," Kate Stone wrote on behalf of herself and her friends.[108]

The Confederacy had been born in a promise to defend elite southerners' way of living, but over the course of the war the rebels proved unable to keep that promise. Instead of a short war, the conflict dragged on, killing and mutilating American men in numbers unrivaled before or since. Southerners of every class experienced increasing want of food, clothing, household goods, and medicines (with the wealthiest deprived the least and the latest). As wartime losses and hardships tested Confederate women's loyalty, their home front experiences with slave management further undermined their flagging spirits. Planter women began to question whether the Confederate cause was worth all they were losing and suffering. As historian Drew Gilpin Faust has shown, the consequences of slaveholding women's doubts were grave. In the last years of the war, women encouraged their men to end their service to the Confederacy, and in the last months of the war they even endorsed desertion, which was already on the rise and proved fatal to the Confederate effort.[109] As well as pressing the Union toward emancipation, slaves' wartime movement helped to weaken the Confederacy from within.

Uses of space by blacks had consequences for other aspects of life on the home front. For every story of slaves helping to hide the family silver, there were cases of those who led Union soldiers to the food, clothing, weapons, and valuables that they sought. Of necessity, often the very people "their masters had put the most confidence in" were in a position to lead the "Yanks" to the "secret place" where they could find "every thing" they might need. Soldiers had either to ransack a plantation or to depend on help from the enslaved, for aside from the Confederate owners of these goods, "no one but the servant[s] knew anything about" such hiding places.[110] Union soldiers were even more dependent on enslaved people for another form of help: guidance through Confederate terrain. The memoirs of escaped Union prisoners of war abound in accounts of the help and support that they found in the quarters.

Joining those southern whites who had traded illegally with enslaved people, Union soldiers and Confederate deserters entered the rival geography. Whites entered that geography in significant numbers for the first time during the Civil War. Enslaved woman Nancy Johnson and her husband were able to help the "Yankee prisoner that got away & came to our house" one night. The couple "kept him hid in my house a whole day," and the following night Johnson's husband "slipped him over" to another man, who in turn "conveyed him off so that he got home." The Johnsons belonged to a "bitter" man who, when he began to suspect illicit activity, threatened to "put my husband to death" if he found out that he had hidden the Yankee. The enemies of slaves' enemies, Union soldiers and deserters alike earned the assistance of bondwomen and men who, like the Johnsons, aided Confederate deserters. "Some of the rebel soldiers deserted & came to our house & we fed them." Though the soldiers had fought for the rebels, the Johnsons felt right about "befriend[ing] them because they were on our side." Nancy Johnson elaborated: "They were opposed to the war & didn't own slaves & said they would rather die than fight. Those who were poor white people, who didn't own slaves were some of them Union people."[111] Both Union prisoners of war and Confederate deserters could find themselves far from home, lost in areas where they knew no one and had no "knowledge of woodcraft, or of the country we had to travel through." Ultimately, though, northerners, more than southerners, were strangers in the South, and they needed and "relied upon the negroes" most of all.[112]

More than before the war, women and men coordinated their efforts ushering strangers through slavery's ground. Bondmen guided the prisoners and deserters to other bondmen who would help them, conveying them along the "devious path[s]" that would take the latter home. Escaped prisoner of war John Bray was discovered hiding in a swamp by an enslaved man who recognized him as a northerner, despite his stolen Confederate gear. The bondman quickly reassured Bray that he would not "tell on" him and, further, that he would be "glad to help" him. The bondman "at once started off at a rapid pace, leading me across the fields, a distance of four miles, to the house of another negro, to whom he explained my situation and wishes."[113] Other escaped prisoners of war also were passed from bondman to bondman, who, more than they had before the war, played a key role in facilitating the movement of others in the rival geography.[114]

Enslaved men guided fugitive whites from place to place, while women continued to do some of the work they had done in the rival geography during the antebellum period, providing the food that sustained escaping and deserting soldiers. Whether the visitor was passing through for a "short rest" or hiding out "for at least one month," bondwomen gave the deserving "something to eat" or perhaps even a "hearty supper" while men "did picket duty." The lifesaving help that enslaved people offered revealed to some earnest northerners "a devotion and a spirit of self-sacrifice that were heroic," one northern correspondent wrote after his ordeal. "God bless negroes!"[115]

Though many grateful prisoners of war idealized the blacks who helped them, in fact many enslaved people were cautious about and even suspicious of the Union men. When escaped prisoner of war Henry L. Estabrooks was slipping through Virginia, he sought the help of enslaved people, who gave it in varying degrees. Estabrooks identified potential collaborators by the looks of their homes, avoiding the "buildings whose appearance warned me not to trust them" and approaching those that appeared to be "negro-cabins." The inhabitants of those could almost always be counted on for sympathy and confidentiality, but not necessarily for more. After telling one family his story, Estabrooks asked "them to conceal me in the cabin." But "they would not hear to that." Instead, the couple gave him "a small piece of miserable stuff called bread, and some sour syrup, which I ate ravenously. The food was

The Escaped Correspondent Enjoying the Negro's Hospitality, from Browne, *Four Years in Secessia*. Enslaved women and men who could not or had not yet run away sometimes helped Union prisoners of war make their way back to federal lines. For the first time, whites entered the rival geography in significant numbers.

not fit for swine; but it was the best they had, and I was very thankful for it." The man of the house then "proposed to hide me in the loft of the stable, under some piles of oat-straw." From there Estabrooks was promised a series of guides who would usher him out of the area. The chain was broken, however, when one man, who did come with "a pail of water and two pieces of warm bread, with a little piece of pork skewered on to the bread," could not fulfill his promise because "he had to work that night." Limitations of time, will, and inclination all constrained the assistance bondpeople offered to escaped Yankees.[116]

In light of the thousands of bondpeople who found their way to Union camps, the Civil War era's geography of containment was much less effective than its predecessor. Slavery slowly dissolved as the Confederacy's cause came undone on the battlefield and on the home front, the result of Union military victories, weaknesses and internal conflicts within the Confederacy, diminishing support among Confederate women at home, and slaves' self-emancipatory movement. Even as planters struggled to maintain and strengthen their hold on their slaves, this confluence of factors eroded the Old South's peculiar regime, and with it the spatial order that had both bolstered and reflected it.

The Civil War's runaways had a history. During their enslavement, women, in ways shared with and distinct from those of bondmen, had created secret forms of knowledge about and uses of southern space. In rage, indignation, and fear they fled the worst of their bondage as truants; they pursued secret amusements at illegal parties among slaves; and in rare but noteworthy cases they used their homes to promote antislavery politics. But the consequences of enslaved people's illicit movement were not all limited to the antebellum period. Indeed, during the Civil War their secret uses of space gained momentous importance. The rival geography created by the enslaved over generations offered, in wartime, the literal roads to freedom.

POSTSCRIPT

In the immediate aftermath of war, emancipated people celebrated by openly coming together in mass meetings and religious services. Congregating in the dozens, hundreds, and thousands, they testified to their former misery, gave speeches and sermons about the historic moment, and offered prayers of thanks for freedom. With their former owners subdued, freedpeople were able to piece together something more than the secret spaces they had forged in bondage. Out of the major social institutions formed under slavery, they were able to create the beginnings of a genuine black public sphere: segregated places of amusement, the idealized home (where black mothers were assigned the race work of raising respectable and industrious young women and men), and the black church. Enslaved people's investments in secular, domestic, and religious spaces proved to have long-lived legacies.

In the postemancipation South, neither the formerly enslaved nor former slaveholders abandoned their long-standing interest in the social value of space. Just as quickly as they could, former planters devised new mechanisms for binding freedpeople to the land. Shortly after the end of war, municipalities passed laws requiring black workers to have yearlong employment contracts, which forced many freedpeople out of the cities and towns and back to farmland. Other laws helped to fix freed black workers to the countryside: breaking a contract was made a criminal (not only a civil) offense, and competing landowners were barred from offering enticing pay to laborers. Though these laws did not survive the Reconstruction era, they were palpably animated by antebellum principles of restraint designed to keep black people in their place—on farms—and at work.

Of longer-lasting importance was the sharecropping system that began to emerge in 1866. The Freedmen's Bureau brokered contracts between cash-strapped landowners and hungry black workers in which freedpeople labored not for wages but for a share of the crop they produced. By keeping cash out of the hands of black farmers for generations and by forcing them into crippling debt to the landowners—from whom they purchased farming supplies and store-bought goods for their own use at a cost of 30 to 50 percent above retail—sharecropping very effectively bound black farmers to the land.

But the spirit of the Old South was made most manifest not in labor relations but in the "New" South's emerging spatial social organization. In the decades after emancipation, former slaveholders and their sons and daughters would create a modern way of managing race relations: segregation. Historians have often viewed segregation as a distinctly new solution to a centuries-old race problem. Segregation and spectacle lynching were innovative forms of racial control that arose in response to new problems: black social and economic mobility and the emergence of a small middle class, young blacks undisciplined by slavery, and novel spaces such as the railroad and streetcar. Yet within this new, distinctly modern form lay some of the spatial worries and investments of the old order: placing black and white people in space and society.

As early as the 1870s and increasing in the 1880s and 1890s, southern towns passed laws segregating blacks and whites in public and private spaces and separating the destinies of each people. Public transportation, parks, libraries, hospitals, mental asylums, swimming pools, beaches, restrooms, and, infamously, water fountains were marked with signs that read "For Whites Only," "For Colored Only," or "No Negroes Allowed." Black and white were separated in private spaces, too: roller skating rinks, pool halls, laundry services, shops, and later, movie theaters. Where the law left gaps, custom filled them in. It was understood that some roads were for white drivers only, that on sidewalks blacks were to defer to whites, and that social contact or even eye contact was dangerous. The rituals of the South's racial etiquette were delicate, unspoken, and vital; the very lives of black southerners depended on convincing performances. Though there were holes—black workers in white homes, for instance—Jim Crow was a thorough system of separation upheld by ruthless violence.[1] Segregation was a modern, state-sponsored response to an old problem, but it was built on established habits. Seen in this light, segregation seems as much tradition in a new form as a modern break from it. Even revolutionary moments bring their past with them. While the times may change, people rarely do as quickly.

As sure as enslaved people had challenged slaveholders' bids to dictate their literal and social place, segregation would be (and continues to be) disputed. The earliest sites of contestation were the railroads and the streetcars. In the 1870s and 1880s these were relatively new spaces where custom had not yet settled in to govern behavior. The railroads were owned and managed by northern companies that were indifferent to white southern sensibilities, especially when those sensibilities demanded expensive additional cars to accommodate first- and second-class passengers of each "race." Thus inconsistency and caprice conducted the seating of blacks who held first-class tickets. Lawsuits followed, and one from Louisiana made its way to the U.S. Supreme Court. The plaintiff Homer Plessy challenged an 1890 Louisiana statute calling for the "equal but separate accommodations for the white, and colored races."[2] The Court infamously ruled in 1896 that separate can be equal and therefore violated none of the citizenship rights guaranteed to black Americans by the Fourteenth Amendment. The *Plessy* decision gave segregation in the South and in the North the imprimatur of constitutionality.

One lone voice from the bench dissented. Justice John Marshall Harlan insisted that, contrary to the majority opinion, separation was not and could not be equal. More precisely, segregation discriminated against black citizens and denied them their freedom. Harlan cited a precedent case in which it was asserted that "personal liberty . . . consists in the power of locomotion, of changing situation, or removing one's person to whatsoever places one's own inclination may direct." Freedom entailed movement, the "power of locomotion." The "restraint" of that free movement, Harlan believed, "infring[ed] the personal liberty" of black people.[3] As black and white southerners had for centuries, Harlan associated liberty with movement, and restraint with its denial. Black Americans in the late nineteenth century fought for full and equal access to public locomotion as one element of freedom. Tragically, their legal battles ended with a ruling that legitimated a curtailed version of mobility—and liberty. The struggle for racial justice would become in large part an effort to disentangle blackness from captivity, and race from place.

NOTES

ABBREVIATIONS

LSU   Special Collections, Hill Memorial Library, Louisiana State
University, Baton Rouge

NCSDA   North Carolina State Department of Archives and History, Raleigh

PHS   Pennsylvania Historical Society, Philadelphia

SC   South Caroliniana Library, University of South Carolina, Columbia

SCL   Special Collections Library, Perkins Library, Duke University, Durham,
N.C.

SHC   Southern Historical Collection, University of North Carolina, Chapel Hill

VHS   Virginia Historical Society, Richmond

INTRODUCTION

1. Exemplifying this trend are Walter Johnson, *Soul by Soul*; Ariela J. Gross, *Double Character*; Baptist and Camp, *New Studies in American Slavery*.

2. I use the term "slave" sparingly because it risks flattening the complex history of slavery and essentializing the personhood of bondpeople. I favor "enslaved person," which implies the active historical processes involved in subjugating those who were enslaved, and "bondperson," which connotes a status rather than a state of being.

3. This study has been influenced by James Scott's work on everyday forms of resistance and by his critics. See James Scott, *Domination and the Arts of Resistance* and *Weapons of the Weak*; O'Hanlon, "Recovering the Subject"; Abu-Lughod, "Romance of Resistance"; Ortner, "Resistance and the Problem of Ethnographic Refusal"; Farnsworth-Alvear, "Orthodox Virginity/Heterodox Memories." Histories of slavery that have profitably used James Scott's theories of everyday resistance include Lichtenstein, "'That Disposition to Theft'"; Kay and Cary, *Slavery in North Carolina*; Costa, *Crowns of Glory*. In the early twentieth century W. E. B. DuBois, in *Black Reconstruction in America*, explored the connection between nonrevolutionary actions and their revolutionary consequences. C. L. R. James, Grace C. Lee, and Pierre Chaulieu pointed out some time ago that "ordinary people are rebelling in ways of

their own invention" in order to "regain control over their own conditions of life and their relations with one another" (James, Lee, and Chaulieu, *Facing Reality*, 5).

4. Phillips, *American Negro Slavery*, 327. Eugene D. Genovese's paternalism thesis has been the subject of intense debate since the publication of his monumental *Roll, Jordan, Roll*. Among the many questions at issue is the extent to which enslaved people could resist bondage and the importance of such resistance. Some historians have agreed that paternalistic, slaveholding hegemony determined the shape of black life and, further, that the lives of bondpeople must be understood primarily in terms of their exploitation and oppression by slaveholders. Slaveholding power, in this view, flattened the possibility of meaningful oppositional activity, except for running away and organized rebellion. Everyday forms of resistance "qualify at best as prepolitical and at worst as apolitical"; see Genovese, *Roll, Jordan, Roll*, 3, 6, 7, 22, 90–91, 125, 143–44, 284, 598 (quotation). See also Fox-Genovese, *Within the Plantation Household*, 30, 49–50, 319; Wyatt-Brown, "Mask of Obedience"; Dusinberre, *Them Dark Days*, 235, 248, 265, 270–71, 273. The focus on hegemony overestimates the extent of consent at the expense of the determining role of force. Other historians in the traditional debate have placed black communities, their struggles, and their sufferings—not slaveholders and their hegemonic aspirations—at the center of bondpeople's lives. This tradition includes Aptheker, *American Negro Slave Revolts*; Rawick, *From Sundown to Sunup*; Blassingame, *Slave Community*; Joyner, *Down by the Riverside*; White and White, *Stylin'*. This study builds on this literature but departs from the debate in its focus on women, gender difference and conflict, and culture, as well as in its attention not to lore or religion (that is, to the intellectual and religious histories of enslaved communities) or to organized rebellion, but to values embodied in the everyday physical use of space, to political belief put into movement.

5. White abolitionists used graphic depictions of the exploited or abused enslaved body to garner support for their cause, while ex-slaves sometimes joined them and sometimes pointedly rejected the focus on the body. See Lapsansky, "Graphic Discord"; Clark, "'Sacred Rights of the Weak'"; Barthelemy introduction; Peterson, *"Doers of the Word"*; DeLombard, "'Eye-witness to the Cruelty.'" Historians who have studied enslaved women's experiences and uses of their bodies include Hine and Wittenstein, "Female Slave Resistance"; Deborah Gray White, *Ar'n't I a Woman?*; Shaw, "Mothering under Slavery in the Antebellum South"; Painter, *Sojourner Truth*; Jennifer L. Morgan, "'Some Could Suckle Over Their Shoulder'"; Schwalm, *Hard Fight for We*.

6. Many southern women's historians are studying the common ground between the personal and the political, as well as between the private and the public. See, for example, Evelyn Brooks Higginbotham, *Righteous Discontent*; Elsa Barkley Brown, "Negotiating and Transforming the Public Sphere"; McCurry, *Masters of Small Worlds*; Kathleen M. Brown, *Good Wives*; Hunter, *To 'Joy My Freedom*; Hall, "'You Must Remember This'"; Nasstrom, "Down to Now"; Fett, *Working Cures*.

7. The separation of "individual" and "collective" is another distinction that is only sometimes instructive. Neither independent individuals nor members of a unified

and harmonious community, enslaved people lived with the complexities and compromises that beset all communities: hierarchy, conflict, difference, and strife. By the same token, even when they acted alone, enslaved people sometimes needed the help of others; when they got it (in the form of assistance or complicity), the distinction between organized, collective action and the self-interested behavior of a single person seems less than useful.

8. Harvey, *Justice, Nature, and the Geography of Difference*, 212.

9. Ibid.; Vlach, *Back of the Big House*, 2; Isaac, *Transformation of Virginia*, 33, "slovens" on 33.

10. Isaac, *Transformation of Virginia*, 38.

11. Ibid., 34–38; Vlach, *Back of the Big House*, 2–6.

12. Harvey, *Justice, Nature, and the Geography of Difference*, 217.

13. McCurry, *Masters of Small Worlds*, 10–11.

14. Ibid., 10–15, esp. 5, 11–13, "boundaries of power" quote on 5, "exclusive use" quote on 11.

15. The term "geography of containment" was coined by Houston Baker in his verbal response to Hanchard, "Temporality, Transnationalism, and Afro-Modernity."

16. Weld, *American Slavery As It Is*, 22.

17. Douglas, *Purity and Danger*, 121. See also Turner, *Ritual Process*, 94; McClintock, *Imperial Leather*, 24.

18. Said, *Culture and Imperialism*, esp. 7, 58. "Rival geography" quote by Said as cited in Godlewska and Smith, "Introduction: Critical Histories of Geography," in *Geography and Empire*, 7–8; Sparke, "Mapped Bodies and Disembodied Maps," 305.

19. Enslaved people's alternative uses of space have been discussed in Rhys Isaac's insightful account of a black "alternative territorial system" in the eighteenth century, and in John Michael Vlach's elegant investigation of slaves' "system of place definition," which was defined by motion. See Isaac, *Transformation of Virginia*, 52–53; Vlach, *Back of the Big House*, 13–14.

20. Raboteau, *Slave Religion*.

21. For discussions of the value of the WPA interviews, see Woodward, "History from Slave Sources," and Charles L. Perdue Jr., introduction to Perdue, Barden, and Phillips, *Weevils*, xi–xlv.

22. For example, Stevenson, *Life in Black and White*; Schwalm, *Hard Fight for We*; Olwell, *Masters, Slaves, and Subjects*; Kerr-Ritchie, *Freedpeople in the Tobacco South*; Baptist, *Creating an Old South*.

23. Greenberg, *Honor and Slavery*: xiii; Thomas D. Morris, *Southern Slavery and the Law*; Berlin, *Many Thousands Gone*; Christopher Morris, "Articulation of Two Worlds."

24. Of these topics, slave religion promises a great deal to women's historians, but the focus here has been secular in the hope that other researchers will explore in greater depth enslaved women's religious lives. Some scholars have already begun to do so; see Moody, *Sentimental Confessions*; Fett, *Working Cures*.

25. James Scott, *Domination and the Arts of Resistance*, 223, 203.

1. This book's perspective on the political significance of space has been informed by the following histories, geographies, and related theories: Bakhtin, *Dialogic Imagination*, 84, 243; Isaac, *Transformation of Virginia*, 17–87; Mike Davis, *City of Quartz*; Vlach, *Back of the Big House*, 1–17; Massey, *Space, Place, and Gender*; McClintock, *Imperial Leather*, 23–25; McCurry, *Masters of Small Worlds*, 5–36; Schmidt, "Mapping an Empire."

2. Jordan, *White over Black* (1968), 55–56.

3. Finley, "Slavery"; Philip D. Morgan, "Bound Labor."

4. On the laws of slavery and movement, see Berlin, *Many Thousands Gone*, 113.

5. Ball, *Slavery in the United States*, 125.

6. Bibb, *Narrative*, 17; Fountain Hughes cited in Berlin, *Remembering Slavery*, 282. Abolitionist Theodore Dwight Weld also found the confinement of jail and that of enslavement to be analogous. He wrote that slaves "have not as much liberty as northern men have, who are in jail for debt" (Weld, *American Slavery As It Is*, 22).

7. Sally Hadden found a shared "need to limit the mobility and actions of their bondsmen" among planters from Virginia, North Carolina, and South Carolina in her study of slave patrols. See Hadden, *Slave Patrols*, 3.

8. Hening, *Statutes at Large*, 2:481.

9. Ibid., 6:107–12, 8:523.

10. Ibid., 6:110–11.

11. Ibid., 8:523.

12. McCord, *Statutes at Large*, 7:343.

13. Ibid., 353, 357, 358.

14. Ibid., 363.

15. Ibid., 343, 352.

16. Ibid.

17. Ibid., 354.

18. Ibid., 352–53.

19. Ibid., 354.

20. General Assembly, *Statutes of the Mississippi Territory*, 382; Howard and Hutchinson, *Statutes of the State of Mississippi*, 156; Howell Cobb, *Compilation of the General and Public Statutes*, 596; Peirce, Taylor, and King, *Consolidation and Revision*, 524; Morehead and Brown, *Digest*, 2:1471; Potter, Taylor, and Yancey, *Laws*, 1:125–126; Thomas R. R. Cobb, *Digest*, 1013.

21. General Assembly, *Laws of the State of Missouri*, 2:748; General Assembly, *Statutes of the Mississippi Territory*, 385; Howard and Hutchinson, *Statutes of the State of Mississippi*, 172; Morehead and Brown, *Digest*, 2:1472; Hening, *Statutes at Large*, 3:460, 6:110–11, 8:523, 11:24, 12:182; Potter, Taylor, and Yancey, *Laws*, 1:165; Martin, *Public Acts*, 2:8, 2:54; Nash, Iredell, and Battle, *Revised Statutes*, 1:577–78.

22. General Assembly, *Laws of the State of Missouri*, 2:748; Howard and Hutchinson, *Statutes of the State of Mississippi*, 156; Howell Cobb, *Compilation of the General*

and Public Statutes, 596–97; Peirce, Taylor, and King, *Consolidation and Revision*, 524; Hening, *Statutes at Large*, 3:460–61, 6:107–11, 8:523.

23. General Assembly, *Laws of the State of Missouri*, 2:742; General Assembly, *Statutes of the Mississippi Territory*, 382; Howard and Hutchinson, *Statutes of the State of Mississippi*, 169; Howell Cobb, *Compilation of the General and Public Statutes*, 596; Peirce, Taylor, and King, *Consolidation and Revision*, 528; Morehead and Brown, *Digest*, 2:1472.

24. Howard and Hutchinson, *Statutes of the State of Mississippi*, 175.

25. General Assembly, *Laws of the State of Missouri*, 2:747–49; General Assembly, *Statutes of the Mississippi Territory*, 384–85; Howard and Hutchinson, *Statutes of the State of Mississippi*, 160–61, 174–75; Howell Cobb, *Compilation of the General and Public Statutes*, 589–90, 599–601, 622–23, 635; Peirce, Taylor, and King, *Consolidation and Revision*, 525, 532–33; Morehead and Brown, *Digest*, 2:1411–12.

26. General Assembly, *Statutes of the Mississippi Territory*, 383; Howard and Hutchinson, *Statutes of the State of Mississippi*, 180, 181; Howell Cobb, *Compilation of the General and Public Statutes*, 601; Morehead and Brown, *Digest*, 2:1302; General Assembly, *Laws of the State of Missouri*, 2:742.

27. Thomas D. Morris, *Southern Slavery and the Law*, 346; General Assembly, *Laws of the State of Missouri*, 2:742; General Assembly, *Statutes of the Mississippi Territory*, 383; Howard and Hutchinson, *Statutes of the State of Mississippi*, 157; Peirce, Taylor, and King, *Consolidation and Revision*, 525; Hening, *Statutes at Large*, 12:182; Nash, Iredell, and Battle, *Revised Statutes*, 1:580.

28. General Assembly, *Laws of the State of Missouri*, 2:747; Morehead and Brown, *Digest*, 1:715–17; Thomas R. R. Cobb, *Digest*, 999–1000.

29. *Code of Virginia*, 492.

30. On history and metaphor, see Painter, "Representing Truth."

31. Harriet Miller in Rawick, *American Slave*, 13(3):128; Andrew Boone in ibid., 14(1):134.

32. Isaac, *Transformation of Virginia*, 34–39; Kay and Cary, *Slavery in North Carolina*, 52–58.

33. Kolchin, *American Slavery*, 93.

34. For more on the shift from slavery's patriarchalism in the colonial era to its paternalism in the antebellum years, see Egerton, *Gabriel's Rebellion*, 4–16; Philip D. Morgan, *Slave Counterpoint*, 258–59, 273–96.

35. Faust, introduction to *Ideology of Slavery*, 1–20; Oakes, *Ruling Race*, 163–64; Greenberg, *Honor and Slavery*, 48; Philip D. Morgan, *Slave Counterpoint*, 284–301; Araby Plantation Journal, n.d. [ca. 1840s], p. 194, Nutt Papers, SCL; Eppes Diary, esp. 29 December 1852, 1 January 1853, Eppes Family Papers, VHS; Barrow, *Plantation Life*, 5 July 1840; Hammond, "Plantation Records for Silver Bluff," Hammond Papers, SC; Cornhill Plantation Book, "Negroes rules for government," Furman Papers, SCL; Rice Memoir, 1, VHS; Richard Blow to George Blow, 6 July 1831, Blow Family Papers, VHS; Plantation Journal, 6 January 1836, Huguenin and Johnston Family Papers, SHC; Flynn Plantation Book, "Plantation Rules," SHC.

36. "Settled arrangement" and "comfortable at Home" quotes in "Rules of Highland Plantation," in Barrow, *Plantation Life*, 407; Hadden, *Slave Patrols*, 111; Genovese, *Roll, Jordan, Roll*, esp. 3–7, "mutual obligations" on 5.

37. Cornhill Plantation Book, "Negroes rules for government," n.d. [ca. 1840s], Furman Papers, SCL.

38. Ball, *Slavery in the United States*, 125.

39. Eppes Diary, 2 September 1859, Eppes Family Papers, VHS.

40. Pass written by Thomas L. Spragins, 4 August 18[18?], Section 86, Spragins Family Papers, VHS. See also passes written by Thomas L. Spragins, 30 August, 5 November 1841, ibid.

41. Plantation Journal, 6 January 1836, "Regulations for the year 1838," Huguenin and Johnston Family Papers, SHC.

42. Pass written by John Bassett, 25 February 1826, Bassett Family Papers, VHS.

43. Pass written by Thomas E. West, 31 August 1843, Spragins Family Papers, VHS.

44. Fountain Hughes cited in Berlin, *Remembering Slavery*, 282–83.

45. Mark M. Smith, "Time, Slavery and Plantation Capitalism," "Old South Time," and *Mastered by the Clock*.

46. Mrs. Nancy Young in Cade, "Out of the Mouths of Ex-Slaves," 314.

47. Eppes Diary, 11 December 1855, Eppes Family Papers, VHS.

48. Eppes Diary for 1858, inside cover, ibid. See also Richard Blow to Samuel Proctor, 21 January 1806, Blow Family Papers, VHS. Blow wrote to Proctor, his overseer, "I wish you to give the Negroes the strictest order, at what time they are to be at their places of work every Monday morning, & not suffer them to be indulged an hour after the time you prefix."

49. Eppes Diary, 14 October 1851, Eppes Family Papers, VHS. See also Flynn Plantation Book, "Plantation Rules," SHC; Richard Blow to Samuel Proctor, 21 January 1806, Blow Family Papers, VHS.

50. William Wells Brown, *Narrative*, 15. See also Harry Smith, *Fifty Years in Slavery*, 10–11.

51. Steward, *Twenty-Two Years a Slave*, 12–13. See also Eppes Diary, 14 October 1851, 28 March 1857, Eppes Family Papers, VHS; Northup, *Twelve Years a Slave*, 171.

52. Northup, *Twelve Years a Slave*, 171. See also William Wells Brown, *Narrative*, 14.

53. Waller Holladay to [?], 31 December 1858, Holladay Family Papers, VHS. See also Kollock Plantation Book for Rosedew Plantation, "Rules," SHC; Mark M. Smith, "Old South Time," 1457, and "Time, Slavery, and Plantation Capitalism," 142–68.

54. Cade, "Out of the Mouths of Ex-Slaves," 321.

55. Ervin Diary, 31 December 1846, SHC.

56. Eppes Diary, 27 March 1852, Eppes Family Papers, VHS. In 1729 the legislators of North Carolina made the singular move of effectively outlawing slave travel at night altogether. The better to stamp out slave "traveling and associating themselves together in great numbers, to the terror and damage of the white people," the assembly reminded blacks and whites that "negroes [who] shall presume to travel in the night"

were liable to be punished with up to forty lashes. See Potter, Taylor, and Yancey, *Laws*, 1:126.

57. Matilda McKinney in Rawick, *American Slave*, 13(3):89.

58. Barrow, *Plantation Life*, 18 February 1840.

59. Jim Allen in Rawick, *American Slave*, supp. ser. 1, 6:59.

60. Judith Page Aylett to William Roane Aylett, 8 April 1851, Aylett Family Papers, VHS. See also Andrew Boone in Rawick, *American Slave*, 14(1):134; Ball, *Slavery in the United States*, 122–23; Eppes Diary, 28 March, 29 December 1857, Eppes Family Papers, VHS.

61. Eppes Diary, 2 January 1853, and List of "Presents," 26 December 1859, Eppes Family Papers, VHS. See also Eppes Diary, 2 September 1859, ibid.

62. Harry Smith, *Fifty Years in Slavery*, 74.

63. G. W. Patillo in Rawick, *American Slave*, 13(3):167.

64. Chock Archie in Cade, "Out of the Mouths of Ex-Slaves," 311.

65. Philip D. Morgan, *Slave Counterpoint*, 389.

66. John Andrew Jackson, *Experience of a Slave*, 11–12.

67. Hadden, *Slave Patrols*, 125–29; Steward, *Twenty-Two Years a Slave*, 19; John Brown, *Slave Life in Georgia*, 13–14; Heard Griffin in Rawick, *American Slave*, 12(2):75.

68. Ben Horry as cited in Joyner, *Down by the Riverside*, 132; Rachel Adams in Rawick, *American Slave*, 12(1):5.

69. Hammond, "Plantation Records for Silver Bluff," 27 May 1832, Hammond Papers, SC. See also Barrow, *Plantation Life*, 11 April 1841.

70. Ball, *Slavery in the United States*, 126.

71. George H. Young to James McDowell, 20 September 1843, McDowell Papers, SCL.

72. "Rules of Highland Plantation," in Barrow, *Plantation Life*, 407.

73. *Southern Cultivator*, cited in Rawick, *American Slave*, 13(4):329–30.

74. Plantation Journal, "Rules and regulations for the management and regulation of my plantation," January 1845, Huguenin and Johnston Family Papers, SHC. See also Flynn Plantation Book, "Plantation Rules," SHC; Knox, *Camp-fire and Cotton-field*, 363.

75. "Rules of Highland Plantation," in Barrow, *Plantation Life*, 410.

76. Plantation Journal, 6 January 1836, Huguenin and Johnston Family Papers, SHC.

77. "Rules of Highland Plantation," in Barrow, *Plantation Life*, 406.

78. Betty Wood, *Women's Work, Men's Work*, 14.

79. Of course, many men knew nothing about boating and navigation techniques, but for examples of those who managed to gain skills ranging from the rudimentary to the expert, see John Brown, *Slave Life in Georgia*, 82; William Wells Brown, *Narrative*, 22; Eppes Diary, 30 November 1851, 2 September 1859, 22 May 1860, Eppes Family Papers, VHS.

80. E.g., Nevitt Diary, 23 January, 5, 12 February, 19, 27 March, 21 May, 12 June, 25

September 1831, SHC; pass written by Larkin Hundley, 8 February 1857, Hundley Family Papers, VHS; George H. Young to James McDowell, 20 September 1843, McDowell Papers, SCL.

81. Pass written by Larkin Hundley, 8 February 1857, Hundley Family Papers, VHS.

82. Hadden, *Slave Patrols*, 111.

83. "Rules of Highland Plantation," in Barrow, *Plantation Life*, 407.

84. Plantation Journal, "Rules and regulations for the management and regulation of my plantation," 1842 and January 1845, Huguenin and Johnston Family Papers, SHC.

85. "Perfect order" quote in Plantation Journal, 6 January 1836, Huguenin and Johnston Family Papers, SHC; "not to marry from Home" quote in Cornhill Plantation Book, "Negroes rules for government," Furman Papers, SCL.

86. Eppes Diary, 2, 12 January 1859, Eppes Family Papers, VHS.

87. Pass written by [?], 30 August 1837, and document by John B. McPhail, 13 January 1845, Spragins Family Papers, VHS.

88. Passes written for Margaret, Maria, Martha, Agnes, Sarah, [?], and Mary by Mary Evelina (Dandridge) Hunter, August and September 1862, Hunter Family Papers, VHS.

89. Pass written by J. B. Jones, 23 December 1853, and pass written by Samuel Jones, 14 October 1858, Jones Family Papers, VHS.

90. Eppes Diary, 1 June 1856, Eppes Family Papers, VHS.

91. Barrow, *Plantation Life*, 15 April 1838. Ira Berlin, Barbara J. Fields, Thavolia Glymph, Joseph P. Reidy, and Leslie S. Rowland came to a similar conclusion in *Freedom*, 11–12.

92. Pilsbury Diary, 25–28 December 1848, SHC.

93. Schwalm, *Hard Fight for We*, 19–46.

94. Georgianna Foster in Rawick, *American Slave*, 14(1):315. See also Henry James Trentham in ibid., 15(2):364.

95. Thomas H. Jones, *Experience*, 7; Hammond, "Plantation Records for Silver Bluff," 3 November 1832, Hammond Papers, SC.

96. "'Round de place" quote by Georgianna Foster in Rawick, *American Slave*, 14(1):316; John Brown, *Slave Life in Georgia*, 7, 13; James Williams in Helen Bradley Foster, *"New Raiments of Self,"* 82; John F. Van Hook in Rawick, *American Slave*, 13(4):80.

97. John F. Van Hook in Rawick, *American Slave*, 13(4):80. See also Hannah Plummer in ibid., 15(2):179; testimony of Nancy Johnson before the Southern Claims Commission, 22 March 1873, in Berlin et al., *Freedom*, 151.

98. John Brown, *Slave Life in Georgia*, 55–56.

99. Northup, *Twelve Years a Slave*, 254–57.

100. Charlie Hudson in Rawick, *American Slave*, 12(2):225. See also Thomas H. Jones, *Experience*, 9; Harry Smith, *Fifty Years in Slavery*, 10; John Brown, *Slave Life in Georgia*, 112–13; William Wells Brown, *Narrative*, 24.

CHAPTER 2

1. Albert, *House of Bondage*, 91–92.

2. This argument builds on the pioneering work of Deborah Gray White, who first pointed out truancy's gender dimensions in her *Ar'n't I a Woman?*, 74–77. Other sources have also discussed truancy in the eighteenth and nineteenth centuries, including Genovese, *Roll, Jordan, Roll*, 648–57; Peter H. Wood, *Black Majority*, 241, 263–68; Fox-Genovese, *Within the Plantation Household*, 319–20; Franklin and Schweninger, *Runaway Slaves*, 98–109, 234. The argument made here departs from the consensus in this literature regarding the limited political significance of truancy.

3. Franklin and Schweninger, *Runaway Slaves*, 211–12. These figures are consistent, though not identical, with those arrived at by Freddie L. Parker for an earlier period. Parker found that between 1775 and 1840, 18 percent of runaway North Carolinians were women. See Parker, *Running for Freedom*, 70–72; see also Deborah Gray White, *Ar'n't I a Woman?*, 74.

4. Deborah Gray White, *Ar'n't I a Woman?*, 76; Fox-Genovese, *Within the Plantation Household*, 320; Malone, *Sweet Chariot*, 15–18, 259–60; Stevenson, *Life in Black and White*, 221–25; King, "'Suffer With Them Until Death'"; Brenda E. Stevenson, "Gender Conventions, Ideals, and Identity among Antebellum Virginia Slave Women," in Gaspar and Hine, *More Than Chattel*, 174–75, 180.

5. Molly Horniblow cited in King, "Mistress and Her Maids," 92.

6. Patience M. Avery in Perdue, Barden, and Phillips, *Weevils*, 14, 16.

7. George Ross, American Freedmen's Inquiry Commission Interviews, 1863, reprinted in Blassingame, *Slave Testimony*, 406.

8. William Wells Brown, *Narrative*, 30–32, 70.

9. Harry Smith, *Fifty Years in Slavery*, 67; Livermore, *My Story of the War*, 353.

10. Bibb, *Narrative*, 16–17.

11. Deborah Gray White, *Ar'n't I a Woman?*, 76; Fox-Genovese, *Within the Plantation Household*, 319.

12. U.S. Census, Schedule 4, Agricultural Census, Adams County, Mississippi, 1850.

13. John Nevitt kept an extraordinarily meticulous log of truants' escapes, mutual assistance, returns, and punishment, providing an important source for the history of truancy. The frequency of absenteeism at Clermont may indicate that enslaved people there engaged in the practice more intensely than did individuals in other places. Yet herein lies the diary's strength. While Nevitt's diary cannot (as no single source can) tell us about truancy everywhere, the heightened activity it documents allows us an unusual glimpse into patterns of gender difference. See Nevitt Diary, SHC.

14. In 1826 and 1829 women's participation was unusually low: no women ran away in 1826 (and only four men did), and only one women ran away (but fifteen men did) in 1829. The percentage of women among truants in the other years was 36 in 1827, 41 in 1828, 30 in 1830, 19 in 1831, and 20 in 1832. See Nevitt Diary, SHC.

15. Rockingham Plantation Journal, SCL.

16. Silver Bluff and Clermont plantations both had even sex ratios; in all likelihood, given the predominance of balanced sex ratios in the antebellum period, Rockingham plantation did as well. See Hammond, "Plantation Records for Silver Bluff," 1831 slave list, Hammond Papers, SC; U.S. Census, Schedule 2, Slave Population, Adams County, Mississippi, 1850.

17. Throughout the plantation Americas, enslaved people tried to escape their shackles by three principal forms of flight: truancy, also known as *petit marronage* in the literature outside the United States; running away to free societies or urban spaces; and *marronage*, the establishment of independent societies. Maroon societies were comparatively rare in the United States, especially by the antebellum period, where flight mainly took the form of escape to the North (or, to a lesser degree, to southern towns and cities) and truancy. The literature on maroons and *petit marronage* in the Americas is immense, but a few canonical studies are Mullin, *Flight and Rebellion*; Price, *Maroon Societies*; Kopytoff, "Early Political Development of Jamaican Maroon Societies"; Heuman, *Out of the House of Bondage*.

18. Lorenzo L. Ivy in Perdue, Barden, and Phillips, *Weevils*, 153; Barrow, *Plantation Life*, 13 August 1839.

19. Albert, *House of Bondage*, 91–92; Hammond, "Plantation Records for Silver Bluff," 22 January 1835, Hammond Papers, SC.

20. Roach Diary, 12, 14 April 1850, VHS.

21. In all years together, the following number of incidents occurred each month: January, 19; February, 14; March, 8; April, 10; May, 5; June, 9; July, 8; August, 7; September, 8; October, 8; November, 14; December, 6; see Nevitt Diary, SHC. For incidents at the beginning of January, see Nevitt's entries for 1 January 1828, 9 January 1829, 6, 11 January 1830, 8 January 1831, and 8 January 1832.

22. George D. Lewis to William L. Lewis, 7 October 1854, Lewis Family Letters, SCL. See also Barrow, *Plantation Life*, 27 October 1838, 16 September 1841; Georgianna Foster in Rawick, *American Slave*, 14(1):317; Weld, *American Slavery As It Is*, 11; Cocke Formbook (1854), 4, VHS.

23. Kemble, *Journal*, 71.

24. "Rules for the management of the negroes at Rock Castle," Rutherford Family Papers, VHS; Cocke Formbook (1854), 4, VHS.

25. Lorenzo L. Ivy in Perdue, Barden, and Phillips, *Weevils*, 154.

26. Hannah Plummer in Rawick, *American Slave*, 15(2):180.

27. Benjamin Johnson in ibid., 12(2):324. See also Veney, *Narrative*, 12.

28. William Brooks in Perdue, Barden, and Phillips, *Weevils*, 57; Virginia Hayes Shepherd in ibid., 259. See also Bibb, *Narrative*, 16, 26; Louise Jones in Perdue, Barden, and Phillips, *Weevils*, 186; Benjamin Johnson in Rawick, *American Slave*, 12(2):324.

29. "Compilation," in Rawick, *American Slave*, 13(4):292. For more examples of working white men's sexual relations with enslaved women, see Eppes Diary, 5 September 1857, Eppes Family Papers, VHS; William Wells Brown, *Narrative*, 24.

30. Anna Baker in Rawick, *American Slave*, 7(2):13.

31. Lizzie F. Partin to [her sister], 24 February 1858, Bain Papers, SCL.

32. Tom Hawkins in Rawick, *American Slave*, 12(2):130; Julia Rush in ibid., 13(3):230; Lueatha Mansfield in Cade, "Out of the Mouths of Ex-Slaves," 311.

33. Roach Diary, 31 July 1850, VHS.

34. Judith Page Aylett to William Roane Aylett, 8 April 1851, Aylett Family Papers, VHS.

35. Benjamin Johnson in Rawick, *American Slave*, 12(2):324.

36. Lue Bradford in Cade, "Out of the Mouths of Ex-Slaves," 321; Sylvia DuBois, *Sylvia DuBois*, 54–55, 64–66.

37. Eppes Diary, 18 January 1858, Eppes Family Papers, VHS.

38. Sylvia DuBois, *Sylvia DuBois*, 54–55, 64–66.

39. M. J. Sims in Cade, "Out of the Mouths of Ex-Slaves," 308.

40. In addition to gender difference and push and pull factors, many local issues shaped truancy. Rebellion plots and scares would have both encouraged and chilled truancy, as would have the vacillations in interpersonal relationships between enslaved people and overseers, drivers, and owners. Changes in black family and community life (such as births, deaths, marriages, and sales) gave reasons to run or to stay in place, depending on the situation. For instance, men who did not live with their families certainly would have run away to visit them for events such as the birth of a child, whether they were given permission or not. Moreover, in all likelihood many of the women and men who attended slave funerals and weddings did not have passes and were thus absentee.

41. Philip D. Morgan's work on runaways in colonial South Carolina also concluded that visiting was an important incentive, especially for men looking for mates; see his "Colonial South Carolina Runaways," 69–74.

42. Gutman, *Black Family in Slavery and Freedom*; Stevenson, *Life in Black and White*.

43. Douglass, *Narrative* (1989), 2. See also Albert, *House of Bondage*, 21.

44. A. R. McCall to George Noble Jones, 21 June 1856, in Phillips and Glunt, *Florida Plantation Records*.

45. Alice Green in Rawick, *American Slave*, 12(2):34.

46. Bibb, *Narrative*, 26–28.

47. Ellen Campbell in Rawick, *American Slave*, 13(4):224–25. See also Nevitt Diary, 12, 20 February 1831, SHC.

48. On slaves' "invisible institution," the black church, see Raboteau, *Slave Religion*.

49. Rev. W. P. Jacobs in Perdue, Barden, and Phillips, *Weevils*, 157. See also Albert, *House of Bondage*, 11.

50. Susan McIntosh in Rawick, *American Slave*, 13(3):84; Fett, *Working Cures*, 60–83.

51. Fett, *Working Cures*, esp. 72, 36–83, 81; "read the woods" quote in ibid., 72; Eppes, *Negro of the Old South*, 98–100.

52. Albert, *House of Bondage*, 96; John Brown, *Slave Life in Georgia*, 74.

53. Hammond, "Plantation Records for Silver Bluff," 24, 26 January 1832, Hammond Papers, SC; Olmsted, *Cotton Kingdom*, 76.

54. Charles Crawley in Perdue, Barden, and Phillips, *Weevils*, 78; Liza Brown in ibid., 63.

55. Albert, *House of Bondage*, 97.

56. Ibid.

57. Olmsted, *Cotton Kingdom*, 76.

58. Veney, *Narrative*, 12. See also Albert, *House of Bondage*, 88.

59. Barrow, *Plantation Life*, 22 September 1841. See also Hammond, "Plantation Records for Silver Bluff," 16 July 1832, Hammond Papers, SC.

60. Document by John B. McPhail, 13 January 1845, and pass written by [?], 30 August 1837, Spragins Family Papers, VHS; Rosalie P. Aylett to William Roane Aylett, 8 April 1851, Aylett Family Papers, VHS.

61. Hammond, "Plantation Records for Silver Bluff," 1831 slave list, 5 July 1835, Hammond Papers, SC.

62. Nevitt Diary, SHC; Hammond, "Plantation Records for Silver Bluff," 24, 26 January 1832, 2 November 1833, Hammond Papers, SC; John Brown, *Slave Life in Georgia*, 74; Barrow, *Plantation Life*, 1 April 1838, 11 April, 22 September 1841, 22 June 1842, 7 May 1843; Albert, *House of Bondage*, 88–89, 94, 96; Liza Brown in Perdue, Barden, and Phillips, *Weevils*, 63; Charles Crawley in Perdue, Barden, and Phillips, *Weevils*, 78; Lorenzo L. Ivy in Perdue, Barden, and Phillips, *Weevils*, 153; Olmsted, *Cotton Kingdom*, 76, 450.

63. Olmsted, *Cotton Kingdom*, 76, 450; Mollie Booker in Perdue, Barden, and Phillips, *Weevils*, 54; Samuel Walter Chilton in Perdue, Barden, and Phillips, *Weevils*, 71; Cecelski, *Waterman's Song*, 121–51. Fugitives appear to have received more assistance from whites—sympathetic Quakers and sailors or labor-hungry timber companies and naval stores—than did truants, who remained within planters' spheres of influence. See Cecelski, *Waterman's Song*, 130–32.

64. Lorenzo L. Ivy in Perdue, Barden, and Phillips, *Weevils*, 154.

65. Mollie Booker in ibid., 54. See also Cornelia Carney in ibid., 67.

66. Rosalie P. Aylett to William Roane Aylett, 8 April 1851, Aylett Family Papers, VHS.

67. Midge Burnett in Rawick, *American Slave*, 14(1):156.

68. Hammond, "Plantation Records for Silver Bluff," 1831 slave list, 18 July 1832, Hammond Papers, SC.

69. Barrow, *Plantation Life*, 25 December 1839.

70. Camilla Jackson in Rawick, *American Slave*, 13(4):257.

71. Olmsted, *Cotton Kingdom*, 76.

72. Nevitt Diary, 20, 28 March 1831, SHC.

73. Lorenzo L. Ivy in Perdue, Barden, and Phillips, *Weevils*, 153–54.

74. Hannah Plummer in Rawick, *American Slave*, 15(2):180–81.

75. William Brooks in Perdue, Barden, and Phillips, *Weevils*, 57.

76. Barrow, *Plantation Life*, 19 October 1843.

77. Nevitt Diary, 18 March 1832, SHC.

78. Olmsted, *Journey in the Back Country*, 48. See also Hammond, "Plantation Records for Silver Bluff," 18, 19 July 1832, Hammond Papers, SC; Blassingame, *Slave Community*, 196; Faust, *James Henry Hammond and the Old South*, 95.

79. Cornelia Carney in Perdue, Barden, and Phillips, *Weevils*, 67.

80. Albert, *House of Bondage*, 70–71.

81. Ibid., 88–89.

82. See Eric Hobsbawm's discussion of social banditry for more on the importance of "individual" protest in the eyes of peasant classes, in his *Primitive Rebels*, 5–17. James Scott discusses the self-interested nature of organized as well as unorganized politics in his *Weapons of the Weak*, 291–303.

83. Albert, *House of Bondage*, 88–92.

84. Hammond, "Plantation Records for Silver Bluff," 1, 18 July 1832, Hammond Papers, SC; Cornhill Plantation Book, "Rules for negroes," [ca. January 1847], Furman Papers, SCL; Faust, *James Henry Hammond and the Old South*, 95.

85. Nevitt Diary, 9 July, 21 August, 2 October, 9, 13 November 1827, 25 January, 2 March, 6 December, 2 September 1828, 24 July, 9 November, 3 December 1830, 2 September 1832, SHC; "brought home" quote in 2 September 1832 entry; "sent him out" and "forgave Rubin" quotes in 2 October 1827 entry; Nevitt paying neighboring bondmen for their services on 24 July 1830 and 3 August 1832. See also Hammond, "Plantation Records for Silver Bluff," 1 November 1833, 11–12 May 1835, Hammond Papers, SC; Peter H. Wood, *Black Majority*, 264.

86. Dennis was accused by local whites of having been involved in a planned rebellion, but Barrow refused to believe it, conferring the blame for the plot on his neighbors' bondmen. See Barrow, *Plantation Life*, 16 April, 17 July 1841; see also 25 December 1839.

87. Testimony of Colonel Higginson before the American Freedmen's Inquiry Commission, June 1863, in Berlin et al., *Freedom*, 138–39.

88. James H. R. Washington to George Paul Harrison, 18 March 1846, Harrison Papers, SCL. See also Elizabeth Sparks in Perdue, Barden, and Phillips, *Weevils*, 274.

89. For more on slave patrols, see Fry, *Nightriders in Black Folk History*; Hadden, *Slave Patrols*.

90. Annie Stephenson in Rawick, *American Slave*, 15(2):314. See also Hammond, "Plantation Records for Silver Bluff," 13 June 1832, 1 August 1834, Hammond Papers, SC; Barrow, *Plantation Life*, 29 September, 1 October 1837, 29 May, 18 July 1840, 26 March 1841.

91. Barrow, *Plantation Life*, 15–16 October, 9 November 1844, 15, 27 October, 11 November 1845. See also Philip Henry Pitts Diary and Account Book, 17 September 1850, SHC; Rev. Ishrael Massie in Perdue, Barden, and Phillips, *Weevils*, 209; William Wells Brown, *Narrative*, 21–22.

92. Barrow, *Plantation Life*, 29 September 1837, 18 July, 4 December 1840, 26 March 1841, 7 May 1843, 15–18 October, 9 November 1844, 28–30 September, 14, 27 October

1845; quotes in entries for 27 October 1845, 4 December 1840. See also Hammond, "Plantation Records for Silver Bluff," 16 July 1832, 12 August, 4 October 1833, 20 July 1844, Hammond Papers, SC; Nevitt Diary, 29 May, 7 June, 13 November 1830, 25, 27 April 1832, SHC; Eppes Diary, 30 November 1851, Eppes Family Papers, VHS; Veney, *Narrative*, 13.

93. Cornelia Carney in Perdue, Barden, and Phillips, *Weevils*, 67.

94. Hammond, "Plantation Records for Silver Bluff," 29 January, 16 February 1847, Hammond Papers, SC.

95. Elizabeth Sparks in Perdue, Barden, and Phillips, *Weevils*, 274.

96. Cornhill Plantation Book, 23 January, 2 December 1847, 26 June 1848, "Runaway Negroes &c." [ca. January 1847], Furman Papers, SCL. Sumterville had an enslaved population of 846 and 10 free blacks in 1850; see U.S. Census Office, *Seventh Census*, 339.

97. Charlie Pye in Rawick, *American Slave*, 13(3):187.

98. Nevitt Diary, SHC.

99. Kemble, *Journal*, 216.

100. Liza McCoy in Perdue, Barden, and Phillips, *Weevils*, 199. See also Weld, *American Slavery As It Is*, 21.

101. John Price, Jason Fussell, J. J. Anderson, [illegible], and G. J. J. Anderson to Montezuma Jones, 5 February 1850, Jones Papers, SHC.

102. Eppes, *Negro of the Old South*, 100.

103. Roswell King to Pierce Butler, 25 November 1803, 25 October 1812, 27 June 1813, 6 July 1817, Butler Family Papers, PHS; Kemble, *Journal*, 230.

104. Lorenzo L. Ivy in Perdue, Barden, and Phillips, *Weevils*, 153.

105. Barrow, *Plantation Life*, 1 April 1838, 13 August 1839, 22 December 1840, 22 June 1842, 15 October 1844. See also Eppes Diary, 11 December 1852, 29 December 1857, Eppes Family Papers, VHS; Gavin Diary, 20 November 1855, 22 January, 14 March 1856, 25 January 1858, SHC.

106. Kali Nicole Gross explores violence as a language in "Dismembered Body of Wakefield Gaines."

107. Alex Woods in Rawick, *American Slave*, 15(2):416–17. See also Henry James Trentham in ibid., 15(2):365.

108. Henry James Trentham in ibid., 15(2):365; Dosia Harris in ibid., 12(2):108; Nevitt Diary, 17 January 1828, SHC; William Wells Brown, *Narrative*, 22.

109. Lizzie Williams in Rawick, *American Slave*, 15(2):396; Eppes Diary, 8 October 1851, Eppes Family Papers, VHS; Nevitt Diary, 21 April 1826, 29 April, 9 November 1827, 17 July 1828, 26 March, 3 April, 18 July, 2 September, 4 November 1832, SHC; John R. Lyons to "Uncle Billy," 4 April 1854, Renwick Papers, SCL; Barrow, *Plantation Life*, 4 October 1839, "scab" quote in 15 September 1840 entry.

110. Cage with bells in John Brown, *Slave Life in Georgia*, 76; "decent smoking" quote in William Wells Brown, *Narrative*, 22; "womens cloths" quote in Barrow, *Plantation Life*, 20 April 1838; see also 21 July 1839. Truants were reported to have been

shot and killed or shot at in Rachel O'Connor to Mary Weeks Moore, 7 May 1844, in Webb, *Mistress of Evergreen Plantation*; Barrow, *Plantation Life*, 16, 19 November, 24 May 1837, 28 September 1838, 11 December 1839, 16 September 1841; Ellen Campbell in Rawick, *American Slave*, 13(4):224–25; Weld, *American Slavery As It Is*, 11.

111. John Brown, *Slave Life in Georgia*, 55–56.

112. Nevitt Diary, 1 January, 23 December 1829, 13 February 1832, SHC; Cornhill Plantation Book, "Negroes" [n.d.], "Runaway Negroes, &c." [ca. January 1847], SCL. See also D. W. Parrish to Charles Johnston, 12 December 1844, Johnston Papers, SHC; John R. Lyons to "Uncle Billy," 4 April 1854, Renwick Papers, SCL; Hammond, "Plantation Records for Silver Bluff," 11–12 May, 7, 18 July 1835, Hammond Papers, SC.

113. Charles Crawley in Perdue, Barden, and Phillips, *Weevils*, 78.

114. *Clagon v. Veasey*, 7 Iredell Eq. (Supreme Court of North Carolina, June 1851), 176.

115. Barrow, *Plantation Life*, 3 October 1839.

116. Virginia Hayes Shepherd in Perdue, Barden, and Phillips, *Weevils*, 259.

117. Kemble, *Journal*, 230, 238; A. R. McCall to George Noble Jones, 21 June 1856, in Phillips and Glunt, *Florida Plantation Records*; Nevitt Diary, 29 April 1827, SHC; Albert, *House of Bondage*, 21. John Mann shot Lydia, the bondwoman he had hired, when she ran away from him. Her owner's prosecution of Mann led to the famous case *State v. Mann*, 12 NC 263 (1829), Supreme Court of North Carolina. Elsa Barkley Brown has suggested that black women may have been subjected to more violence in the postbellum years than has been appreciated by historians; see her "Negotiating and Transforming the Public Sphere."

118. Eppes Diary, 8 October 1851, Eppes Family Papers, VHS. See also Albert, *House of Bondage*, 92.

119. Albert, *House of Bondage*, 20.

120. Harry Smith, *Fifty Years in Slavery*, 71.

121. Olmsted, *Cotton Kingdom*, 453–56.

122. Nevitt Diary, SHC. Nevitt used the word "forgave" in the 20 July, 10 August, 2 October 1827, and 5 February 1831 entries.

123. John R. Lyons to "Uncle Billy," 4 April 1854, Renwick Papers, SCL. See also Fannie Berry in Perdue, Barden, and Phillips, *Weevils*, 34.

124. Nevitt Diary, 31 August 1832, SHC; Hammond, "Plantation Records for Silver Bluff," 22 January 1835, Hammond Papers, SC.

125. Olmsted, *Cotton Kingdom*, 75.

126. "Playing possum" in Eppes Diary, 18 January 1858, Eppes Family Papers, VHS.

127. Hammond, "Plantation Records for Silver Bluff," 10 October 1839, Hammond Papers, SC; Diary of Francis Cope Yarnall, "Letters of Slavery," 1853, Yarnall Papers, SCL; Plantation Journal, "Regulations for the year 1838," Huguenin and Johnston Family Papers, SHC; Barrow, *Plantation Life*, 22 June 1842.

128. Bacot Diary, 11 February 1861, SC.

1. Nancy Williams in Perdue, Barden, and Phillips, *Weevils*, 316. Williams was fourteen years old when the Civil War began. Before slavery ended, however, she had reached young adulthood; she told her interviewer that she had "growed up" when she left the slaveholding house for field work. Many enslaved people came of age at this point in their lives. About the same time, she "start[ed] dis cou'tin.'" Like many, but not all, formerly enslaved interviewees in the 1930s, Williams had more than a child's memory of bondage. She offers, as do other interviewees in the Works Progress Administration collection, the rich testimony of a young adult.

2. Bondpeople living on farms, in neighborhoods, and in states (such as Florida and Delaware) with small numbers of other enslaved people would certainly have enjoyed far fewer illegal parties, if they managed to organize any at all. Conversely, South Carolina's black majority no doubt had greater decision-making power over the frequency and quality of their parties. But South Carolinians were not the only enslaved people to know life in a black majority. In 1850 about half (50.6 percent) of all bondpeople lived on farms that owned at least 20 people. A significant minority of 13.1 percent lived on holdings of 50 to 100 people. See Gray, *History of Agriculture*, 1:530. Locally, then, many enslaved people inhabited communities among and near enough others to make independent socializing in the form of secret parties viable.

3. My analysis here builds on Albert Raboteau's work on slave Christianity and its proto-institutional qualities, as well as on George Rawick's and Charles Joyner's studies of the "off times" hours between "sundown to sunup." See Raboteau, *Slave Religion*; Rawick, *From Sundown to Sunup*; Joyner, *Down by the Riverside*.

4. Work, *American Negro Songs*, 43, 144.

5. Ariela J. Gross, *Double Character*, 124.

6. On slaves' commodification, see Walter Johnson, *Soul by Soul*; Edward E. Baptist, " 'Cuffy,' 'Fancy Maids,' and 'One-Eyed Men.' "

7. Ida B. Wells as cited in Fett, *Working Cures*, 1.

8. Many works have theorized the social significance of the body, including Fanon, *Black Skin, White Masks*, 109–40; Douglas, *Natural Symbols*, 65–81; Foucault, *Discipline and Punish*, esp. 3–31, 73–103. Recent historical scholarship has demonstrated that the black body has been more than a site of racial subjugation and suffering; see, for example, Kelley, *Race Rebels*; Hunter, *To 'Joy My Freedom*; Helen Bradley Foster, *"New Raiments of Self"*; White and White, *Stylin'*.

9. Dorinda Outram, *Body and the French Revolution*, 1; James, Lee, and Chaulieu, *Facing Reality*, 5; James Scott, *Weapons of the Weak*, 289–99. Dagmar Herzog and Uta Poiger have demonstrated that German feminist analyses connecting the personal and the political grew out of broader German New Left efforts to do the same. American and German feminist movements in the 1970s may have popularized the concept and applied it in especially relevant ways to women's lives, but they did not invent it. See Dagmar Herzog, " 'Pleasure, Sex and Politics Belong Together' "; Poiger, *Jazz, Rock and Rebels*, 219, 269 n. 32.

10. Hine and Wittenstein, "Female Slave Resistance"; Deborah Gray White, *Ar'n't I a Woman*; Fox-Genovese, *Within the Plantation Household*; Painter, *Sojourner Truth*; Schwalm, *Hard Fight for We*; Fett, *Working Cures*.

11. White abolitionists used graphic representations of the exploited, abused, or degraded enslaved body to garner support for the antislavery cause. See Lapsansky, "Graphic Discord"; Clark, " 'Sacred Rights of the Weak.' " Scholars of slave narratives have demonstrated that black writers—especially women—used rhetorical strategies to draw attention away from their bodies in order to emphasize their political voices rather than titillate white audiences. See Barthelemy introduction; Peterson, *"Doers of the Word,"* esp. 22; DeLombard, " 'Eye-witness to the Cruelty.' "

12. Jennifer L. Morgan, " 'Some Could Suckle over Their Shoulder,' " esp. 170, 171, 179, 181, 184.

13. Kathleen M. Brown, *Good Wives*, 116–19, 125, 135. For more on the origins of notions of racial difference and their relation to the expansion of the African slave trade and American slavery, see Edmund S. Morgan, *American Slavery, American Freedom*, 295–337; Jordan, *White over Black* (1969); Vaughn, "Origins Debate"; Kolchin, *American Slavery*, 11–12, 17.

14. James T. Alexander to William Roane Aylett, 20 December 1855, and William Roane Aylett to Alice Roane (Brockenbrough) Aylett, 10 February 1864, Aylett Family Papers, VHS; Eppes Diary, 1 September 1859, List of "Presents," 26 December 1859, 2 January 1860, 4 December 1865, Eppes Family Papers, VHS; Robert C. Henderson to Peter Saunders, 11 January 1862, Saunders Family Papers, VHS; Nevitt Diary, 25–26 December 1827, 25–27 December 1828, 26 December 1829, 24, 26 December 1831, SHC; Colin Clarke to Maxwell Troax Clarke, 20 September 1854, 14 September 1862, Clarke Papers, SHC; Ellen McCollam to Andrew McCollam Jr., 5 October 1860, 26 March 1863, McCollam Papers, SHC; Hammond, "Plantation Records for Silver Bluff," 4 November 1833, 5 June, 9, 10 October 1839, 8 May 1840, 23 February 1847, Hammond Papers, SC; Barrow, *Plantation Life*, 13 September 1839, 11 April 1840, 2 October 1841, 19 October 1843, 11 October, 28 November 1844; Charles Lewellyn to P. C. Cameron, 28 September 1848, Cameron Family Papers, SHC; Ervin Diary, 25 April 1846, SHC.

15. Martha Allen in Rawick, *American Slave*, 14(1):14.

16. Rev. Ishrael Massie in Purdue et al., *Weevils*, 207.

17. Carrie Mason in Rawick, *American Slave*, 13(3):112–13. Interracial sex was generally treated as an open secret, scandalous only when publicly acknowledged. See Joshua D. Rothman, "James Callendar and Social Knowledge of Interracial Sex in Antebellum Virginia," in Lewis and Onuf, *Sally Hemings and Thomas Jefferson*, 87–113.

18. Webb, *Mistress of Evergreen Plantation*, 2 April 1834.

19. *"Wickedness"* in Webb, *Mistress of Evergreen Plantation*, 2 April 1834; "prostitutes" in Chesnut, *Diary from Dixie*, 14 March 1861.

20. Webb, *Mistress of Evergreen Plantation*, 20 November 1833, 19 February, 2 April 1834. For other examples of white men's sexual violence against enslaved women, see John Brown, *Slave Life in Georgia*, 112–13; "Compilation" in Rawick, *American Slave*,

13(4):292; Douglass, *Narrative* (1960), 24; Kemble, *Journal*, 230; Veney, *Narrative*, 26. For scholarship on sexual contact between white men and enslaved women in the colonial and Old South, see Faust, *James Henry Hammond and the Old South*, 314–19; McLaurin, *Celia*; Gordon-Reed, *Thomas Jefferson and Sally Hemings*; Philip D. Morgan, *Slave Counterpoint*, 398–412; Block, "Lines of Color, Sex, and Service"; Lewis and Onuf, *Sally Hemings and Thomas Jefferson*; Baptist, " 'Cuffy,' 'Fancy Maids,' and 'One-Eyed Men.' " For an example of how notions of black women's hyperactive sexuality infused everyday southern culture, see the raunchy verse penned by the University of North Carolina college student Young Allen, n.d., folder 10, ser. 3, Young Allen Papers, SHC.

21. Eppes Diary, 24 December 1853, Eppes Family Papers, VHS; Anna Baker in Rawick, *American Slave*, 7(2):12.

22. Midge Burnett in Rawick, *American Slave*, 14(1):157; Genovese, *Roll, Jordan, Roll*, 3–7, 570, 577–80, 584. Roger Abrahams has shown how bondpeople sometimes turned paternalistic events like cornshuckings into rituals of their own meaning. See Abrahams, *Singing the Master*, esp. 83–106.

23. Barrow, *Plantation Life*, 3 January 1840.

24. Ibid., 31 December 1837.

25. As cited in Hazzard-Gordon, *Jookin'*, 18.

26. Lenneth Jones in Rawick, *American Slave*, 16(1):23. See also George Fleming in ibid., supp. ser. 1, 11:128.

27. Nevitt Diary, 25, 30 December 1827, 27 December 1828, 25 December 1829, 27 December 1830, SHC.

28. Neal Upson in Rawick, *American Slave*, 13(4):68; Bill Heard in ibid., 12(2):142.

29. "Bio-text" is John O'Neill's term in *Communicative Body*, 3.

30. Thomas H. Jones, *Experience*, 5.

31. Fanon, *Black Skin, White Masks*, 110–11. Hortense Spillers described the distinction between "body" and "flesh" as the "central one between liberated and captive subject-positions" (Spillers, "Mama's Baby, Papa's Maybe," 457).

32. Edmund S. Morgan, "Slavery and Freedom" and *American Slavery, American Freedom*, 295–337; Faust, *James Henry Hammond and the Old South*; Greenberg, *Honor and Slavery*, 48; Walter Johnson, *Soul by Soul*; Ariela J. Gross, *Double Character*, 131.

33. The lyrics, as Bob Ellis remembered them, were

> Keep yo' eye on de sun,
> See how she run,
> Don't let her catch you with your work undone.
> I'm a trouble, I'm a trouble,
> Trouble don' las' always.

See Ellis in Perdue, Barden, and Phillips, *Weevils*, 88; Charlie Crump in Rawick, *American Slave*, 14(1):213. For another version, see George White in Perdue, Barden, and Phillips, *Weevils*, 308.

34. Ebenezer Pettigrew as cited in Cecelski, *Waterman's Song*, 66.

35. Charlie Crump in Rawick, *American Slave*, 14(1):213; Midge Burnett in ibid., 14(1):156.

36. Charlie Crump in ibid., 14(1):213; Midge Burnett in ibid., 14(1):156; Kitty Hill in ibid., 14(1):424; Isaac, *Transformation of Virginia*, 53.

37. Jefferson Franklin Henry in Rawick, *American Slave*, 12(2):188.

38. Steward, *Twenty-Two Years a Slave*, 19–22.

39. Ibid., 20.

40. Ibid., 15, 21.

41. Ibid., 20–24.

42. Ibid., 23–24.

43. Mrs. Bird Walton in Perdue, Barden, and Phillips, *Weevils*, 297; Charlie Crump in Rawick, *American Slave*, 14(1):213; Minnie Folkes in Perdue, Barden, and Phillips, *Weevils*, 93; Perry Lewis in Rawick, *American Slave*, 16(8):49–50; John F. Van Hook in Rawick, *American Slave*, 13(4):80; Fry, *Nightriders in Black Folk History*, 93; Hadden, *Slave Patrols*, 109.

44. John C. Van Hook in Rawick, *American Slave*, 13(4):80.

45. Roy Redfield in ibid., 13(4):306; Fannie Moore in ibid., 15(2):132.

46. George Fleming in ibid., supp. ser. 1, 11:127.

47. Hungerford, *Old Plantation*, 61–63.

48. Elder, *Life of Samuel Hall*, 29.

49. Roy Redfield in Rawick, *American Slave*, 13(4):306; Fannie Moore in ibid., 15(2):132; Rhodus Walton in ibid., 13(4): 40, 64, 124; Nancy Williams in Perdue, Barden, and Phillips, *Weevils*, 316; Phil Towns in Rawick, *American Slave*, 13(4):40; Neal Upson in Rawick, *American Slave*, 13(4):64; George Fleming in Rawick, *American Slave*, supp. ser. 1, 11:128.

50. Dosia Harris in Rawick, *American Slave*, 12(2):110.

51. Mollie Williams in ibid., 7(2):161.

52. James Singleton in ibid. 7(2):126.

53. Mollie Williams in ibid., 7(2):162.

54. Ibid., 7(2):161.

55. White and White, *Stylin'*, 73. "Hugged up" and "indecent" in Eliza Washington interview in Rawick, *American Slave*, 11(7):52.

56. Liza Mention in Rawick, *American Slave*, 13(3):124; Fannie Berry in Perdue, Barden, and Phillips, *Weevils*, 49–50.

57. Fannie Berry in Perdue, Barden, and Phillips, *Weevils*, 49; George Fleming in Rawick, *American Slave*, supp. ser. 1, 11:127; Hazzard-Gordon, *Jookin'*, 19.

58. Philip D. Morgan, *Slave Counterpoint*, 586.

59. Hazzard-Gordon, *Jookin'*, 20; Nancy Williams in Perdue, Barden, and Phillips, *Weevils*, 316; Jane Smith Hill Harmon in Rawick, *American Slave*, 12(2):99.

60. Barrow, *Plantation Life*, 30 December 1838.

61. Stevenson, *Life in Black and White*, 255, 23; Christopher Morris, *Becoming Southern*, 63; *State v. Thornton* (NC) Busbee 252, June 1853; *State v. Jarot* (NC) I

Iredell, 76, June 1840; Indictments of Daniel Keese [et al.], December 1849, Craven County, County Criminal Records, NCSDA; James Cornelius in Rawick, *American Slave*, 7(2):30. Dora Franks remembered singing "Old Dan Tucker" with other enslaved youth in Mississippi; see Dora Franks in Rawick, *American Slave*, 7(2):53.

62. *State v. Isaac, a slave*, 29 August 1859, Granville County CR, 1857–1863, folder 1859, NCSDA.

63. Stone, *Brokenburn*, 2 March 1863.

64. Addie Vinson in Rawick, *American Slave*, 13(4):104.

65. For more on black style under slavery, see Patricia Hunt, "Struggle to Achieve Individual Expression"; Helen Bradley Foster, *"New Raiments of Self"*; White and White, *Stylin'*.

66. Joyner, *Down by the Riverside*, 107.

67. Olmsted, *Cotton Kingdom*, 82; Rachel Adams in Rawick, *American Slave*, 12(1):4; Charity McCallister in Rawick, *American Slave*, 15(2):62; Fannie Dunn in Rawick, *American Slave*, 14(1):272.

68. Roswell King to Pierce Butler, 6 July 1817, Butler Family Papers, PHS.

69. Faust, *James Henry Hammond and the Old South*, 100–103; Genovese, *Roll, Jordan, Roll*, 5–7; Eppes Diary, Eppes Family Papers; Roswell King to Pierce Butler, 7 December 1812, 20 April 1816, 6 July 1817, Butler Family Papers PHS; Jacobs, *Incidents in the Life of a Slave Girl*, 11.

70. Ann Clark in Rawick, *American Slave*, 4(1):223; George Fleming in ibid., supp. ser. 1, 11:130. See also Annie Osborne in ibid., supp. ser. 2, 8:2990. As other historians have pointed out, this "masculinization" of bondwomen at work was never complete, and rarely did it define enslaved women's gender identities. At work in their specialized labor, their gender-segregated or gender-specific agricultural labor, and the reproductive labor they performed for their families, enslaved women constructed their own meanings and expressions of womanhood. See Deborah Gray White, *Ar'n't I a Woman?*; Jacqueline Jones, *Labor of Love, Labor of Sorrow*; Schwalm, *Hard Fight for We*.

71. On the South Carolina slave economy, see Phillip D. Morgan, *Slave Counterpoint*; Olwell, *Masters, Slaves, and Subjects*, 166–80; Lockley, "Trading Encounters." Enslaved South Carolinians' independent economy has gained the most scholarly attention, but bondpeople everywhere in the South traded goods and owned property. See Penningroth, "Slavery, Freedom, and Social Claims," 409.

72. Olmsted, *Cotton Kingdom*, 82; Charlie Meadow as cited in Helen Bradley Foster, *"New Raiments of Self,"* 111; Marie Askin Simpson as cited in Helen Bradley Foster, *"New Raiments of Self,"* 112; Jennie Kendricks in Rawick, *American Slave*, 13(3):2; Charlie Pye in Rawick, *American Slave*, 13(3):186; Olmsted, *Cotton Kingdom*, 82; Charlie Hudson in Rawick, *American Slave*, 12(2):228; Susan McIntosh in Rawick, *American Slave*, 13(3):81; Hannah Plummer in Rawick, *American Slave*, 15(2):179; Betty Brown in Rawick, *American Slave*, 11(2):53; Nancy Williams in Perdue, Barden, and Phillips, *Weevils*, 316–17; Mary A. Hicks in Rawick, *American Slave*, 14(1):184;

Joyner, *Down by the Riverside*, 74; Schwalm, *Hard Fight for We*, 60; Buchanan, "Slave Mississippi," 175–84.

73. For recipes, see Page Commonplace Book, VHS; Helen Bradley Foster, *"New Raiments of Self,"* app. 3; Susan McIntosh in Rawick, *American Slave*, 13(3):81.

74. Jennie Kendricks in Rawick, *American Slave*, 13(3):2; Charlie Pye in ibid., 13(3):186.

75. Morris Sheppard and Catherine Slim in Helen Bradley Foster, *"New Raiments of Self,"* 114; Helen Bradley Foster, *"New Raiments of Self,"* 112, app. 3; Nancy Williams in Perdue, Barden, and Phillips, *Weevils*, 316–17; Mary A. Hicks in Rawick, *American Slave*, 14(1):184; Betty Brown in Rawick, *American Slave*, 11(2):52–53; Olmsted, *Cotton Kingdom*, 82.

76. Henry James Trentham in Rawick, *American Slave*, 15(2):364.

77. Isaac Williams, *Aunt Sally*, 47; John Hook in Rawick, *American Slave*, 13(4):80; Hannah Plummer in Rawick, *American Slave*, 15(2):179; Charlie Grant in Rawick, *American Slave*, supp. ser. 1, 1:165; Betty Cofer in Rawick, *American Slave*, 14(1):169.

78. Isaac Williams, *Aunt Sally*, 47; John Goodwin in Albert, *House of Bondage*, 64; Bill Collins as cited in Helen Bradley Foster, *"New Raiments of Self,"* 104; Ed McCree in Rawick, *American Slave*, 13(3):60.

79. Tempie Herndon Durham in Rawick, *American Slave*, 14(1):286.

80. Anna Mitchell in ibid., 15(2):114.

81. "Aunt Martha" and Sina Banks as cited in Helen Bradley Foster, *"New Raiments of Self,"* 104; Coles Diary, 162, VHS; Betty Cofer in Rawick, *American Slave*, 14(1):169. Leslie Schwalm has shown that South Carolina rice planters did not consider specialized women's work to be skilled; they reserved that designation for men's work. "Skilled" status brought rewards to the worker, but because most women specialists were denied recognition, their work brought them "none of the relative advantages enjoyed by slave men in skilled jobs—not the mobility, not the option of earning cash for extra work, not the prestige or power accrued by drivers." But their specialized labor did grant women a "degree of independence, an escape from direct supervision, and a means of avoiding the demanding, treacherous labor of the rice fields." See Schwalm, *Hard Fight for We*, 21, 32–33, 45.

82. Amanda McDaniel in Rawick, *American Slave*, 13(3):73; Isaac Williams, *Aunt Sally*, 47; Albert, *House of Bondage*, 64; Henry James Trentham in Rawick, *American Slave*, 15(2):364. See also Susan McIntosh in Rawick, *American Slave*, 13(4):183; Fannie Moore in Rawick, *American Slave*, 15(2):129; Bill Collins as cited in Helen Bradley Foster, *"New Raiments of Self,"* 104.

83. George Womble in Rawick, *American Slave*, 13(4):183; Charlie Pye in ibid., 13(3):183.

84. Hannah Plummer in ibid., 15(2):179; Fannie Moore in ibid., 15(2):129; Isaac Williams, *Aunt Sally*, 32.

85. Bill Collins as cited in Helen Bradley Foster, *"New Raiments of Self,"* 104; Amanda McDaniel in Rawick, *American Slave*, 13(3):72; George Womble in Rawick,

American Slave, 13(4):183; Fannie Moore in Rawick, *American Slave*, 15(2):129; Hannah Plummer in Rawick, *American Slave*, 15(2):179; Charlie Pye in Rawick, *American Slave*, 13(3):186; "Aunt" Adeline in Rawick, *American Slave*, 13(4):212; John F. Van Hook in Rawick, *American Slave*, 13(4):80.

86. Schwalm, *Hard Fight for We*, 59; Georgianna Foster in Rawick, *American Slave*, 14(1):315; Hannah Plummer in Rawick, *American Slave*, 15(2):179.

87. Nancy Williams in Perdue, Barden, and Phillips, *Weevils*, 316–17; Robert Shepherd in Rawick, *American Slave*, 13(3):253.

88. Annie Wallace in ibid., 294.

89. Salena Taswell in Rawick, *American Slave*, 17:306; Faust, *Mothers of Invention*, 223; Camilla Jackson in Rawick, *American Slave*, 12(2):297; Ebeneezer Brown in Rawick, *American Slave*, 6(1):249.

90. George Abraham in Rawick, *American Slave*, 11(1):57.

91. Isaac, *Transformation of Virginia*, 43.

92. Harvey, *Justice, Nature, and the Geography of Difference*, 220.

93. "Aunt" Adeline in Rawick, *American Slave*, 13(4):220.

94. Helen Bradley Foster, *"New Raiments of Self,"* 252–53; White and White, "Slave Hair," 70.

95. Helen Bradley Foster, *"New Raiments of Self,"* 252; White and White, "Slave Hair," 70–71; George F. Abrams summarized by interviewer G. L. Summer in Rawick, *American Slave*, supp. ser. 1, 11:57; Henry Lewis and Frances Willingham as cited in Helen Bradley Foster, *"New Raiments of Self,"* 115.

96. George F. Abrams summarized by interviewer G. L. Summer in Rawick, *American Slave*, supp. ser. 1, 1:1:57; Henry Lewis and Frances Willingham in Helen Bradley Foster, *"New Raiments of Self,"* 115, 252; Louise Jones in Perdue, Barden, and Phillips, *Weevils*, 186; White and White, "Slave Hair," 70–71.

97. Fett, *Working Cures*, 70.

98. Kemble, *Journal*, 93.

99. White and White, *Stylin'*, 17–24. Maude Southwell Wahlman and John Scully argued that the motivation of black quilt makers' use of color was "to create unpredictability and movement" (as cited in White and White, *Stylin'*, 24).

100. Clothing distribution lists, 1802, Page Commonplace Book, VHS; "List of negroes who received clothes," April, November 1846, Kollock Plantation Book for Rosedew Plantation, SHC; Helen Bradley Foster, *"New Raiments of Self,"* 243–44; W. L. Bost in Rawick, *American Slave*, 14:139.

101. Henry James Trentham in Rawick, *American Slave*, 15(2):364.

102. Nancy Williams in Perdue, Barden, and Phillips, *Weevils*, 316. For more on women's use of clothing to exhibit their individuality, see Patricia Hunt, "Struggle to Achieve Individual Expression."

103. Mary Wyatt in Perdue, Barden, and Phillips, *Weevils*, 333.

104. Diary of Frances (Scott) Miller, 3, 5 July 1858, 7 February 1857, Armistead-Blanton-Wallace Family Papers, VHS.

105. Ibid.

106. Ibid.

107. Rorabaugh, *Alcoholic Republic*, esp. ix–xiv, 5–21, 61.

108. *Smith v. Commonwealth* (Kentucky, 6 B. Mon., September 1845), 22; *Mayo v. James* (12 Grattan, Court of Appeals of Virginia, January 1855), 7–8; Eppes Diary, 30 November 1851, Eppes Family Papers, VHS; Olmsted, *Cotton Kingdom*, 39, 66; Elkanah Talley to Benjamin Brand, 10 September 1809, Brand Papers, VHS; Granville County, CR 1857–63, folder 1860, NCSDA; Wade, *Slavery in the Cities*, 144; Bynum, *Unruly Women*, 99.

109. Elbert Hunter in Rawick, *American Slave*, 14(1):459.

110. Lucy McCullough in ibid., 13(3):69–70.

111. Eppes Diary, 30 November 1851, Eppes Family Papers, VHS; Barrow, *Plantation Life*, 11 April 1841.

112. Hammond, "Plantation Records for Silver Bluff," 16 October 1835, Hammond Papers, SC.

113. Barrow, *Plantation Life*, 23 January 1838.

114. Ball, *Fifty Years in Chains*, 145, 157. See also John Blackford Diary, 10 October 1837, Blackford Family Papers, VHS.

115. Sylvia DuBois, *Sylvia DuBois*, 61–62. For directions on how to make peach brandy, see ibid., 68.

116. Charlie Tye Smith in Rawick, *American Slave*, 13(1):276; Julia Larken in ibid., 13(3):39.

117. Paul Gilroy has suggested that "more authentic freedoms . . . can only be enjoyed in non-work time. The black body is here celebrated as an instrument of pleasure rather than an instrument of labor. The nighttime becomes the right time, and the space allocated for recovery and recuperation is assertively and provocatively occupied by the pursuit of leisure and pleasure" (Gilroy, "One Nation Under a Groove," 274).

118. Olmsted, *Cotton Kingdom*, 70.

119. Jefferson Franklin Henry in Rawick, *American Slave*, 12(2):188–89. Fatigue and its effects on plantation production was a problem after paternalist frolics as well. Some slaveholders accounted for this and allowed time for naps on the day following frolics. For example, Addie Vinson remembered how after a dance given by her owner, "niggers dat had done danced half de night would be so sleepy when de bugle sounded dey wouldn't have time to cook breakfast. Den 'bout de middle of de mawnin' dey would complain 'bout bein' so weak and hongry dat de overseer would fetch 'em in and have 'em fed. He let 'em rest 'bout an hour and a half; den he marched 'em back to de field and wuked 'em 'til slap black dark" (Rawick, *American Slave*, 13[4]:109).

120. Work, *American Negro Songs*, 193.

121. *Preamble and Regulations* (adopted 21 November 1846), 3–4. For Hammond's complaints about drinking and theft among the enslaved population at Silver Bluff,

see Hammond, "Plantation Records for Silver Bluff," 16 October 1835, Hammond Papers, SC. Lawrence McDonnell studied this document and discusses its complaints in "Money Knows No Master."

122. *Preamble and Regulations*, 3–5, 8. Richard Eppes made similar complaints: "The absence of the negroes at night from their houses has become intolerable and finding that talking and threatening had no effect I was resolved to put a stop to it by administering in full effect our plantation laws. . . . Upon ringing my bell this evening found servants all absent walked down to Madison's & told him that it must not occur again" (Eppes Diary, 2 September 1859, Eppes Family Papers, VHS).

123. *Preamble and Regulations*, 3, 5. Slaveholders' fears about the effects of slave drinking were not strictly racial in nature; elites attempted to curb poor white drinking as well. Many antebellum Americans believed that regular or excessive drinking impinged upon a person's productivity and stimulated flashes of anger. One newspaper editorialist opined, for example, that "in proportion as men become drunkards, they cease to be useful to themselves, to their families, or to society. . . . When a common laborer becomes a drunkard, his family is soon reduced to the utmost need. The more he drinks the less he works, and the greater are his expenditures." Furthermore, the journalist warned, "an early effect of habitual drinking . . . is IRASCIBILITY OF TEMPER" (Natchez, Mississippi, *Southern Galaxy*, 17 July 17 1828). There were, nonetheless, racial aspects to slaveholders' extreme concern regarding slave drinking. Decreased productivity in a working white man only indirectly cost others; the worker "ceas[ed] to be useful" to "society" generally. But an enslaved person's decreased productivity directly cost her or his owner. Moreover, unlike its effects on whites, when imbibed by a black body, alcohol was widely believed to disinhibit blacks' impulses—that is, innate African savagery and violence—otherwise repressed under slavery's ostensible civilizing influence. See Herd, "Paradox of Temperance."

124. *Preamble and Regulations*, 3–5. Everywhere in the slave South that blacks traded for and drank alcohol, slaveholders worried, as the Savannah River neighbors did, about the stability of slave "subordination." Kentucky's supreme court tellingly worried in 1845 that trading liquor to bondpeople would "tempt them to petty larcenies, by way of procuring the means necessary to buy." Equally important, access to alcohol threatened to "lead them to dissipation, insubordination and vice, and obstruct the good government, well being and harmony of society." Many southerners, even those in the cities, would have concurred with the conclusion arrived at by the Savannah River Anti–Slave Traffick Association that black-marketing and drinking gave bondpeople ideas inappropriate to their station and inspired behavior threatening to those who sought to maintain black "subordination." For example, in 1846 one Charleston jury said, "The unrestrained intercourse and indulgence of familiarities between the black and white . . . are destructive of the respect and subserviency which our laws recognize as due from the one to the other and which form an essential feature in our institutions." Just a few years later, in 1851 another Charleston jury argued that slave black-marketing brought "the negro in such familiar contact with the white man, as to . . . invite the assertion of equality, or draw from

him exhibitions of presumption and insubordination" (*Smith v. Commonwealth* [6 B. Mon., Kentucky, September 1845], 22; Charleston juries quoted in Wade, *Slavery in the Cities*, 157).

125. *Preamble and Regulations*, 3–5.

CHAPTER 4

1. Thomas H. Jones, *Experience*, 7.

2. "Double character" coined by Thomas Reade Cobb and analyzed in Ariela J. Gross in *Double Character*; "person with a price" quote in Walter Johnson, *Soul by Soul*, 1.

3. Gutman, *Black Family in Slavery and Freedom*; Webber, *Deep Like the Rivers*; Vlach, *Back of the Big House*; King, *Stolen Childhood* and " 'Suffer With Them Until Death' "; Stevenson, *Life in Black and White*; Schwartz, *Born in Bondage*.

4. For elegant arguments on the importance of the home to the nascence of political struggles, see Steedman, *Landscape for a Good Woman*, 13–14; Faue, *Community of Suffering and Struggle*, 15–16.

5. Pacquette, "Jacobins of the Lowcountry," 192; William H. Lee to Jefferson Davis, 4 May 1861, in Berlin et al., *Free at Last*, 4.

6. E.g., Jordan, *Tumult and Silence at Second Creek*; Costa, *Crowns of Glory*, esp. 170–71; Egerton, *He Shall Go Out Free*, xiii–xvi; Michael P. Johnson, "Denmark Vesey and His Co-Conspirators," 915–76; Pearson, "Trials and Errors"; Egerton, "Forgetting Denmark Vesey"; Thomas J. Davis, "Conspiracy and Credibility"; Pacquette, "Jacobins of the Lowcountry," esp. 187–88; Michael P. Johnson, "Reading Evidence."

7. Dumas Malone, ed., *Dictionary of American Biography* (New York: Charles Scribner's Sons, 1946), 30–31; George H. Young to James McDowell, McDowell Papers, SCL.

8. Young to McDowell, 1 January 1842, McDowell Papers, SCL.

9. Agreement between Young and McDowell, April 1843, Documents folder, McDowell Papers, SCL.

10. Young to McDowell, 1 January 1842, McDowell Papers, SCL.

11. Agreement between Young and McDowell, April 1843, Documents folder, McDowell Papers, SCL.

12. Young to McDowell, 20 September 1843, McDowell Papers, SCL.

13. Agreement between Young and McDowell, April 1843, Documents folder, McDowell Papers, SCL.

14. Young to McDowell, 17 February 1846, McDowell Papers, SCL.

15. Agreement between Young and McDowell, April 1843, Documents folder, McDowell Papers, SCL.

16. Young to McDowell, 10 December 1845, McDowell Papers, SCL.

17. Young to McDowell, 17 February 1846, McDowell Papers, SCL.

18. Young to McDowell, 24 July 1847, McDowell Papers, SCL.

19. Ibid.

20. Bolster, *Black Jacks*, 199–200; Buchanan, "Slave Mississippi," 175–77, 183–84; Cecelski, *Waterman's Song*, 66.

21. Young to McDowell, 24 July 1847, McDowell Papers, SCL.

22. Young to McDowell, 15 August 1845, McDowell Papers, SCL.

23. Lehuu, *Carnival on the Page*, 3; Dahl, *History of the Book*, 220–21.

24. Hudson, *Journalism in the United States*, 416–27, 587–89, "helped make newspaper readers" quote on 417; Lehuu, *Carnival on the Page*, 17, 24; Mott, *American Journalism*, 228–44; Dahl, *History of the Book*, 220–21; Moore, *Historical, Biographical, and Miscellaneous Gatherings*, 35–39.

25. Lehuu, *Carnival on the Page*, 103.

26. Lapsansky, "Graphic Discord," esp. 201–3.

27. Ibid., 202.

28. William J. Anderson's title cited in Clark, "'Sacred Rights of the Weak,'" 469. John W. Blassingame found that less than 20 percent of slave narratives were published by antislavery societies; see Blassingame, *Slave Testimony*, xxix.

29. Dillon, *Slavery Attacked*, 178; Savage, *Controversy*, ix, 3.

30. Savage, *Controversy*, 3, 9, 14.

31. Walker, *Appeal to the Colored Citizens of the World*, 13, 18, 22.

32. Bolster, *Black Jacks*, 197–98; Hinks, *To Awaken My Afflicted Brethren*, 118, 134, 137–39, 149; "fellow named Derry" and "brought some of those pamphlets" quotes by J. Burgwyn as cited in Hinks, *To Awaken My Afflicted Brethren*, 39.

33. George W. Prescott to Bracket L. Prescott, 10 December 1835, Prescott Papers, SHC.

34. Elder, *Life of Samuel Hall*, 28.

35. Savage, *Controversy*, 56–57.

36. Howard and Hutchinson, *Statutes of the State of Mississippi*, 672–73.

37. Ibid., 720.

38. Thomas R. R. Cobb, *Digest*, 999.

39. Bolster, *Black Jacks*, 198.

40. Thomas R. R. Cobb, *Digest*, 999–1000.

41. Savage, *Controversy*, 56–57.

42. Bolster, *Black Jacks*, 198; Cecelski, *Waterman's Song*, 146.

43. Howell Cobb, *Compilation of the General and Public Statutes*, 603; Thomas R. R. Cobb, *Digest*, 999, 1001.

44. Thomas R. R. Cobb, *Digest*, 830.

45. Bolster, *Black Jacks*, 211.

46. Cecelski, *Waterman's Song*, 146, 121–51.

47. "Vigilance" to the *Richmond Inquirer*, 1857, Ware Family Papers, VHS.

48. E. A. Andrews cited in Herbert, *Abolitionist Crusade and Its Consequences*, 79.

49. Anna (Howe) Whitteker to Emily (Howe) Dupuy, 23 August 1835, Dupuy Papers, VHS. See also Savage, *Controversy*, 2; Dillon, *Slavery Attacked*, 68; Joseph S. Hartly to Captain C. H. Bonham, 15 May 1849, Miscellaneous Letters Collection, SHC.

50. Savage, *Controversy*, 15–22.

51. Grimké, "Appeal to the Christian Women of the South."

52. Ibid.

53. Rice Memoir, 2, VHS.

54. Horton, *Free People of Color*, 66–67; Buchanan, "Slave Mississippi." Black abolitionist and rebellion organizer Denmark Vesey obtained abolitionist books and pamphlets, which he studied along with the Bible, in his Charleston home. See Egerton, *He Shall Go Out Free*, 98.

55. Sarah Bruce Seddon to Charles Bruce, 4 August 1850, Bruce Family Papers, VHS.

56. Painter, "Representing Truth," 474.

57. Benedict Anderson discusses the role of print culture in general and the newspaper in particular in the formation of imagined national communities; see his *Imagined Communities*.

58. Philpot, *Facts for White Americans*, 26, 27, 51–52.

59. Avirett, *Old Plantation*, viii.

60. Mattie J. Jackson, *Story of Mattie J. Jackson*, 13.

61. Ibid., 13–14.

62. Ibid., 14.

63. Ibid., 19–20.

CHAPTER 5

1. Houston H. Holloway as cited in Foner, *Reconstruction*, 77.

2. Lewis, *Out of the Ditch*, 9.

3. Charlie Davenport in Rawick, *American Slave*, supp. ser. 1, 7(2):565.

4. As cited in Foner, *Reconstruction*, 80.

5. Ibid.

6. For more on American freedom's spatial (and expansionist) dimensions, see Foner, *Story of American Freedom*, 47–55.

7. Saville, *Work of Reconstruction*, 18–19, 40–45.

8. "Feel of freedom" quote and Richard Edwards as cited in Litwack, *Been in the Storm So Long*, 292. For more on postwar movement, see ibid., 292–332.

9. W. E. B. DuBois, *Black Reconstruction in America*, 81–82; Ira Berlin, Barbara J. Fields, Thavolia Glymph, Joseph P. Reidy, and Leslie S. Rowland, "The Destruction of Slavery," in Berlin et al., *Freedom*, 1–56; Foner, *Reconstruction*, xxv, 1–11, 81.

10. Edwards, *Scarlett Doesn't Live Here Anymore*, 105.

11. Testimony of C. B. Wilder before the Freedmen's Inquiry Commission, 9 May 1863, in Berlin et al., *Freedom*, ser. 1, 1:90. See also Elder, *Life of Samuel Hall*, 22.

12. Edmondson Diary, 4 May 1864, SHC.

13. "The negro movement" in 4 May 1865 entry, Mordecai Diary, SHC; "stampede" in "Excerpts from proceedings of a general court-martial in the case of George, Robert, Stephen, Peter, and William," 6–8 April 1862, in Berlin et al., *Freedom*, ser. 1, 1:789; "great stampede" in Armstrong Diary, 29 April 1863, VHS.

14. James Scott, *Domination and the Arts of Resistance*, 202–3, 223; Berlin et al., introduction to *Freedom*, xvi–xvii.

15. Stone, *Brokenburn*, 19 June 1861.

16. Eliza Walker as cited in Faust, *Mothers of Invention*, 74. See also Stone, *Brokenburn*, 22 March 1863.

17. Broun Diary, 29 April 1863, SHC.

18. "Les esclaves et la proclamation du président Lincoln," *Le Monde Illustré*, 21 March 1863, 180–82.

19. Mohr, *On the Threshold of Freedom*, 95.

20. Stone, *Brokenburn*, 5 March 1863.

21. "Fannie" to "My dear Husband," 10 January 1863, Huntington Library.

22. Stone, *Brokenburn*, 27 April 1863.

23. Hopley, *Life in the South*, 2:217.

24. Charles Manigault as cited in Foner, *Nothing But Freedom*, 80–81.

25. Hopley, *Life in the South*, 2:217.

26. Ibid., 216.

27. Joseph Ramsy to General Rousseau, 16 March 1864, in Berlin et al., *Freedom*, ser. 1, 1:320.

28. Josephine N. Pugh as cited in Jung, " 'Coolies' and Cane," 11.

29. Mordecai Diary, 21 April 1865, SHC.

30. Ibid.

31. Stone, *Brokenburn*, 22, 24 March, 25 April 1863. See also Alice Roane (Brockenbrough) Aylett to William Roane Aylett, 29 October 1861, Aylett Family Papers, VHS.

32. Stone, *Brokenburn*, 22 May 1863.

33. Elder, *Life of Samuel Hall*, 24.

34. Berlin et al., "Tidewater Virginia and North Carolina," in *Freedom*, ser. 1, 1:61–62.

35. Breckenridge, *Lucy Breckenridge of Grove Hill*, 31 August 1862.

36. Foster Diary, 25 July 1863, SCL. See also 28 July 1863.

37. Testimony of C. B. Wilder before the American Freedmen's Inquiry Commission, 9 May 1863, in Berlin et al., *Freedom*, ser. 1, 1:89–90.

38. Ibid.; Pugh Civil War Account, n.d., 3, LSU; "front of Battle" in O. S. Glisson to Silas H. Stringham, 15 July 1861, in Berlin et al., *Freedom*, ser. 1, 1:75–76; Jas. W. Cooke to J. M. Mason, 27 August 1861, in Berlin et al., *Freedom*, ser. 1, 1:77.

39. "Fannie" to "My dear Husband," 10 January 1863, Huntington Library.

40. Colin Clarke to Maxwell Troax Clarke, 10 May 1862, Clarke Papers, SHC.

41. Stone, *Brokenburn*, 22 March, 25 April 1863.

42. Testimony of Captain C. B. Wilder before the American Freedmen's Inquiry Commission, 9 May 1863, in Berlin et al., *Freedom*, ser. 1, 1:89.

43. Colin Clarke to Maxwell Troax Clarke, 24 August 1862, Clarke Papers, SHC.

44. Ibid., 5 May 1863.

45. Ibid., 10 August 1862, 21 May 1863.

46. Ibid., 10 August 1862.

47. Maxwell Troax Clarke to Powhatan Clarke, 17 August 1862, Clarke Papers, SHC.

48. "Deported Negroes," 21 July 1861, Jones Family Papers, VHS; Robert C. Henderson to Peter Saunders, 11 January 1862, Saunders Family Papers, VHS; Stone, *Brokenburn*, 29–30 June, 5 July 1862, 3 March 1863.

49. Schwalm, *Hard Fight for We*, 90.

50. Slightly more than half of the population of freedpeople in three federally held counties (54 percent) were men, while just less than half (46 percent) were women. See Census Return, 20 August 1863, in Berlin et al., *Freedom*, ser. 1, 1:91.

51. Dulany Diary, 2 August 1862, VHS. See also Foster Diary, 28 July 1863, SCL.

52. "Marion" to [cousin Anne], n.d. [1863/65?], Kuntz Collection, Tulane University. See also Broun Diary, 29 April 1863, SHC; Foster Diary, 28 July 1863, SCL.

53. Testimony of C. B. Wilder in Berlin et al., *Freedom*, ser. 1, 1:89–90.

54. Colin Clarke to Maxwell Troax Clarke, 10 August 1862, Clarke Papers, SHC.

55. Edmondson Diary, 5, 15 February 1864, SHC.

56. Colyer, *Report of the Services*, 33, 41; Brockett and Vaughn, *Woman's Work*, 147; Kirkland, *Pictorial Book*, 574; Sidney Andrews, *South Since the Civil War*, 24–25.

57. Colyer, *Report of the Services*, 33.

58. Brockett and Vaughn, *Woman's Work*, 147.

59. Foster Diary, 4 July 1863, SCL.

60. Colyer, *Report of the Services*, 47–48, 51.

61. Nourse Diary, 31 August 1862, VHS.

62. Mary Amis Hooper to "My dear children," 27 May [1862?], Blanchard Papers, SHC.

63. Edmund S. Morgan, "Slavery and Freedom" and *American Slavery, American Freedom*, 295–337; Walter Johnson, *Soul by Soul*, esp. 78–116.

64. Colin Clarke to Maxwell Troax Clarke, 15, 17 August 1862, 16 July 1863, Clarke Papers, SHC; Edwards, *Scarlett Doesn't Live Here Anymore*, 82–83.

65. Nordhoff, *Freedmen of South-Carolina*, 20–21.

66. Testimony of Colonel Higginson before the American Freedmen's Inquiry Commission, June 1863, in Berlin et al., *Freedom*, ser. 1, 1:138–39.

67. Hadden, *Slave Patrols*, 167–87; C. C. Jones as cited in ibid., 169.

68. Jere Pearsall to Jefferson Davis, 25 November 1863, in Berlin et al., *Freedom*, ser. 1, 1:94.

69. Henry L. Wood to "Colonel," 30 April 1863, Jerrard Papers, LSU.

70. Roark, *Masters without Slaves*, 74.

71. Susie Burns in Perdue, Barden, and Phillips, *Weevils*, 64.

72. "Caged up" and "locked . . . up" quotes in "Célina" to [Henri Roman], 29 December 1862, Roman Family Papers, Tulane University; Berlin et al., *Freedom*, ser. 1, 1:673.

73. "Célina" to [Henri Roman], 25 February 1863, Roman Family Papers, Tulane University.

74. Testimony of Franklin A. Dick, 1 December 1863, before the American Freedmen's Inquiry Commission, in Berlin et al., *Freedom*, ser. 1, 1:474.

75. Lieutenant J. Glendy Sproston to Lieutenant D. Ammen, 8 November 1861, in ibid., 115. See also Nourse Diary, 24 April 1862, VHS; Colyer, *Report of the Services*, 5; Broun Diary, 21 June 1863, SHC.

76. Edmondson Diary, 15 February 1864, SHC.

77. As cited in Roark, *Masters without Slaves*, 74.

78. "Les esclaves et la proclamation du président Lincoln," *Le Monde Illustré*, 21 March 1863, 182; Stone, *Brokenburn*, 14 August 1865.

79. Knox, *Camp-fire and Cotton-field*, 363–64.

80. Frederick Douglass and New Orleans newspaper as cited in McPherson, *Battle Cry of Freedom*, 711; William Wells Brown, *Negro in the American Rebellion*, 177, 179, 184.

81. Knox, *Camp-fire and Cotton-field*, 372.

82. Roark, *Masters without Slaves*, 37, 76, 80.

83. As cited in ibid., 47.

84. "Demoralized" in Stone, *Brokenburn*, 2 July 1861, 27 April 1863.

85. Ellen McCollam to Andrew McCollam, 26 March 1863, McCollam Papers, SHC.

86. Stone, *Brokenburn*, 29 June, 2 July 1861.

87. Berlin et al., *Freedom*, ser. 1, 1:42.

88. Stone, *Brokenburn*, 5 March 1863.

89. Henry L. Wood to "Colonel," 30 April 1863, Jerrard Papers, LSU.

90. Célina to [Henri Roman], 29 December 1862, Roman Family Papers, Tulane University.

91. Cocke Formbook (1854), 4, VHS; the *Southern Cultivator*, quoted in Rawick, *American Slave*, 13(4):330–31. See also Knox, *Camp-fire and Cotton-field*, 363.

92. Faust, *Mothers of Invention*, 30–35, 51, 53–79; Drew Gilpin Faust, " 'Trying to do a Man's Business': Gender, Violence, and Slave Management in Civil War Texas," in Faust, *Southern Stories*, 174–92. See also Bethell Diary, 5 January 1865, SHC.

93. Testimony of C. B. Wilder before the American Freedman's Inquiry Commission, 9 May 1863, in Berlin et al., *Freedom*, ser. 1, 1:89.

94. "Fannie" to "My dear Husband," 10 January 1863, Huntington Library.

95. Mordecai Diary, 21 April 1865, SHC.

96. Dulany Diary, 2 August 1862, VHS.

97. Stone, *Brokenburn*, 5 July 1862.

98. Sam McCullum in Rawick, *American Slave*, 7(2):102–3.

99. "Fannie" to "My dear Husband," 10 January 1863, Huntington Library.

100. Stone, *Brokenburn*, 29 June 1861.

101. Ibid., 3, 8 March 1863.

102. "Célina" to [Henri Roman], 7 January, 25 February 1863, Roman Family Papers, Tulane University.

103. Stone, *Brokenburn*, 20 September 1863.

104. "Marion" to [cousin Anne], n.d., Kuntz Collection, Tulane University.

105. Foster Diary, 25 July 1863, SCL.

106. Edmondson Diary, 2, 26 March, 31 May 1864, SHC.

107. Alice Roane (Brockenbrough) Aylett to William Roane Aylett, 1863, Aylett Family Papers, VHS.

108. Foster Diary, 16 July 1863, SCL. See also Broun Diary, 1 May 1864, SHC.

109. Faust, *Mothers of Invention*, 238–44.

110. Broun Diary, 1 May 1864, SHC.

111. Testimony of Nancy Johnson before the Southern Claims Commission, 22 March 1873, in Berlin et al., *Freedom*, ser. 1, 1:150.

112. Kirkland, *Pictorial Book*, 612–13; Captain Alured Larke and Captain R. H. Day to the Provost Marshal of the Department of the South, 7 December 1864, in Berlin et al., *Freedom*, ser. 1, 1:809; Browne, *Four Years in Secessia*, 361, 370–71.

113. Kirkland, *Pictorial Book*, 612–13.

114. Captain Alured Larke and Captain R. H. Day to the Provost Marshal of the Department of the South, 7 December 1864, in Berlin et al., *Freedom*, ser. 1, 1:809; Browne, *Four Years in Secessia*, 367–70.

115. Kirkland, *Pictorial Book*, 612–13; "did picket duty," Junius Henri Brown as cited in William Wells Brown, *Negro in the American Rebellion*, 319; Captain Alured Larke and Captain R. H. Day to the Provost Marshal of the Department of the South, 7 December 1864, in Berlin et al., *Freedom*, ser. 1, 1:809; Browne, *Four Years in Secessia*, 367–70; Junius Henri Brown as cited in William Wells Brown, *Negro in the American Rebellion*, 320.

116. Estabrooks, *Adrift in Dixie*, 74–78.

POSTSCRIPT

1. McMillen, *Dark Journey*; Ayers, *Southern Crossing*; Litwack, *Trouble in Mind*.

2. Brook Thomas, ed., *Plessy v. Ferguson: A Brief History with Documents* (Boston: Bedford Books, 1997), 41.

3. Ibid., 55.

BIBLIOGRAPHY

PRIMARY SOURCES

Manuscript Collections

Huntington Library, Los Angeles, Calif.
    "Fannie" to "My dear Husband," 10 January 1863 (call no. HM 58079)
North Carolina State Department of Archives and History, Raleigh
    County Criminal Records Concerning Slaves and Free Persons of Color
        Craven County, Davidson County, Gates County, Granville County
    State v. Horace H. Rowland and Thomas T. Davis
Pennsylvania Historical Society, Philadelphia
    Butler Family Papers
        Letters of Roswell King and Roswell King Jr. to Pierce Butler
    Wister Family Papers
        Butler section
South Caroliniana Library, University of South Carolina, Columbia
    Ada Bacot Diary
    James Henry Hammond Papers
        James Henry Hammond. "Plantation Records for Silver Bluff Plantation (1831 to
            1855)." Microfilm: Records of Ante-Bellum Southern Plantations, ser. A, pt. 1,
            reel 1.
Southern Historical Collection, University of North Carolina, Chapel Hill
    George Washington Allen Papers
        Correspondence of George Washington Allen and Alexander A. Allen
    Young Allen Papers
    Everard Green Baker Diaries
    Mary E. Bateman Diary
    Battle Family Papers
    Mary Jeffreys Bethell Diary
    John Houston Bills Diary
    Elizabeth Hooper Blanchard Papers

Catherine Barbara Broun Diary, 1861–68

Burgwyn Family Papers
   Plantation accounts, diary, slave lists, and correspondence of Henry King Brown

John Ewing Calhoun Papers

Cameron Family Papers

Carmichael Family Papers
   Mary Eliza (Eve) Carmichael Diary

Farrish Carter Papers

Maxwell Troax Clarke Papers

Elizabeth Collier Diary, 1862–65

William Cooper Diaries

Calvin Josiah Cowles Papers

Cupola House Papers

Mathew Smart Davis Papers

Belle Edmondson Diary

Ethelbert William Ervin Diary

Andrew Flynn Plantation Book, 1840

Foscue Family Papers

David Gavin Diary

Record Book for Green Valley Plantation

John Berkley Grimball Diary

Margaret Ann Meta (Morris) Grimball Diary

William Henry Holcombe Diary

Hubbard Family Papers

Huguenin and Johnston Family Papers
   Plantation Journal

Charles C. W. Johnston Papers

Calvin Jones Papers

Mary Susan Ker Papers
   Diary and photographs

George J. Kollock Plantation Journals

Lester-Gray Collection of Documents Relating to Joseph Clover Baldwin
   Photograph album

Benjamin Franklin Little Papers, 1806, 1833–1935

Manly Family Papers

Louis Marshall Papers

Andrew McCollam Papers

William Parsons McCorkle Papers
   Lucilla Agnes Gamble McCorkle Diary

James S. Milling Papers, 1852–1883

Miscellaneous Letters Collection

Emma Mordecai Diary

George W. Mordecai Papers
    Correspondence and slave records
John Nevitt Diary
Rebecca S. C. Pilsbury Diary
Philip Henry Pitts Papers
Polk and Yeatman Family Papers
Helen M. Prescott Papers
Quitman Family Papers, 1784–1978
Roach and Eggleston Family Papers
    Diary of Mahala P. Eggleston
William Conrad Schutte Papers
Singleton Family Papers
Edward Wasmuth Diary
Wilson and Hairson Family Papers
    Memorandum book
Special Collections, Hill Memorial Library, Louisiana State University, Baton Rouge
Simon G. Jerrard Papers
Josephine N. Pugh Civil War Account
Special Collections Library, Perkins Library, Duke University, Durham, N.C.
William C. Adams Diary
William T. Bain Papers
Absalom F. Dantzler Papers
Maria Dyer Davies Diary
Thomas Davis Papers
    Diary and commonplace book
Devereux Family Papers
    Personal correspondence and plantation accounts
George Coke Dromgoole and Richard B. Robinson Papers
Kate D. Foster Diary
McDonald Furman Papers
    Cornhill Plantation Book
Ann Henshaw Gardiner Papers
William D. Gibbons Papers
Margaret Davidson Gwyn Diary and Daybook
George Paul Harrison Papers
Edward Thomas Heriot Papers
Elizabeth Sherman Hoar Journal
Lewis Family Letters
Manigault Family Diaries
James McDowell Papers
James McPherson Papers
Jacob Rhett Mott Papers

Haller Nutt Papers

A. M. Reed Papers

William Renwick Papers

Rockingham Plantation Journal

Abraham Jr. and James H. Shepherd Papers

Samuel Smaw Papers

James Henry Rusell Washington Papers

Francis Cope Yarnall Papers

Tulane Manuscripts Department, Tulane University, New Orleans, La.

Rosemonde E. and Emile Kuntz Collection

Roman Family Papers

Virginia Historical Society, Richmond

Mark Alexander Diary

Allen Family Papers

Diaries of Robert Henderson Allen

Armistead-Blanton-Wallace Family Papers

Diary of Frances (Scott) Miller

Sally Armstrong Diary

Aylett Family Papers

Letters of William Roane Aylett

Elizabeth Lumpkin Motley Bagby Account Book

Eliza Lavalette Barksdale Diary

Barbour Family Papers

Agreements and bonds

Baskerville Family Papers

Bassett Family Papers

Margaret Stanely Beckwith Memoir

Blackford Family Papers

John Blackford Diary

Gay Robertson Blackford Memoir

Blow Family Papers

Benjamin Brand Papers

Brand Family Papers

Correspondence of Elkanah Talley to Benjamin Brand

Bruce Family Papers

Correspondence of Sarah Bruce Seddon to Charles Bruce

Moore Fauntleroy Carter Account Book

Amanda Virginia Edmonds Chappelar Diary

Ann Webster Gordon Christian Diary

Civil War Pictorial Envelopes Collection

Clarke Family Papers

Correspondence of Frederick Clarke to John Clarke

Daniel William Cobb Diaries

Philip St. George Cocke Formbook for Belmead Plantation

Elizabeth Coles Diary

Amanda Jane Cooley Diary

Dame Family Papers

   Correspondence of Jonathan Dame and Mary Dame

Mary Eliza (Powell) Dulany Diary

Emily (Howe) Dupuy Papers

   Letters of Anna (Howe) Whitteker

Sarah Dandridge Cooke Duvall Papers

Frederick Deane Goodwin Diaries

Eppes Family Papers

   Diaries of Dr. Richard Eppes

Nancy Johns Turner Hall. "The Imaginist." Unpublished manuscript.

Higginbotham Family Papers

Holladay Family Papers

Hundley Family Papers

Hunter Family Papers

   Bonds and accounts

   Commonplace book of Jane Swann Hunter

Jones Family Papers, 1819–1864

Massie Family Papers

   Commonplace book, account book, and slave lists of Thomas Eugene Massie

John Peter Mettauer Papers

Myers Family Papers

Nash Family Papers

Margaret Tilloston (Kemble) Nourse Diary

Jane Frances Walker Page Commonplace Book

Peckatone Family Papers

Preston Family Papers

   Correspondence of Jane Craighead Marshall and John Preston

Marie Gordon Pryor Rice Memoir

Mahala Perkins Eggleston Roach Diary

Amanda Jane Cooley Roberts

Rutherford Family Papers

   Commonplace book of John Coles Rutherford

Saunders Family Papers

Selden Family Papers

   Diary of John Armistead Selden

Ann Virginia Page Slaughter Diary

Spragins Family Papers

Margaret Stanley Memoir

Taliaferro Family Accounts

Temple Family Papers

    Loose accounts and account books

Tennant Family Papers

    Account book of David Dunlop Brydon

Elizabeth Louisa Van Lew Album

William Macon Waller Papers

    Letters of William Waller

Ware Family Papers

John Augustine Washington

Judith Gates Winfree Memoir

Books, Periodicals, Articles, and Dissertations

Sources that can be found in rare book repositories are so noted.

Albert, Octavia V. Rogers. *The House of Bondage; or, Charlotte Brooks and Other Slaves.* Edited by Henry Louis Gates Jr. 1890. Reprint, New York: Oxford University Press, 1988.

Allen, William Francis, Charles Pickard Ware, and Lucy McKim Garrison, eds. *Slave Songs of the United States.* New York: A. Simpson and Co., 1867.

Alvord, John Watson. *Letters from the South Relating to the Condition of the Freedmen.* Washington, D.C.: Howard University Press, 1870. Library Company of Philadelphia, Philadelphia, Pa.

Anderson, John. *The Story of the Life of John Anderson, the Fugitive Slave.* London: W. Tweedie, 1863. Library Company of Philadelphia, Philadelphia, Pa.

Andrews, Eliza Frances. *The War-time Journal of a Georgia Girl, 1864–65.* Edited by Spencer Bidwell King Jr. Atlanta: Cherokee Publishing Co., 1976.

Andrews, Sidney. *The South Since the Civil War: As shown by Fourteen Weeks of travel and Observation in Georgia and the Carolinas.* Boston: Ticknor and Fields, 1866. Library Company of Philadelphia, Philadelphia, Pa.

Avary, Myrta Lockett, ed. *Recollections of Alexander H. Stephens, His Diary Kept When a Prisoner at Fort Warren, Boston Harbor, 1865; Giving Incidents and Reflections of His Prison Life and Some Letters and Reminiscences.* New York: Doubleday, Page, 1910.

Avirett, James Battle. *The Old Plantation: How We Lived in Great House and Cabin Before the War.* New York: F. Tennyson Nelly, 1901. Library Company of Philadelphia, Philadelphia, Pa.

Ball, Charles. *Fifty Years in Chains; or, the Life of an American Slave.* New York: H. Dayton, 1859. Library Company of Philadelphia, Philadelphia, Pa.

——. *Slavery in the United States: A Narrative of the Life and Adventures of Charles Ball, A Black Man.* Lewistown, Pa.: John W. Shugert, 1836. Library Company of Philadelphia, Philadelphia, Pa. Reprint, Detroit: Negro History Press, 1970.

Barrow, Bennet. *Plantation Life in the Florida Parishes of Louisiana, 1836–1846, as*

Reflected in the Diary of Bennet H. Barrow. Edited by Edwin Adams Davis. New York: Columbia University Press, 1943. Reprint, New York: AMS Press, 1967.

Bayley, Solomon. *Incidents in the Life of Solomon Bayley*. Philadelphia: Tract Association of Friends, [1859?]. Library Company of Philadelphia, Philadelphia, Pa.

Beaumont, Betty Bentley. *Twelve Years of My Life*. Philadelphia: T. B. Peterson & Bros., 1888. Library Company of Philadelphia, Philadelphia, Pa.

Berlin, Ira, Barbara J. Fields, Thavolia Glymph, Joseph P. Reidy, and Leslie S. Rowland, eds. *Freedom: A Documentary History of Emancipation, 1861–1867*. Ser. 1, vol. 1. Cambridge: Cambridge University Press, 1985.

Bibb, Henry. *Narrative of the Life and Adventures of Henry Bibb, Written by Himself*. New York: Published by the Author, 1849. Beinecke Rare Book and Manuscript Library, New Haven, Conn.

Blassingame, John. *Slave Testimony: Two Centuries of Letters, Speeches, Interviews, and Autobiographies*. Baton Rouge: Louisiana State University Press, 1977.

Breckenridge, Lucy Gilmer. *Lucy Breckenridge of Grove Hill: The Journal of a Virginia Girl, 1862–1864*. Edited by Mary D. Robertson. Kent, Ohio: Kent State University Press, 1979.

Brockett, L. P., and Mrs. Mary C. Vaughn. *Woman's Work in the Civil War: A Record of Heroism, Patriotism and Patience*. Philadelphia: Zeigler, McCrudy and Co., 1867. Library Company of Philadelphia, Philadelphia, Pa.

Brown, Henry Box. *Narrative of Henry Box Brown*. Boston: Brown and Stearns, 1849. Library Company of Philadelphia, Philadelphia, Pa.

Brown, John. *Slave Life in Georgia: A Narrative of the Life, Sufferings, and Escape of John Brown, A Fugitive Slave*. 1855. Reprint, Savannah: Beehive Press, 1972. Library Company of Philadelphia, Philadelphia, Pa.

Brown, William Wells. *My Southern Home; or, The South and Its People*. Boston: A. G. Brown, 1880. Beinecke Rare Book and Manuscript Library, New Haven, Conn.

———. *Narrative of the Life of William W. Brown, A Fugitive Slave*. Boston: Anti-Slavery Society Office, 1848. Beinecke Rare Book and Manuscript Library, New Haven, Conn.

———. *The Negro in the American Rebellion: His Heroism and his Fidelity*. Boston: Lee and Shepard, 1867. Library Company of Philadelphia, Philadelphia, Pa.

Browne, Junius Henri. *Four Years in Secessia: Adventures Within and Beyond the Union Lines*. Hartford: O. D. Case and Co., 1865.

Burwell, Letitia M. *A Girl's life in Virginia Before the War*. New York: Frederick A. Stokes, 1895. Library Company of Philadelphia, Philadelphia, Pa.

Cade, John. "Out of the Mouths of Ex-Slaves." *Journal of Negro History* 20 (July 1935): 294–337.

Callaway, Joshua K. *The Civil War Letters of Joshua K. Callaway*. Edited by Judith Lee Hallock. Athens: University of Georgia Press, 1997.

Cobb, Howell. *A Compilation of the General and Public Statutes of the State of Georgia*. New York: Edward O. Jenkins, 1859. Lillian Goldman Library, Yale School of Law, New Haven, Conn.

——. *A Compilation of the Penal Code of the State of Georgia*. Macon: Joseph M. Boardman, 1850. Lillian Goldman Library, Yale School of Law, New Haven, Conn.

Cobb, Thomas R. R., comp. *A Digest of the Statute laws of the State of Georgia in Force Prior to the Session of the General Assembly of 1851*. Athens: Christy, Kelsea and Burke, 1851. Lillian Goldman Library, Yale School of Law, New Haven, Conn.

The Code of Virginia: Including Legislation to the Year 1860. Richmond: Ritchie, Dunnavant and Co., 1860.

Coffin, Charles Carleton. *Four Years of Fighting: A Volume of Personal Observation With the Army and Navy*. Boston: Ticknor and Fields, 1866. Library Company of Philadelphia, Philadelphia, Pa.

Colyer, Vincent. *Report of the Services Rendered by the Freed People to the United States Army, in North Carolina in the Spring of 1862, After the Battle of Newbern*. New York: Vincent Colyer, 1864. Library Company of Philadelphia, Philadelphia, Pa.

Criswell, Robert. *"Uncle Tom's Cabin" Contrasted with Buckingham Hall, the Planter's Home*. New York: D. Fanshaw, 1852. Library Company of Philadelphia, Philadelphia, Pa.

Davis, Noah. *A Narrative of the Life of Rev. Noah Davis, A Colored Man, Written by Himself, at the Age of Fifty-four*. Baltimore: J. F. Weishampel Jr., 1859. Beinecke Rare Book and Manuscript Library, New Haven, Conn.

Dawson, William C. *A Compilation of the Laws of the State of Georgia*. Milledgeville: Grantland and Orme, 1831. Lillian Goldman Library, Yale School of Law, New Haven, Conn.

Delaney, A. Lucy. *From the Darkness Cometh the Light; or, Struggles for Freedom*. 1891. In *Six Women's Slave Narratives*, edited by Henry Louis Gates Jr. New York: Oxford University Press, 1988.

Devereux, Margaret. *Plantation Sketches*. Cambridge, Mass.: n.p., 1906. Library Company of Philadelphia, Philadelphia, Pa.

Douglass, Frederick. *Narrative of the Life of Frederick Douglass an American Slave, Written by Himself*. 1845. Reprint, Cambridge, Mass.: Harvard University Press, 1960; New York: Anchor, 1989.

DuBois, Sylvia. *Sylvia DuBois: A Biografy of the Slav Who Whipt Her Mistress and Gand Her Freedom*. Edited by Henry Louis Gates Jr. 1883. Reprint, New York: Oxford University Press, 1988.

Elder, Orville. *The Life of Samuel Hall, A Slave for Forty-Seven Years*. Washington, Iowa: Journal Print, 1912. Beinecke Rare Book and Manuscript Library, New Haven, Conn.

Elson, Henry W. *The Civil War: Through the Camera*. 16 vols. Springfield, Mass.: Patriot Publishing, 1912. Library Company of Philadelphia, Philadelphia, Pa.

Eppes, Susan Bradford. *The Negro of the Old South: A Bit of Period History*. Macon, Ga.: J. W. Burke, 1941.

Estabrooks, Henry L. *Adrift in Dixie; or, A Yankee Officer Among the Rebels*. New York: Carleton, 1866. Library Company of Philadelphia, Philadelphia, Pa.

General Assembly. *Laws of the State of Missouri; Revised and Digested by Authority of the General Assembly*. St. Louis: E. Charles, 1825. Lillian Goldman Library, Yale School of Law, New Haven, Conn.

——. *The Revised Statutes of the State of Missouri, Revised and Digested by the Eighth General Assembly*. 3rd ed. St. Louis: Chambers and Knapp, Republican Office, 1835. Lillian Goldman Library, Yale School of Law, New Haven, Conn.

——. *The Revised Statutes of the State of Missouri, Revised and Digested by the Thirteenth Assembly*. St. Louis: J. W. Dougherty, 1845. Lillian Goldman Library, Yale School of Law, New Haven, Conn.

——. *Statutes of the Mississippi Territory*. Natchez: Peter Isler, 1816.

Gielow, Martha S. *Old Plantation Days*. New York: R. H. Russell, 1902. Library Company of Philadelphia, Philadelphia, Pa.

Goodell, Abner Cheney Jr. *The Trial and Execution for Petit Treason, of Mark and Philis, Slaves of Capt. John Codman*. Cambridge: John Wilson and Son, University Press, 1883. Library Company of Philadelphia, Philadelphia, Pa.

Greene, William. *Narrative of Events in the Life of William Greene*. Springfield, Mass.: L. M. Guerney, 1853. Library Company of Philadelphia, Philadelphia, Pa.

Grimké, Angelina. "Appeal to the Christian Women of the South." In *The Public Years of Sarah and Angelina Grimké: Selected Writings, 1835–1839*, edited by Larry Ceplair, 74–75. New York: Columbia University Press, 1989.

Hague, Parthenia Antoinette. *A Blockaded Family: Life in Southern Alabama During the Civil War*. Boston: Houghton, Mifflin, 1888. Library Company of Philadelphia, Philadelphia, Pa.

Hardin, Charles H. *The Revised Statutes of the State of Missouri, Revised and Digested by the Eighteenth General Assembly*. 2 vols. Jefferson: James Lusk, 1856. Lillian Goldman Library, Yale School of Law, New Haven, Conn.

Harper's New Monthly Magazine. Vols. 1–45. New York: Harper and Bros., 1850–72. Library Company of Philadelphia, Philadelphia, Pa.

Hawkins, William George. *Lunsford Lane; or, Another Helper from North Carolina*. Boston: Crosby and Nichols, 1863. Beinecke Rare Book and Manuscript Library, New Haven, Conn.

Hayden, William. *Narrative of William Hayden*. Cincinnati: Published for the author, 1846. Library Company of Philadelphia, Philadelphia, Pa.

Hening, William Waller. *The Statutes at Large: Being a Collection of all the Laws of the Year 1619*. Richmond: Samuel Pleasants, 1809–23. Lillian Goldman Library, Yale School of Law, New Haven, Conn.

Henson, Josiah. *The Life of Josiah Henson*. London: C. Gilpin, 1851. Library Company of Philadelphia, Philadelphia, Pa.

Hopley, Catherine C. *Life in the South: From the Commencement of the War*. 2 vols. London: Chapman and Hall, 1863. Library Company of Philadelphia, Philadelphia, Pa.

Howard, James H. W. *Bond and Free: A True Tale of Slave Times*. Harrisburg, Pa.: Edwin K. Meyers, 1886. Library Company of Philadelphia, Philadelphia, Pa.

Howard, V. E., and A. Hutchinson, comps. *Statutes of the State of Mississippi of a*

Public and General Nature. New Orleans: E. Johns and Co., Stationers' Hall, 1840. Lillian Goldman Library, Yale School of Law, New Haven, Conn.

Hughes, Louis. *Thirty Years a Slave, From Bondage to Freedom*. Milwaukee: South Side Printing, 1897. Library Company of Philadelphia, Philadelphia, Pa.

Hungerford, James. *The Old Plantation and What I Gathered There in an Autumn Month*. New York: Harper and Brothers, 1859. Library Company of Philadelphia, Philadelphia, Pa.

Hutchinson, A. *Code of Mississippi: Being an Analytic Compilation of the Public and General Statutes of the Territory and State*. Jackson: Price and Fall, 1848.

Jackson, John Andrew. *The Experience of a Slave in South Carolina*. London: Passmore and Alabaster, 1862. Library Company of Philadelphia, Philadelphia, Pa.

Jackson, Mattie J. *The Story of Mattie Jackson*. 1866. In *Six Women's Slave Narratives*, edited by Henry Louis Gates Jr. New York: Oxford University Press, 1988.

Jacobs, Harriet Ann. *Incidents in the Life of a Slave Girl, Written by Herself*. Edited by Jean Fagan Yellin. 1861. Reprint, Cambridge, Mass.: Harvard University Press, 1987.

Jones, Thomas H. *The Experience of Thomas Jones, Who Was a Slave for Forty-Three Years. Written by a Friend, as Given to Him by Brother Jones*. Springfield, Mass.: H. S. Taylor, 1854. Beinecke Rare Book and Manuscript Library, New Haven, Conn.; Library Company of Philadelphia, Philadelphia, Pa.

Keckley, Elizabeth. *Behind the Scenes*. New York: Carleton, 1868. Library Company of Philadelphia, Philadelphia, Pa.

Kemble, Frances Ann. *Journal of a Residence on a Georgian Plantation in 1838–39*. Edited by John A. Scott. New York: New American Library, 1975.

Kirkland, Frazar. *The Pictorial Book of Anecdotes and Incidents of the War of the Rebellion*. Hartford, Conn.: Hartford Publishing Co., 1866. Library Company of Philadelphia, Philadelphia, Pa.

Knox, Thomas W. *Camp-fire and Cotton-field: Southern Adventure in the Time of War. Life with the Union Armies, and Residence on a Louisiana Plantation*. New York: Blelock and Company, 1865. Library Company of Philadelphia, Philadelphia, Pa.

Leigh, Edwin. *Bird's Eye View of Slavery in Missouri*. St. Louis: Keith and Woods, C. C. Bailey, James M. Crawford, C. Witter, 1862. Library Company of Philadelphia, Philadelphia, Pa.

Leigh, Frances Butler. *Ten Years of a Georgian Plantation*. London: Richard Bentley and Son, 1883. Library Company of Philadelphia, Philadelphia, Pa.

Lewis, J. Vance. *Out of the Ditch: A True Story of an Ex-Slave*. Houston: Rein and Sons, 1910. Beinecke Rare Book and Manuscript Library, New Haven, Conn.

Lines, Amelia Akehurst. *To Raise Myself a Little: The Diaries and Letters of Jennie, A Georgia Teacher, 1851–1886*. Edited by Thomas Dyer. Athens: University of Georgia Press, 1982. Library Company of Philadelphia, Philadelphia, Pa.

Livermore, Mary A. *My Story of the War: A Woman's Narrative of Four Years Personal Experience*. Hartford, Conn.: A. D. Worthington, 1889. Library Company of Philadelphia, Philadelphia, Pa.

Martin, Francois Xavier. *The Public Acts of the General Assembly of North Carolina.* 2 vols. New Bern: Martin and Ogden, 1804.

McCord, David J. *The Statutes at Large of South Carolina.* 10 vols. Columbia: A. S. Johnston, 1840. Lillian Goldman Library, Yale School of Law, New Haven, Conn.

Memoir of Old Elizabeth, a coloured woman: With a short account of her last sickness and death. Philadelphia: David Heston, 1866. Library Company of Philadelphia, Philadelphia, Pa.

Morehead, C. S., and Mason Brown. *Digest of the Statute Laws of Kentucky, of a Public and Permanent Nature.* 2 vols. Frankfort: Albert G. Hodges, 1834. Lillian Goldman Library, Yale School of Law, New Haven, Conn.

Nash, Frederick, James Iredell, and William H. Battle, eds. *The Revised Statutes of the State of North Carolina, passed by the General Assembly at the Session of 1836–37.* Raleigh: Turner and Hughes, 1837.

Nordhoff, Charles. *The Freedmen of South-Carolina: Some Account of Their Appearance, Character, Condition, and Peculiar Customs.* New York: Charles T. Evans, 1863. Library Company of Philadelphia, Philadelphia, Pa.

Northup, Solomon. *Twelve Years a Slave. Narrative of Solomon Northup, A Citizen of New-York.* New York: Miller, Orton and Mulligan, 1855.

Olmsted, Frederick Law. *The Cotton Kingdom.* Edited by Arthur M. Schlesinger Sr. 1861. Reprint, New York: Modern Library, 1984.

——. *A Journey in the Back Country.* New York: Mason Brothers, 1860. Library Company of Philadelphia, Philadelphia, Pa.

——. *A Journey in the Seabord Slave States, With Remarks on Their Economy.* New York: Dix and Edwards, 1856. Library Company of Philadelphia, Philadelphia, Pa.

Pember, Phoebe. *A Southern Woman's Story.* New York: Carleton, 1879.

Perdue, Charles L., Thomas E. Barden, and Robert K. Phillips, eds. *Weevils in the Wheat: Interviews with Virginia Ex-Slaves.* Bloomington: Indiana University Press, 1980.

Phillips, U. B. *The Revised Statutes of Louisiana.* New Orleans: John Clairborne, 1856. Lillian Goldman Library, Yale School of Law, New Haven, Conn.

Phillips, Ulrich B., and James David Glunt, eds. *Florida Plantation Records from the Papers of George Noble Jones.* St. Louis: Missouri Historical Society, 1927.

Philpot, Francis. *Facts for White Americans, with a plain hint for dupes, and a bone to pick for white nigger demagogues and amalgamation abolitionists, including the parentage, brief career, and execution, of amalgamation abolitionism, whose funeral sermon was preached at Washington on the 7th of February, 1839.* Philadelphia: By the author, 1839.

Picquet, Louisa. *Louisa Picquet, The Octoroon: A Tale of Southern Slave Life.* 1861. In *Collected Black Women's Narratives,* edited by Henry Louis Gates Jr. New York: Oxford University Press, 1988.

Peirce, Levi, Miles Taylor, and William W. King, eds. *The Consolidation and Revision of the Statutes of the State, of a General Nature.* New Orleans: Bee Office, 1852. Lillian Goldman Library, Yale School of Law, New Haven, Conn.

Potter, Henry, J. L. Taylor, and Bart Yancey, eds. *Laws of the State of North Carolina*. 2 vols. Raleigh: J. Gales, 1821.

Preamble and Regulations of the Savannah River Anti–Slave Traffick Association. N.p., n.d.

Prince, Oliver H. *Digest of the Laws of the State of Georgia*. Milledgeville: Grantland and Orme, 1822. Lillian Goldman Library, Yale School of Law, New Haven, Conn.

Rawick, George P., ed. *The American Slave: A Composite Autobiography*. 19 vols. Westport, Conn.: Greenwood, 1972.

Redpath, John R., ed. *The Roving Editor, or Talks with Slaves in the Southern States*. University Park: Pennsylvania State University Press, 1996.

The Revised Code of the Statute Laws of the State of Mississippi. Jackson: E. Barksdale, 1857.

Roper, Moses. *A Narrative of the Adventures and Escape of Moses Roper*. London: Harvey and Darton, 1839. Library Company of Philadelphia, Philadelphia, Pa.

Schoolcraft, Mrs. Henry Rowe. *The Black Gauntlet: A Tale of Plantation Life in South Carolina*. 1852. Philadelphia: Lippincott, 1861. Library Company of Philadelphia, Philadelphia, Pa. Reprint, New York: Negro Universities Press, 1969.

Seabury, Caroline. *The Diary of Caroline Seabury, 1854–1863*. Edited by Suzanne L. Bunkers. Madison: University of Wisconsin Press, 1991.

Shepherd, Samuel. *The Statutes at Large of Virginia*. 3 vols. Richmond: Samuel Shepherd, 1835. Lillian Goldman Library, Yale School of Law, New Haven, Conn.

Sims, J. Marion. *Silver Sutures in Surgery: The Anniversary Discourse Before the New York Academy of Medicine*. New York: Samuel S. and William Woods, 1858. Library Company of Philadelphia, Philadelphia, Pa.

———. *The Story of My Life*. Edited by his son, H. Marion Sims. New York: Appleton, 1884. Library Company of Philadelphia, Philadelphia, Pa.

Smallwood, Thomas. *A Narrative of Thomas Smallwood (Coloured Man)*. Edited, annotated, and with an introduction by Richard Almonte. Toronto: Mercury Press, 2000.

Smith, Harry. *Fifty Years in Slavery in the United States of America*. 1891. Reprint, Grand Rapids, Mich.: Clark Historical Library, 1973.

Steward, Austin. *Twenty-Two Years a Slave and Forty Years a Freeman*. 1857. Reprint, Reading, Mass.: Addison-Wesley, 1969.

Stone, Kate. *Brokenburn: The Journal of Kate Stone, 1861–1868*. Edited by John Q. Anderson. Baton Rouge: Louisiana State University Press, 1955.

Taylor, Susie King. *Reminiscences of My Life in Camp*. 1902. In *Collected Black Women's Narratives*, edited by Henry Louis Gates Jr. New York: Oxford University Press, 1988.

Thompson, John. *The Life of John Thompson, a Fugitive Slave; Containing his History or 25 Years in Bondage, and His Providential Escape*. 1856. Reprint, New York: Negro Universities Press, 1968.

Toulmin, Harry. *Digest of the Laws of the State of Alabama*. Cahawba: Ginn and Curtis, 1823. Lillian Goldman Library, Yale School of Law, New Haven, Conn.

Truth, Sojourner. *Narrative of Sojourner Truth*. 1850. Edited by Margaret Washington. Reprint, New York: Vintage, 1993.

U.S. Census Office. *The Seventh Census of the United States, 1850*. New York: Arno Press, 1976.

Veney, Bethany. *The Narrative of Bethany Veney: A Slave Woman*. 1889. In *Collected Black Women's Narratives*, edited by Henry Louis Gates Jr. New York: Oxford University Press, 1988.

Vermeule, Elizabeth. *Narrative of Elizabeth Vermeule*. New York: American Tract Society, 1846.

Walker, David. *David Walker's Appeal to the Colored Citizens of the World*. Edited by Peter P. Hinks. College Park: Pennsylvania State University Press, 2000.

Watson, Henry. *Narrative of Henry Watson, a Fugitive Slave*. 1848. Reprint, Millwood, N.Y.: Kraus Reprint, 1973. Library Company of Philadelphia, Philadelphia, Pa.

Webb, Allie Bayne Windham, ed. *Mistress of Evergreen Plantation: Rachel O'Connor's Legacy of Letters, 1823–1845*. Albany: State University of New York Press, 1983.

Weld, Theodore Dwight. *American Slavery As It Is: Testimony of a Thousand Witnesses*. 1839. Reprint, New York: Arno Press, 1968.

Williams, Isaac. *Aunt Sally; or, The Cross the Way Freedom. A Narrative of the Slave-Life and Purchase of the Mother of Rev. Isaac Williams, of Detroit, Michigan*. Cincinnati: American Reform Tract and Book Society, 1858. Library Company of Philadelphia, Philadelphia, Pa.

Work, John W. *American Negro Songs: A Comprehensive Collection of 230 Folk Songs, Religious and Secular*. New York: Howell, Soskin, 1940.

SECONDARY SOURCES

Abrahams, Roger D. *Singing the Master: The Emergence of African American Culture in the Plantation South*. New York: Penguin, 1992.

Abu-Lughod, Lila. "The Romance of Resistance: Tracing Transformations of Power through Bodouin Women." In *Beyond the Second Sex: New Directions in the Anthropology of Gender*, edited by Peggy Reeves Sanday and Ruth Gallagher Goodenough, 313–37. Philadelphia: University of Pennsylvania Press, 1990.

Alexander, Adele Logan. *Ambiguous Lives: Free Women of Color in Rural Georgia, 1789–1879*. Fayetteville: University of Arkansas Press, 1991.

Alexander, Jeffrey C., and Steven Seidman. *Culture and Society: Contemporary Debates*. Cambridge: Cambridge University Press, 1990.

Anderson, Benedict. *Imagined Communities: Reflections of the Origin and Spread of Nationalism*. London: Verso, 1983.

Andrews, William L. "The First Fifty Years of the Slave Narrative, 1760–1810." In *The Art of Slave Narrative: Original Essays in Criticism and Theory*, edited by John Sekora and Darwin T. Turner, 6–24. Macomb: Western Illinois University Press, 1982.

Aptheker, Herbert. *Abolitionism: A Revolutionary Movement*. Boston: Twayne, 1989.

———. *American Negro Slave Revolts.* 1943. Reprint, New York: International Publishers, 1969.

Ardener, Shirley. *Women and Space: Ground Rules and Social Maps.* New York: St. Martin's Press, 1981.

Ayers, Edward L. *Southern Crossing: A History of the American South, 1877–1906.* New York: Oxford University Press, 1995.

Bakhtin, M. M. *The Dialogic Imagination: Four Essays by M. M. Bakhtin.* Edited by Michael Holquist. Austin: University of Texas Press, 1981.

Baptist, Edward E. *Creating an Old South: Middle Florida's Plantation Frontier before the Civil War.* Chapel Hill: University of North Carolina Press, 2002.

———. "'Cuffy,' 'Fancy Maids,' and 'One-Eyed Men': Rape, Commodification, and the Domestic Slave Trade in the United States." *American Historical Review* 106 (December 2001): 1619–50.

Baptist, Edward E., and Stephanie M. H. Camp, eds. *New Studies in American Slavery.* Athens: University of Georgia Press, forthcoming.

Barthelemy, Anthony G. Introduction to *Collected Black Women's Narratives,* edited by Henry Louis Gates Jr., xxix–xlviii. New York: Oxford University Press, 1988.

Bauer, Raymond, and Alice H. Bauer. "Day to Day Resistance to Slavery." *Journal of Negro History* 27 (October 1942): 388–419.

Bayliss, John F. *Black Slave Narratives.* New York: Collier, 1970.

Beckles, Hilary McD. *Afro-Caribbean Women and Resistance to Slavery in Barbados.* London: Karnak House, 1988.

———. *Natural Rebels: A Social History of Enslaved Black Women in Barbados.* New Brunswick: Rutgers University Press, 1989.

Berlin, Ira. *Many Thousands Gone: The First Two Centuries of Slavery in North America.* Cambridge, Mass.: Harvard University Press, 1998.

———, ed. *Remembering Slavery: African Americans Talk about Their Personal Experiences of Slavery and Emancipation.* New York: New Press, 1998.

Berlin, Ira, and Philip Morgan, eds. *Cultivation and Culture: Labor and the Shaping of Slave Life in the Americas.* Charlottesville: University of Virginia Press, 1993.

———. *The Slaves' Economy: Independent Production by Slaves in the Americas.* London: Frank Cass and Co., 1991.

Berlin, Ira, Barbara J. Fields, Steven F. Miller, Joseph P. Reidy, and Leslie S. Rowland, eds. *Free at Last: A Documentary History of Slavery, Freedom, and the Civil War.* New York: Free Press, 1992.

Blassingame, John. *The Slave Community: Plantation Life in the Antebellum South.* New York: Oxford University Press, 1972.

Block, Sharon. "Lines of Color, Sex, and Service: Comparative Sexual Coercion in Early America." In *Sex, Love, Race: Crossing Boundaries in North American History,* edited by Martha Hodes, 141–63. New York: New York University Press, 1999.

Bolster, Jeffrey W. *Black Jacks: African American Seaman in the Age of Sail.* Cambridge, Mass.: Harvard University Press, 1997.

Bonnell, Victoria E., and Lynn Hunt, eds. *Beyond the Cultural Turn: New Directions in the Study of Society and Culture*. Berkeley: University of California Press, 1999.

Bourdieu, Pierre. *In Other Words: Essays towards a Reflexive Sociology*. Stanford: Stanford University Press, 1990.

——. *Outline of a Theory of Practice*. 1972. Reprint, Cambridge: Cambridge University Press, 1977.

Bracey, John H., August Meier, and Elliot Rudwick, eds. *American Slavery: The Question of Resistance*. Belmont, Calif.: Wadsworth, 1971.

Breeden, James O. *Advice among Masters: The Ideal of Slave Management in the Old South*. Westport, Conn.: Greenwood, 1980.

Brown, Elsa Barkley. "Negotiating and Transforming the Public Sphere: African American Political Life in the Transition from Slavery to Freedom." *Public Culture* 7 (Winter 1994): 107–46.

Brown, Kathleen M. *Good Wives, Nasty Wenches, and Anxious Patriarchs: Gender, Race, and Power in Colonial Virginia*. Chapel Hill: University of North Carolina Press, 1996.

Buchanan, Thomas C. "The Slave Mississippi: African-American Steamboat Workers, Networks of Resistance, and the Commercial World of the Western Rivers, 1811–1880." Ph.D. diss., Carnegie Mellon University, 1998.

Bynum, Victoria. *Unruly Women: The Politics of Social and Sexual Control in the Old South*. Chapel Hill: University of North Carolina Press, 1992.

Carby, Hazel V. *Race Men*. Cambridge, Mass.: Harvard University Press, 1998.

——. *Reconstructing Womanhood: The Emergence of the Afro-American Woman Novelist*. New York: Oxford University Press, 1987.

Cecelski, David S. *The Waterman's Song: Slavery and Freedom in Maritime North Carolina*. Chapel Hill: University of North Carolina Press, 2001.

Chesnut, Mary Boykin. *A Diary from Dixie by Mary Boykin Chesnut*. Edited by Ben Ames Williams. 1949; Cambridge, Mass.: Harvard University Press, 1976.

Clark, Elizabeth B. "'The Sacred Rights of the Weak': Pain, Sympathy, and the Culture of Individual Rights in Antebellum America." *Journal of American History* 82 (September 1995): 463–93.

Coryell, Janet L., Martha H. Swain, Sandra Gioia Treadway, and Elizabeth Hayes Turner, eds. *Beyond Image and Convention: Explorations in Southern Women's History*. Columbia: University of Missouri Press, 1998.

Costa, Emilia Viotti da. *Crowns of Glory, Tears of Blood: The Demarara Slave Rebellion of 1823*. New York: Oxford University Press, 1994.

Craton, Michael. *Testing the Chains: Resistance to Slavery in the British West Indies*. Ithaca: Cornell University Press, 1982.

Cunningham, George. "'Called Into Existence': Desire, Gender and Voice in Frederick Douglass's Narrative of 1845." *differences* 1, no. 3 (1989): 108–36.

Dahl, Svend. *History of the Book*. New York: Scarecrow Press, 1958.

Davenport, Cyril. *The Book: Its History and Development*. New York: Van Nostrand, 1908.

Davis, Mike. *City of Quartz: Excavating the Future in Los Angeles*. London: Verso, 1990.

Davis, Nathalie Zemon. *The Return of Martin Guerre*. Cambridge, Mass.: Harvard University Press, 1983.

Davis, Thomas J. "Conspiracy and Credibility: Look Who's Talking, about What—Law Talk and Loose Talk." *William and Mary Quarterly*, 3rd ser., 59, no. 1 (January 2002): 167–74.

——. *A Rumor of Revolt: The "Great Negro Plot" in Colonial New York*. Amherst: University of Massachusetts Press, 1985.

de Certeau, Michel. *The Practice of Everyday Life*. Berkeley: University of California Press, 1984.

DeLombard, Jeannine. " 'Eye-witness to the Cruelty': Southern Violence and Northern Testimony in Frederick Douglass' 1845 Narrative." In "Violence, the Body, and 'the South,' " edited by Houston A. Baker Jr. and Dana D. Nelson. Special issue, *American Literature*, July 2001, 245–75.

Dew, Charles B. *Bond of Iron: Master and Slave at Buffalo Forge*. New York: Norton, 1994.

Dillon, Merton. *Slavery Attacked: Southern Slaves and Their Allies, 1619–1865*. Baton Rouge: Louisiana State University Press, 1990.

Douglas, Mary, ed. *Constructive Drinking: Perspectives in Drink from Anthropology*. Cambridge: Cambridge University Press, 1987.

——. *Natural Symbols: Explorations in Cosmology*. New York: Pantheon, 1970.

——. *Purity and Danger: An Analysis of Concepts of Pollution and Taboo*. London: Routledge and Kegan Paul, 1966.

DuBois, W. E. B. *Black Reconstruction in America, 1860–1880*. Edited by David Levering Lewis. 1935. Reprint, New York: Simon and Schuster, 1992.

Duncan, N. *BodySpace: Destabilizing Geographies of Gender and Sexuality*. London: Routledge, 1996.

Dusinberre, William. *Them Dark Days: Slavery in the American Rice Swamps*. New York: Oxford University Press, 1996.

Eaton, Clement. "The Resistance of the South to Northern Radicalism." *New England Quarterly*, June 1935, 215–31.

Edwards, Laura F. *Scarlett Doesn't Live Here Anymore: Southern Women in the Civil War Era*. Urbana: University of Illinois Press, 2000.

Egerton, Douglas R. "Forgetting Denmark Vesey; or, Oliver Stone Meets Richard Wade." *William and Mary Quarterly*, 3rd ser., 59, no. 1 (January 2002): 143–52.

——. *Gabriel's Rebellion: The Virginia Slave Conspiracies of 1800 and 1802*. Chapel Hill: University of North Carolina Press, 1993.

——. *He Shall Go Out Free: The Lives of Denmark Vesey*. Madison, Wis.: Madison House, 1999.

Elkins, Stanley. *Slavery: A Problem in American Institutional and Intellectual Life*. Chicago: University of Chicago Press, 1976.

Ellis, A. B. *The Tshi-Speaking Peoples of the Gold Coast of West Africa. Their Religion, Manners, Customs, Laws, Language, Etc.* London: Chapman and Hall, 1887.

Ellison, Mary. "Resistance to Oppression: Black Women's Response to Slavery in the United States." *Slavery and Abolition* 4, no. 1 (1983): 56–63.

Eltis, David. *The Rise of African Slavery in the Americas.* Cambridge: Cambridge University Press, 2000.

Ernst, Robert T., and Lawrence Hugg, eds. *Black America: Geographic Perspectives.* Garden City, N.Y.: Anchor, 1976.

Fanon, Frantz. *Black Skin, White Masks.* 1952. Reprint, New York: Grove Weidenfeld, 1967.

——. *The Wretched of the Earth.* 1961. Reprint, New York: Grove Weidenfeld, 1963.

Farge, Arlette, and Jacques Revel. *The Vanishing Children of Paris: Rumor and Politics before the French Revolution.* Cambridge, Mass.: Harvard University Press, 1991.

Farnsworth-Alvear, Ann. "Orthodox Virginity/Heterodox Memories: Understanding Women's Stories of Mill Discipline in Medellin, Columbia." *Signs* 23 (Autumn 1997): 71–102.

Faue, Elizabeth. *Community of Suffering and Struggle: Women, Men, and the Labor Movement in Minneapolis, 1915–1945.* Chapel Hill: University of North Carolina Press, 1991.

Faust, Drew Gilpin. *The Ideology of Slavery: Pro-Slavery Thought in the Antebellum South, 1830–1860.* Baton Rouge: Louisiana State University Press, 1981.

——. *James Henry Hammond and the Old South: A Design for Mastery.* Baton Rouge: Louisiana State University Press, 1982.

——. *Mothers of Invention: Women of the Slaveholding South in the American Civil War.* Chapel Hill: University of North Carolina Press, 1996.

——. *Southern Stories: Slaveholders in Peace and War.* Columbia: University of Missouri Press, 1992.

Fede, Andrew. "Legitimized Violent Slave Abuse in the American South, 1619–1865: A Case Study of Law and Social Change in Six Southern States." *American Journal of Legal History* 29, no. 2 (1985): 93–105.

Fett, Sharla M. *Working Cures: Healing, Health, and Power on Southern Slave Plantations.* Chapel Hill: University of North Carolina Press, 2002.

Finkelman, Paul. *African Americans and the Law.* New York: Garland, 1992.

——. *Women and the Family in a Slave Society.* New York: Garland, 1989.

Finley, Moses. "Slavery." In *International Encyclopedia of the Social Sciences,* edited by David L. Sills, 14:307–13. New York: Macmillan, 1968.

Fogel, William, and Stanley L. Engerman. *Time on the Cross: The Economics of American Negro Slavery.* Boston: Little, Brown, 1974.

Foner, Eric. *Nothing But Freedom: Emancipation and Its Legacy.* Baton Rouge: Louisiana State University Press, 1983.

——. *Reconstruction: America's Unfinished Revolution, 1863–1877.* New York: Harper and Row, 1988.

——. *A Short History of Reconstruction.* New York: Harper and Row, 1984.

——. *The Story of American Freedom*. New York: Norton, 1998.

Foster, Helen Bradley. *"New Raiments of Self": African American Clothing in the Antebellum South*. New York: Oxford University Press, 1997.

Foster, Frances Smith. Introduction to *The House of Bondage; or, Charlotte Brooks and Other Slaves*. 1890. Reprint, New York: Oxford University Press, 1988.

Foucault, Michel. *Discipline and Punish: The Birth of the Prison*. 1975. Reprint, New York: Vintage, 1979.

——. *The History of Sexuality: An Introduction*. Vol. 1. 1976. New York: Vintage, 1978.

Fox-Genovese, Elizabeth. *Within the Plantation Household: Black and White Women of the Old South*. Chapel Hill: University of North Carolina Press, 1988.

Fox-Genovese, Elizabeth, and Eugene Genovese. *Fruits of Merchant Capital: Slavery and Bourgeois Property in the Rise and Expansion of Capitalism*. New York: Oxford University Press, 1983.

Franklin, John Hope. *The Free Negro in North Carolina, 1790–1860*. Chapel Hill: University of North Carolina Press, 1943.

——. "Runaway Slaves." *American Visions* 6 (February 1991): 30–31.

Franklin, John Hope, and Loren Schweninger. *Runaway Slaves: Rebels on the Plantation*. New York: Oxford University Press, 1999.

Frederickson, George M. *The Black Image in the White Mind: The Debate on Afro-American Character and Destiny, 1817–1914*. Middletown, Conn.: Wesleyan University Press, 1971.

Fry, Gladys-Marie. *Nightriders in Black Folk History*. Knoxville: University of Tennessee Press, 1975.

Gaspar, David Berry. *Bondmen and Rebels: A Case Study of Master-Slave Relations in Antigua, with Implications for Colonial British America*. Baltimore: Johns Hopkins University Press, 1985.

Gaspar, David Barry, and Darlene Clark Hine, eds. *More Than Chattel: Black Women and Slavery in the Americas*. Bloomington: Indiana University Press, 1996.

Genovese, Eugene D. *From Rebellion to Revolution: Afro-American Slave Revolts in the Making of the Modern World*. Baton Rouge: Louisiana State University Press, 1979.

——. *In Red and Black: Marxian Explorations in Southern and Afro-American History*. Knoxville: University of Tennessee Press, 1984.

——. *The Political Economy of Slavery: Studies in the Economy and Society of the Slave South*. New York: Vintage, 1965.

——. *Roll, Jordan, Roll: The World the Slaves Made*. New York: Vintage, 1972.

Gilroy, Paul. *The Black Atlantic*. London: Verso, 1993.

——. "One Nation under a Groove: The Cultural Politics of 'Race' and Racism in Britain." In *Anatomy of Racism*, edited by David Theo Goldberg, 263–82. Minneapolis: University of Minnesota Press, 1990.

Glassman, Jonathon. "The Bondsman's New Clothes: The Contradictory Consciousness of Slave Resistance on the Swahili Coast." *Journal of African History* 32 (1991): 277–312.

——. *Feasts and Riots*. Portsmouth, N.H.: Heineman, 1995.

Glenn, Susan. *Daughters of the Shtetl: Life and Labor in the Immigrant Generation*. Ithaca: Cornell University Press, 1990.

Godlewska, Anne, and Neil Smith, eds. *Geography and Empire*. Oxford: Blackwell, 1994.

Goldfield, David. *Region, Race, and Cities: Interpreting the Urban South*. Baton Rouge: Louisiana State University Press, 1997.

Gordon-Reed, Annette. *Thomas Jefferson and Sally Hemings: An American Controversy*. Charlottesville: University of Virginia Press, 1997.

Gorn, Elliot J. "'Gouge and Bite, Pull Hair and Scratch': The Social Significance of Fighting in the Southern Backcountry." *American Historical Review* 90 (February 1985): 18–43.

Graff, Harvey J. *The Labyrinths of Literacy: Reflections of Literacy Past and Present*. Philadelphia: Falmer Press, 1987.

Gramsci, Antonio. *Selections from the Prison Notebooks*. Edited by Quintin Hoare and Geoffrey Nowell. New York: International Publishers, 1971.

Gray, Lewis Cecil. *History of Agriculture in the South United States to 1860*. 2 vols. Washington, D.C.: Carnegie Institution of Washington, 1933.

Greenberg, Kenneth S. *Honor and Slavery: Lies, Duels, Noses, Masks, Dressing as a Woman, Gifts, Strangers, Humanitarianism, Death, Slave Rebellions, the Proslavery Argument, Baseball, Hunting, Gambling in the Old South*. Princeton: Princeton University Press, 1996.

Griffin, Farah Jasmine. *"Who Set You Flowin'?": The African-American Migration Narrative*. New York: Oxford University Press, 1995.

Grimstead, David. *American Mobbing, 1828–1861: Toward Civil War*. New York: Oxford University Press, 1998.

Gross, Ariela J. *Double Character: Slavery and Mastery in the Antebellum Southern Courtroom*. Princeton: Princeton University Press, 2000.

Gross, Kali Nicole. "The Dismembered Body of Wakefield Gaines and Other Tales of African American Female Criminality in Philadelphia, 1880–1910." Ph.D. diss., University of Pennsylvania, 1999.

Guha, Ranajit. *Elementary Aspects of Peasant Insurgency in Colonial India*. Delhi: Oxford, 1983.

Gutman, Herbert. *The Black Family in Slavery and Freedom, 1750–1925*. New York: Vintage, 1976.

Hadden, Sally Elizabeth. *Slave Patrols: Law and Violence in Virginia and the Carolinas*. Cambridge, Mass.: Harvard University Press, 2001.

Hall, Jacquelyn Dowd. "'You Must Remember This': Autobiography as Social Critique." *Journal of American History* 85 (September 1998): 439–66.

Hanchard, Michael. "Temporality, Transnationalism, and Afro-Modernity." Paper presented to the "Reshaping Afro-American Studies" seminar, Center for the Study of Black Literature and Culture, University of Pennsylvania, 27 March 1997.

Harding, Vincent. *There Is a River: The Black Struggle for Freedom in America*. 1981. Reprint, New York: Vintage, 1983.

Harris, Seale. *Woman's Surgeon: The Life Story of J. Marion Sims*. New York: Macmillan, 1950.

Harrold, Stanley. *The Abolitionists and the South, 1831–1861*. Lexington: University Press of Kentucky, 1995.

Harvey, David. *Justice, Nature, and the Geography of Difference*. Oxford: Blackwell, 1996.

Hazzard-Gordon, Katrina. *Jookin': The Rise of Cultural Dance Formations in African-American Culture*. Philadelphia: Temple University Press, 1990.

Herbert, Hilary A. *The Abolition Crusade and Its Consequences: Four Periods in American History*. New York: Charles Scribner's Sons, 1912.

Herd, Denise. "The Paradox of Temperance: Blacks and the Alcohol Question in Nineteenth-Century America." In *Drinking: Behavior and Belief in Modern History*, edited by Susanna Barrows and Robin Room, 354–75. Berkeley: University of California Press, 1991.

Herzog, Dagmar. "'Pleasure, Sex and Politics Belong Together': Post-Holocaust Memory and the Sexual Revolution in West Germany." *Critical Inquiry* 24 (Winter 1998): 393–444.

Heuman, Gad, ed. *Out of the House of Bondage: Runaways, Resistance, and Marronage in Africa and the New World*. London: Frank Cass, 1986.

Higginbotham, A. Leon. *In the Matter of Color: Race and the American Legal Process: The Colonial Period*. New York: Oxford University Press, 1978.

Higginbotham, Evelyn Brooks. "African-American Women's History and the Metalanguage of Race." *Signs* 17 (Winter 1992): 251–74.

——. *Righteous Discontent: The Women's Movement in the Black Baptist Church*. Cambridge, Mass.: Harvard University Press, 1992.

Hine, Darlene Clark. "Rape and the Inner Lives of Black Women in the Middle-West: Preliminary Thoughts on the Culture of Dissemblance." *Signs* 14 (Summer 1989): 912–20.

Hine, Darlene Clark, and Kate Wittenstein. "Female Slave Resistance: The Economics of Sex." In *The Black Woman Cross-Culturally*, edited by Filomena Steady, 289–91. Cambridge, Mass.: Schenkman, 1981.

Hinks, Peter P. *To Awaken My Afflicted Brethren: David Walker and the Problem of Antebellum Slave Resistance*. University Park: Pennsylvania State University Press, 1997.

Hobsbawm, Eric. "Peasants and Politics." *Journal of Peasant Studies* 1, no. 1 (1973): 3–22.

——. *Primitive Rebels: Studies in Archaic Forms of Social Movements in the Nineteenth and Twentieth Centuries*. New York: Norton, 1959.

Hodes, Martha. *White Women, Black Men: Illicit Sex in the Nineteenth-Century South*. New Haven: Yale University Press, 1997.

——, ed. *Sex, Love, Race: Crossing Boundaries in North American History*. New York: New York University Press, 1999.

Hollander, Anne. *Seeing through Clothes*. Berkeley: University of California Press, 1975.

Holt, Sharon Ann. "Symbol, Memory, and Service: Resistance and Family in Nineteenth-Century African America." In *Working toward Freedom: Slave Society and Domestic Economy in the American South*, edited by Larry E. Hudson Jr., 192–210. Rochester, N.Y.: University of Rochester Press, 1994.

Horton, James. *Free People of Color: Inside the African American Community*. Washington, D.C.: Smithsonian Institution Press, 1993.

Hudson, Frederic. *Journalism in the United States from 1690 to 1872*. New York: Harper and Brothers, 1873.

Hunt, Lynn, ed. *The New Cultural History*. Berkeley: University of California Press, 1989.

Hunt, Patricia. "The Struggle to Achieve Individual Expression through Clothing and Adornment: African-American Women under and after Slavery." In *Discovering the Women in Slavery: Emancipating Perspectives on the American Past*, edited by Patricia Morton, 227–40. Athens: University of Georgia Press, 1996.

Hunter, Tera. *To 'Joy My Freedom: Southern Black Women's Lives and Labors after the Civil War*. Cambridge, Mass.: Harvard University Press, 1997.

Isaac, Rhys. *The Transformation of Virginia, 1740–1790*. 1982. Reprint, New York: Norton, 1988.

James, C. L. R. *The Black Jacobins: Toussaint L'Ouverture and the San Domingo Revolution*. 1963. Reprint, New York: Vintage, 1989.

James, C. L. R., Grace Lee, and Pierre Chaulieu. *Facing Reality*. 1958. Reprint, Detroit: Benwick, 1974.

Jennings, Thelma. " 'Us Colored Women Had to go Through a Plenty': Sexual Exploitation of African-American Women." *Journal of Women's History* 1, no. 3 (Winter 1990): 45–74.

Johnson, Michael P. "Denmark Vesey and His Co-Conspirators." *William and Mary Quarterly*, 3rd ser., 58, no. 4 (October 2001): 913–76.

——. "Reading Evidence." *William and Mary Quarterly*, 3rd ser., 59, no. 1 (January 2002): 193–202.

——. "Runaway Slaves and the Slave Communities in South Carolina, 1799–1830." *William and Mary Quarterly*, 3rd ser., 38, no. 3 (July 1981): 418–41.

——. "Smothered Infants: Were Slave Mothers at Fault?" *Journal of Southern History* 47, no. 4 (November 1981): 493–520.

Johnson, Walter. *Soul by Soul: Life inside the Antebellum Slave Market*. Cambridge, Mass.: Harvard University Press, 1999.

Jones, Howard. *Mutiny on the Amistad*. New York: Oxford University Press, 1987.

Jones, Jacqueline. *Labor of Love, Labor of Sorrow: Black Women, Work, and the Family, From Slavery to the Present*. New York: Vintage, 1985.

Jordan, Winthrop. *Tumult and Silence at Second Creek: An Inquiry into a Civil War Slave Conspiracy*. Baton Rouge: Louisiana State University Press, 1993.

——. *White over Black: American Attitudes toward the Negro, 1550–1812*. Chapel Hill: University of North Carolina Press, 1968. Reprint, New York: Penguin, 1969.

Joyner, Charles. *Down by the Riverside: A South Carolina Slave Community*. Urbana: University of Illinois Press, 1984.

Jung, Moon-Ho. "'Coolies' and Cane: Race, Labor, and Sugar Production in Louisiana, 1852–1877." Ph.D. diss., Cornell University, 2000.

Kay, Marvin L., and Lorin Lee Cary. *Slavery in North Carolina, 1748–1775*. Chapel Hill: University of North Carolina Press, 1995.

Kelley, Robin D. G. *Race Rebels: Culture, Politics, and the Black Working Class*. New York: Free Press, 1994.

Kerber, Linda. *Women of the Republic: Intellect and Ideology in Revolutionary America*. New York: Norton, 1986.

Kerr-Ritchie, Jeffrey R. *Freedpeople in the Tobacco South: Virginia, 1860–1900*. Chapel Hill: University of North Carolina Press, 1999.

King, Wilma. "The Mistress and Her Maids: White and Black Women in a Louisiana Household, 1858–1868." In *Discovering the Women in Slavery: Emancipating Perspectives on the American Past*, edited by Patricia Morton, 82–106. Athens: University of Georgia Press, 1996.

———. "'Rais Your Children Up Rite': Parental Guidance and Child Rearing Practices among Slaves in the Nineteenth Century South." In *Working toward Freedom: Slave Society and Domestic Economy in the American South*, edited by Larry E. Hudson Jr., 143–62. Rochester, N.Y.: University of Rochester Press, 1994.

———. *Stolen Childhood: Slave Youth in Nineteenth-Century America* (Bloomington: Indiana University Press, 1995).

———. "'Suffer With Them Until Death': Slave Women and Their Children in Nineteenth-Century America." In *More Than Chattel: Black Women and Slavery in the Americas*, edited by David Barry Gaspar and Darlene Clark Hine, 147–68. Bloomington: Indiana University Press, 1996.

Kolchin, Peter. *American Slavery, 1619–1877*. New York: Hill and Wang, 1993.

Kopytoff, Barbara Klamon. "The Early Political Development of Jamaican Maroon Societies." *William and Mary Quarterly*, 3rd ser., 35, no. 2 (April 1978): 287–307.

Kratz, Corinne A. *Affecting Performance: Meaning, Movement, and Experience in Okiek Women's Initiation*. Washington, D.C.: Smithsonian Institution Press, 1994.

Lapsansky, Phillip. "Graphic Discord: Abolitionist and Antiabolitionist Images." In *The Abolitionist Sisterhood: Women's Political Culture in Antebellum America*, edited by Jean Fagan Yellin and John C. Van Horne, 201–30. Ithaca: Cornell University Press, 1994.

Lebsock, Suzanne. *The Free Women of Petersburg: Status and Culture in a Southern Town, 1784–1860*. New York: Norton, 1984.

LeFevbre, Henri. *Critique of Everyday Life*. 1947. Reprint, London: Verso, 1958.

Lefler, Hugh Talmage, and Albert Ray Newsome. *North Carolina: The History of a Southern State*. Chapel Hill: University of North Carolina Press, 1954.

Lehuu, Isabelle. *Carnival on the Page: Popular Print Media in Antebellum America*. Chapel Hill: University of North Carolina Press, 2000.

Levine, Lawrence W. *Black Culture and Black Consciousness: Afro-American Folk Thought from Slavery to Freedom*. New York: Oxford University Press, 1977.

Lewis, Jan Ellen, and Peter S. Onuf, eds. *Sally Hemings and Thomas Jefferson: History, Memory, and Civic Culture*. Charlottesville: University of Virginia Press, 1999.

Lichtenstein, Alex. "'That Disposition to Theft With Which They Have Been Branded': Moral Economy, Slave Management, and the Law." *Journal of Social History* 22 (Spring 1988): 413–40.

Lipsitz, George. *A Life in the Struggle: Ivory Perry and the Culture of Opposition*. Philadelphia: Temple University Press, 1988.

Litwack, Leon. *Been in the Storm So Long: The Aftermath of Slavery*. New York: Vintage, 1979.

——. *Trouble in Mind: Black Southerners in the Age of Jim Crow*. New York: Knopf, 1998.

Lockley, Timothy J. "Trading Encounters between Non-Elite Whites and African Americans in Savannah, 1790–1860." *Journal of Southern History* 66, no. 1 (February 2000): 25–48.

Malone, Ann Paton. *Sweet Chariot: Slave Family and Household Structure in Nineteenth-Century Louisiana*. Chapel Hill: University of North Carolina Press, 1996.

Marx, Anthony W. *Making Race and Nation: A Comparison of the United States, South Africa, and Brazil*. Cambridge: Cambridge University Press, 1998.

Massey, Doreen. *Space, Place, and Gender*. Minneapolis: University of Minnesota Press, 1994.

Masuzawa, Tomoko. "Troubles with Materiality: The Ghost of Fetishism in the Nineteenth Century." *Comparative Studies in Society and History* 42 (April 2000): 242–67.

Mbembe, Achille. "The Banality of Power in the Postcolony." *Public Culture* 4 (Spring 1992): 1–30.

McClintock, Anne. *Imperial Leather: Race, Gender and Sexuality in the Colonial Contest*. New York: Routledge, 1995.

McCurry, Stephanie. *Masters of Small Worlds: Yeoman Households, Gender Relations, and the Political Culture of the Antebellum South Carolina Low Country*. New York: Oxford University Press, 1995.

McDonnell, Lawrence T. "Money Knows No Master: Market Relations and the American Slave Community." In *Developing Dixie: Modernization in a Traditional Society*, edited by Winfred B. Moore Jr., Joseph F. Tripp, and Lyon G. Tyler Jr., 31–44. New York: Greenwood, 1988.

McGregor, Deborah Kuhn. *Sexual Surgery and the Origins of Gynecology: J. Marion Sims, His Hospital and His Patients*. New York: Garland, 1989.

McLaurin, Melton. *Celia, a Slave: A True Story of Violence and Retribution in Antebellum America*. Athens: University of Georgia Press, 1991.

McMillen, Neil. *Dark Journey: Black Mississippians in the Age of Jim Crow*. 1989. Reprint, Urbana: University of Illinois Press, 1990.

McPherson, James. *Battle Cry of Freedom: The Civil War Era*. 1988; Reprint, New York: Ballantine Books, 1989.

Meillasoux, Claude. *The Anthropology of Slavery: The Womb of Iron and Gold*. 1986. Reprint, Chicago: University of Chicago Press, 1991.

Miller, Joseph C. *Way of Death: Merchant Capitalism and the Angolan Slave Trade, 1730–1830*. Madison: University of Wisconsin Press, 1988.

Mintz, Sidney W., and Richard Price. *The Birth of African-American Culture: An Anthropological Perspective*. 1976. Reprint, Boston: Beacon Press, 1992.

Mohr, Clarence L. *On the Threshold of Freedom: Masters and Slaves in Civil War Georgia*. Athens: University of Georgia Press, 1986.

Moody, Joycelyn. *Sentimental Confessions: Spiritual Narratives of Nineteenth-Century African American Women*. Athens: University of Georgia Press, 2001.

Moore, John W. *Historical, Biographical, and Miscellaneous Gatherings, in the Form of Disconnected Notes Relative to Printers, Printing, Publishing, and Editing of Books, Newspapers, Magazines, and Other Literary Productions*. Concord, N.H.: Republican Press Association, 1886.

Morgan, Edmund S. *American Slavery, American Freedom: The Ordeal of Colonial Virginia*. New York: Norton, 1975.

———. "Slavery and Freedom: The American Paradox." *Journal of American History* 59 (June 1972): 5–29.

Morgan, Jennifer L. "'Some Could Suckle Over Their Shoulder': Male Travelers, Female Bodies, and the Gendering of Racial Ideology, 1500–1770." *William and Mary Quarterly*, 3rd ser., 54, no. 1 (January 1997): 167–92.

Morgan, Philip D. "Bound Labor." In *Encyclopedia of the North American Colonies*, edited by Jacob Cooke, 2:17–31. New York: S. Scribner's Sons, 1993.

———. "Colonial South Carolina Runaways: Their Significance for Slave Culture." In *Out of the House of Bondage: Runaways, Resistance, and Marronage in Africa and the New World*, edited by Gad Heuman, 57–78. London: Frank Cass, 1986.

———. *Slave Counterpoint: Black Culture in the Eighteenth-Century Chesapeake and Lowcountry*. Chapel Hill: University of North Carolina Press, 1998.

Morris, Christopher. "The Articulation of Two Worlds: The Master-Slave Relationship Reconsidered." *Journal of American History* 85 (December 1998): 982–1007.

———. *Becoming Southern: The Evolution of a Way of Life: Warren County and Vicksburg, Mississippi, 1770–1860*. New York: Oxford University Press, 1995.

Morris, Thomas D. *Southern Slavery and the Law, 1619–1860*. Chapel Hill: University of North Carolina Press, 1996.

Morton, Patricia, ed. *Discovering the Women in Slavery: Emancipating Perspectives on the American Past*. Athens: University of Georgia Press, 1996.

———. *Disfigured Images: The Historical Assault on Afro-American Women*. New York: Greenwood, 1991.

Mott, Frank Luther. *American Journalism: A History of Newspapers in the United States through 260 Years, 1690 to 1950*. New York: Macmillan, 1950.

Mullin, Gerald. *Flight and Rebellion: Slave Resistance in Eighteenth-Century Virginia*. New York: Oxford University Press, 1972.

Nasstrom, Kathryn L. "Down to Now: Memory, Narrative, and Women's Leadership in the Civil Rights Movement in Atlanta, Georgia." *Gender and History* 11, no. 1 (April 1999): 113–44.

Oakes, James. "The Political Significance of Slave Resistance." *History Workshop Journal* 22 (Fall 1986): 89–107.

——. *The Ruling Race: A History of American Slaveholders*. 1982. Reprint, New York: Vintage, 1983.

O'Hanlon, Rosalind. "Recovering the Subject: *Subaltern Studies* and Histories of Resistance in Colonial South Asia." *Modern Asian Studies* 22, no. 1 (1988): 189–224.

Olwell, Robert. *Masters, Slaves, and Subjects: The Culture of Power in the South Carolina Low Country*. Ithaca: Cornell University Press, 1998.

O'Neill, John. *The Communicative Body: Studies in Communicative Philosophy, Politics, and Sociology*. Evanston, Ill.: Northwestern University Press, 1989.

Ortner, Sherry. "Resistance and the Problem of Ethnographic Refusal." *Comparative Studies in Society and History* 37 (Spring 1995): 163–93.

Oshinsky, David M. *"Worse Than Slavery": Parchman Farm and the Ordeal of Jim Crow Justice*. 1996. Reprint, New York: Free Press, 1997.

Outram, Dorinda. *The Body and the French Revolution: Sex, Class, and Political Culture*. New Haven: Yale University Press, 1989.

Pacquette, Robert L. "Jacobins of the Lowcountry: The Vesey Plot on Trial." *William and Mary Quarterly*, 3rd ser., 59, no. 1 (January 2002): 185–92.

——. "Social History Update: Slave Resistance and Social History." *Journal of Social History* 24 (Spring 1991): 681–85.

Painter, Nell Irvin. "Representing Truth: Sojourner Truth's Knowing and Becoming Known." *Journal of American History* 81 (September 1994): 461–92.

——. *Sojourner Truth: A Life, a Symbol*. New York: Norton, 1996.

——. *Soul Murder and Slavery*. Waco, Tex.: Markam Press Fund, Baylor University Press, 1995.

Parish, Peter J. *Slavery: History and Historians*. New York: Harper and Row, 1989.

Parker, Freddie L. *Running for Freedom: Slave Runaways in North Carolina, 1775–1840*. New York: Garland, 1993.

Pearson, Edward A., "Trials and Errors: Denmark Vesey and His Historians." *William and Mary Quarterly*, 3rd ser., 59, no. 1 (January 2002): 137–42.

Peiss, Kathy, and Christina Simmons, eds. *Passion and Power: Sexuality in History*. Philadelphia: Temple University Press, 1989.

Penningroth, Dylan. "Slavery, Freedom, and Social Claims to Property among African Americans in Liberty County, Georgia, 1850–1880." *Journal of American History* 84 (September 1997): 405–36.

Peterson, Carla L. *"Doers of the Word": African-American Women Speakers and Writers of the North, 1830–1880*. New York: Oxford University Press, 1995.

Phillips, Ulrich B. *American Negro Slavery: A Survey of the Supply, Employment, and Control of Negro Labor as Determined by the Plantation Regime*. 1918. Reprint, Baton Rouge: Louisiana State University Press, 1966.

Poiger, Uta G. *Jazz, Rock, and Rebels: Cold War Politics and American Culture in a Divided Germany* Berkeley: University of California Press, 2000.

Pratt, Mary Louise. *Imperial Eyes: Travel Writing and Transculturation*. London: Routledge, 1992.

Price, Richard, ed. *Maroon Societies: Rebel Slave Communities in the Americas*. Garden City, N.Y.: Anchor, 1973.

Raboteau, Albert J. *Slave Religion: The "Invisible Institution" in the Antebellum South*. New York: Oxford University Press, 1978.

Rawick, George. *From Sundown to Sunup: The Making of the Black Community*. Westport, Conn.: Greenwood, 1972.

Rediker, Marcus. *Between the Devil and the Deep Blue Sea: Merchant Seamen, Pirates, and the Anglo-American Maritime World, 1700–1750*. Cambridge: Cambridge University Press, 1987.

Roark, James L. Notes to *Masters without Slaves: Southern Plantations in the Civil War and Reconstruction*. New York: Norton, 1977.

Rorabaugh, William. *Alcoholic Republic: An American Tradition*. New York: Oxford University Press, 1979.

Rosenthal, Judy. *Possession, Ecstasy, and Law in Ewe Voodoo*. Charlottesville: University of Virginia Press, 1998.

Said, Edward. *Culture and Imperialism*. New York: Knopf, 1993.

Savage, W. Sherman, *The Controversy over the Distribution of Abolition Literature, 1830–1860*. Washington, D.C.: Association for the Study of Negro Life and History, 1938.

Saville, Julie. *The Work of Reconstruction: From Slave to Wage Laborer in South Carolina, 1860–1870*. Cambridge: Cambridge University Press, 1994.

Schmidt, Benjamin. "Mapping an Empire: Cartographic and Colonial Rivalry in Seventeenth-Century Dutch and English North America." *William and Mary Quarterly*, 3rd ser., 54, no. 3 (July 1997): 549–78.

Schwalm, Leslie. *A Hard Fight for We: Women's Transition from Slavery to Freedom in South Carolina*. Urbana: University of Illinois Press, 1997.

Schwartz, Marie Jenkins. *Born in Bondage: Growing Up Enslaved in the Antebellum South*. Cambridge, Mass.: Harvard University Press, 2000.

Schwarz, Philip J. *Twice Condemned: Slaves and the Criminal Laws of Virginia, 1705–1865*. Baton Rouge: Louisiana State University Press, 1988.

Scott, James. *Domination and the Arts of Resistance: Hidden Transcripts*. New Haven: Yale University Press, 1990.

——. *Weapons of the Weak: Everyday Forms of Peasant Resistance*. New Haven: Yale University Press, 1985.

Scott, Joan Wallach. *Gender and the Politics of History*. New York: Columbia University Press, 1988.

——. "Gender: A Useful Category of Historical Analysis." *American Historical Review* 96 (December 1991): 1053–75.

Sedgwick, Eve Kosofsky. *Epistemology of the Closet*. Berkeley: University of California Press, 1990.

Shaw, Stephanie. "Mothering under Slavery in the Antebellum South." In *Mothering: Ideology, Experience, and Agency*, edited by Evelyn Nakano Glenn, Grace Chang, and Linda Renine Forcey, 237–58. New York: Routledge, 1994.

Smith, Mark M. *Mastered by the Clock: Time, Slavery, and Freedom in the American South*. Chapel Hill: University of North Carolina Press, 1997.

——. "Old South Time in Comparative Perspective." *American Historical Review* 101 (December 1996): 1432–96.

——. "Time, Slavery, and Plantation Capitalism in the Ante-bellum American South." *Past and Present* 150 (February 1996): 142–68.

Smith-Rosenberg, Carroll. *Disorderly Conduct: Visions of Gender in Victorian America*. New York: Knopf, 1985.

Sparke, Matthew. "Mapped Bodies and Disembodied Maps: (Dis)placing Cartographic Struggle in Colonial Canada." In *Places through the Body*, edited by Heidi J. Nast and Steve Pile, 305–36. London: Routledge, 1998.

Spelman, Elizabeth. *Inessential Woman: Problems of Exclusion in Feminist Thought*. Boston: Beacon Press, 1988.

Spillers, Hortense. "Mama's Baby, Papa's Maybe: An American Grammar Lesson." In *Within the Circle: An Anthology of African American Literary Criticism from the Harlem Renaissance to the Present*, edited by Angelyn Mitchell, 454–81. 1987. Reprint, Durham, N.C.: Duke University Press, 1994.

Stallybrass, Peter. "Marx's Coat." In *Border Fetishisms: Material Objects in Unstable Places*, edited by Patricia Spyer, 183–207. New York: Routledge, 1998.

Stampp, Kenneth. *The Peculiar Institution: Slavery in the Antebellum South*. New York: Vintage, 1956.

Stansell, Christine. *City of Women: Sex and Class in New York, 1789–1860*. Urbana: University of Illinois Press, 1987.

Steedman, Carolyn Kay. *Landscape for a Good Woman: A Story of Two Lives*. New Brunswick: Rutgers University Press, 1987.

Sterling, Dorothy, ed. *We Are Your Sisters: Black Women in the Nineteenth Century*. New York: Norton, 1984.

Stevenson, Brenda E. *Life in Black and White: Family and Community in the Slave South*. New York: Oxford University Press, 1996.

Thompson, E. P. *The Making of the English Working Class*. 1963. Reprint, New York: Vintage, 1966.

Thornton, John. *Africa and Africans in the Making of the Atlantic World, 1400–1800*. 1992. Reprint, Cambridge: Cambridge University Press, 1998.

Tobin, Beth. *Picturing Imperial Power: Colonial Subjects in Eighteenth-Century British Painting*. Durham, N.C.: Duke University Press, 1999.

Turner, Victor. *The Ritual Process: Structure and Anti-Structure*. Chicago: University of Chicago Press, 1969.

Vaughn, Alden T. *By the Work of Their Hands: Studies in Afro-American Folklife*. Ann Arbor: University of Michigan Research Press, 1991.

———. "The Origins Debate: Slavery and Racism in Seventeenth-Century Virginia." *Virginia Magazine of History and Biography* 97, no. 3 (July 1989): 311–54.

Vlach, John Michael. *Back of the Big House: The Architecture of Plantation Slavery*. Chapel Hill: University of North Carolina Press, 1993.

Wade, Richard C. *Slavery in the Cities: The South, 1820–1860*. New York: Oxford University Press, 1964.

Webber, Thomas L. *Deep Like the Rivers: Education in the Slave Quarter Community, 1831–1865*. New York: Norton, 1978.

White, Deborah Gray. *Ar'n't I a Woman? Female Slaves in the Plantation South*. New York: Norton, 1985.

White, Shane. "A Question of Style: Blacks in and around New York City in the Late 18th Century." *Journal of American Folklore* 102 (January/March 1989): 23–44.

White, Shane, and Graham White. "Slave Clothing and African-American Culture in the Eighteenth and Nineteenth Centuries." *Past and Present* 148 (August 1995): 149–86.

———. "Slave Hair and African-American Culture in the Eighteenth and Nineteenth Centuries." *Journal of Southern History* 61, no. 1 (February 1995): 45–76.

———. *Stylin': African American Expressive Culture from Its Beginnings to the Zoot Suit*. Ithaca: Cornell University Press, 1998.

Williams, Eric. *Capitalism and Slavery*. 1944. Reprint, New York: Capricorn Books, 1966.

Williams, Raymond. *The Long Revolution*. New York: Harper and Row, 1961.

Windley, Lathan Algerna. *Profile of Runaway Slaves in Virginia and South Carolina from 1730 through 1787*. New York: Garland, 1995.

Wood, Betty. "Some Aspects of Female Resistance to Chattel Slavery in Low Country Georgia, 1763–1815." *Historical Journal* 30, no. 3 (1987): 603–22.

———. *Women's Work, Men's Work: The Informal Slave Economies of Lowcountry Georgia*. Athens: University of Georgia Press, 1995.

Wood, Peter H. *Black Majority: Negroes in Colonial South Carolina from 1670 through the Stono Rebellion*. New York: Norton, 1974.

Woodward, C. Vann. "History from Slave Sources: A Review Article." *American Historical Review* 79 (April 1974): 470–81.

Wyatt-Brown, Bertram. "The Mask of Obedience: Male Slave Psychology in the Old South." *American Historical Review* 93 (December 1988): 1228–52.

———. *Southern Honor: Ethics and Behavior in the Old South*. New York: Oxford University Press, 1982.

Yee, Shirley. *Black Women Abolitionists: A Study in Activism*. Knoxville: University of Tennessee Press, 1992.

Young, Jeffrey Robert. *Domesticating Slavery: The Master Class in Georgia and South Carolina, 1670–1837*. Chapel Hill: University of North Carolina Press, 1999.

INDEX

Abolitionism, 94; and texts, 95; in the eighteenth century, 100–101; visual culture of, 100–101, 107–8, 109; and representations of violence, 101–2, 144 (n. 5); Postal Campaign of, 102; in the South, 102–3, 106–7; southern laws prohibiting, 104; during the Civil War, 114–16

Abolitionists, black, 105–6

African women, 63–64

Albert, Octavia, 35

Alcohol, 66, 87, 166 (nn. 123, 124); and violence, 77; women's production of, 88

"Amalgamation prints," 98–99, 111–14

American Anti-Slavery Society, 101

Ball, Charles, 13, 19, 88

Barrow, Bennet, 52, 53

Berlin, Ira, 119

Bibb, Henry, 13, 45, 65

Bolster, Jeffrey W., 103

Brown, Kathleen M., 63

Brown, William Wells, 130

California (enslaved woman), 96–99, 109–11

Captivity, slavery as a form of, 12

Charly (enslaved man), 20, 21

Clarke, Colin, 124, 127

Clermont plantation, 39

Clothing: and status, 78–79; procuring, 79–80, 85; making, 80; and second shift, 80–81; and temporal order, 80–81; hoopskirts, 83; accessories, 84; shoes, 84–85; as celebration of emancipation, 121; procuring during the Civil War, 121

Contamination: abolitionist texts as, 104–5; black watermen as, 104–5; abolitionists as, 109

Contrabands: kidnaped during the Civil War, 126

Dance, 75–76

Douglas, Mary, 6

Douglass, Frederick, 44, 130

Dress. See Clothing

DuBois, Sylvia, 88

DuBois, W. E. B., 118, 143 (n. 3)

Edwards, Laura, 119

Edwards, the Reverend Richard, 118

Emancipation, 117; spatial and temporal aspects of, 117–19

Emancipation Proclamation, 116, 118, 120

Eppes, Richard, 20–22, 57

Ervin, William Ethelbert, 24

Estabrooks, Henry L., 136

Family: as binding women to the South, 37–38; gender roles in, 37–38; and truancy, 44; and courtship, 45; visiting, 45; and life in the quarters, 93–94

Faust, Drew Gilpin, 83, 135

Fences, 5

Fett, Sharla, 46

Geography of containment, 6, 16–17; and women, 6; enforcement of, 24–25, 33; and plantation discipline, 27; and mastery, 27–28; and gender difference, 28–34; and plantation frolics, 65; and abolitionism, 108; during the Civil War, 128–30, 137–38; and the Union army, 129–30

Georgian style of architecture, 4

Grimké, Angelina, 107

Hairstyles, 84

Hammond, James Henry, 26, 39, 47, 48, 51, 88

Harlan, Justice John Marshall, 141

Harvey, David, 4, 5

Hiring, 96–98

Hoopskirts, 83

Hughes, Fountain, 20

Isaac (enslaved man), 96–99

Ivy, Lorenzo L., 40, 42, 48

Jackson, Mattie, 114–16

James, C. L. R., 62, 143 (n. 3)

Kemble, Frances, 84

Lincoln, Abraham: illustration of, 115; and Emancipation Proclamation, 118

Literacy, laws against, 103–4

Litwack, Leon, 118

Magazines, 100

Manhattan Anti-Slavery Society, 105–6

Mariah (enslaved woman), 44–45

McCurry, Stephanie, 5

McDowell, James, 96

Miller, Frances, 86

Miller, John Blount, 18–19, 51, 53, 56

Mobility: gender differences, 37–38, 124–25; during the Civil War, 123, 125, 128

Morgan, Jennifer L., 63

Musicians (enslaved), 73

Nevitt, John, 39, 52, 56–57

Newspaper. See Penny papers

Northup, Solomon, 22, 33

Olmsted, Frederick Law, 49, 50, 57, 89

Outram, Dorinda, 62

Overseers: as enforcers of geography of containment, 26; sexual exploitation by, 42

Painter, Nell Irvin, 109

Parties (slave), 68–92; preparing for, 67–70, 72; and passes, 72; and alcohol, 72, 87; music and musicians and, 73, 74–75; dance and, 74–76; and violence, 76–78; and clothing, 78–87

Passes: laws governing in Virginia, 13; laws governing, 13–16; laws governing in South Carolina, 14–15; spatial and temporal aspects of, 19–20, 24; general, 28–29; enslaved men's access to, 28–30; for women, 30–31; women denied access to, 30–32; and alcohol, 72; and parties, 72

Paternalism, 3, 17, 144 (n. 4); and shift from patriarchalism, 17–18; and space, 18

Patriarchalism, 17

Penny papers, 100

Philpot, Francis, 112

Pickets, Confederate, 128
Plessy v. Ferguson, 141
Postal Campaign, 102
Powell, William P., 105
Principles of restraint, 12–16
Print technology, 99–100
Proslavery: and depictions of abolition-
    ism, 111–13; *Facts for White
    Americans . . .* (pamphlet), 112

Racial etiquette, 122, 131
Religion, 61
Resistance: everyday, 3; individual and
    collective distinction, 3, 50–51, 144
    (n. 6); personal and political, 3, 51,
    94, 144 (n. 6); hidden and visible dis-
    tinction, 3, 94
Rival geography: movement in, 6, 7;
    planters' responses to, 7; and truancy,
    35–59; and slave quarters, 48; and
    parties, 61–62; during the Civil War,
    135–37
Roach, Mahala P. Eggleston, 40, 43
Rockingham plantation, 39
Rose (enslaved woman), 86
Rubin and Jerry (enslaved men), 52
Runaways: laws regarding, 13–14

Savannah River Anti–Slave Traffick
    Association, 90–92
Scientific agriculture, 20
Scott, James C., 2, 119, 143 (n. 3)
Second shift, 32–33, 80–82
Segregation, 140–41
Sexual exploitation: by overseers, 42; by
    enslaved men, 43; by slaveholders,
    64–65
Shoes, 84–85
Slaveholding women: violence by, 43;
    during the Civil War, 131–35
Slave patrols, 25–26, 71, 113–14; and
    women, 72; during the Civil War, 128
Slavery and freedom, 127

Smith, Mark M., 20
Smith, Sallie, 35, 50, 51
Space: significance of, 4, 6; and gender,
    5; and paternalism, 18; and women's
    work, 32
Steward, Austin, 22, 69–71
Stone, Kate, 133
Suicide, 58

Three bodies, 62–68
Tickets (South Carolina). *See* Passes,
    laws governing in South Carolina
Time: and passes, 19–20; and contain-
    ment, 19–24; regulating women's
    work, 22; night, 24
Truancy: terminology of, 35; definition
    of, 36; intraregional differences in,
    39–40; and household work, 40; and
    work, 40, 58; seasonal timing of, 41;
    and violence, 41–44; and family, 44;
    and the church, 45; and healers, 46;
    and surviving in the woods, 46–47;
    women's support of, 47; and negoti-
    ated returns, 49; punishment of, 51–
    53, 55–59, 57; average length of
    absence, 54; returning from, 54; and
    order, 58
Truants: compared with percentages of
    female fugitives, 36; capture of, 53

Union soldiers, 126
Urana (enslaved woman), 88

Veney, Bethany, 46
Violence, 77–78, 157 (n. 117); and tru-
    ancy, 41–44; by slaveholding women,
    43; and alcohol, 77; at parties, 78;
    abolitionist representations of, 101–
    2; male slaveholders' ideal of "cool,"
    132
Virginia: laws regarding runaways, 13–
    14

Walker, David, 102–3

Watermen, black, 98, 105–6, 108; and contamination, 104

Wilder, C. B., 123

Williams, Nancy, 60, 85

Work, women's specialized, 81, 163 (n. 81)

Works Progress Administration interviews of formerly enslaved people, 8

Wyatt, Mary, 85

Young, George H., 96, 111–14

GENDER & AMERICAN CULTURE

Closer to Freedom: Enslaved Women and Everyday Resistance in the Plantation South, by Stephanie M. H. Camp (2004).

Masterful Women: Slaveholding Widows from the American Revolution through the Civil War, by Kirsten E. Wood (2004).

Manliness and Its Discontents: The Black Middle Class and the Transformation of Masculinity, 1900–1930, by Martin Summers (2004).

Citizen, Mother, Worker: Debating Public Responsibility for Child Care after the Second World War, by Emilie Stoltzfus (2003).

Women and the Historical Enterprise in America: Gender, Race, and the Politics of Memory 1880–1945, by Julie Des Jardins (2003).

Free Hearts and Free Homes: Gender and American Antislavery Politics, by Michael D. Pierson (2003).

Ella Baker and the Black Freedom Movement: A Radical Democratic Vision, by Barbara Ransby (2003).

Signatures of Citizenship: Petitioning, Antislavery, and Women's Political Identity, by Susan Zaeske (2003).

Love on the Rocks: Men, Women, and Alcohol in Post–World War II America, by Lori Rotskoff (2002).

The Veiled Garvey: The Life and Times of Amy Jacques Garvey, by Ula Yvette Taylor (2002).

Working Cures: Health, Healing, and Power on Southern Slave Plantations, by Sharla Fett (2002).

Southern History across the Color Line, by Nell Irvin Painter (2002).

The Artistry of Anger: Black and White Women's Literature in America, 1820–1860, by Linda M. Grasso (2002).

Too Much to Ask: Black Women in the Era of Integration, by Elizabeth Higginbotham (2001).

Imagining Medea: Rhodessa Jones and Theater for Incarcerated Women, by Rena Fraden (2001).

Painting Professionals: Women Artists and the Development of Modern American Art, 1870–1920, by Kirsten Swinth (2001).

Remaking Respectability: African American Women in Interwar Detroit, by Victoria W. Wolcott (2001).

Ida B. Wells-Barnett and American Reform, 1880–1930, by Patricia A. Schechter (2001).

Taking Haiti: Military Occupation and the Culture of U.S. Imperialism, 1915–1940, by Mary A. Renda (2001).

Before Jim Crow: The Politics of Race in Postemancipation Virginia, by Jane Dailey (2000).

Captain Ahab Had a Wife: New England Women and the Whalefishery, 1720–1870, by Lisa Norling (2000).

Civilizing Capitalism: The National Consumers' League, Women's Activism, and Labor Standards in the New Deal Era, by Landon R. Y. Storrs (2000).

Rank Ladies: Gender and Cultural Hierarchy in American Vaudeville, by M. Alison Kibler (1999).

Strangers and Pilgrims: Female Preaching in America, 1740–1845, by Catherine A. Brekus (1998).

Sex and Citizenship in Antebellum America, by Nancy Isenberg (1998).

Yours in Sisterhood: Ms. Magazine and the Promise of Popular Feminism, by Amy Erdman Farrell (1998).

We Mean to Be Counted: White Women and Politics in Antebellum Virginia, by Elizabeth R. Varon (1998).

Women Against the Good War: Conscientious Objection and Gender on the American Home Front, 1941–1947, by Rachel Waltner Goossen (1997).

Toward an Intellectual History of Women: Essays by Linda K. Kerber (1997).

Gender and Jim Crow: Women and the Politics of White Supremacy in North Carolina, 1896–1920, by Glenda Elizabeth Gilmore (1996).

Delinquent Daughters: Protecting and Policing Adolescent Female Sexuality in the United States, 1885–1920, by Mary E. Odem (1995).

U.S. History as Women's History: New Feminist Essays, edited by Linda K. Kerber, Alice Kessler-Harris, and Kathryn Kish Sklar (1995).

Common Sense and a Little Fire: Women and Working-Class Politics in the United States, 1900–1965, by Annelise Orleck (1995).

How Am I to Be Heard?: Letters of Lillian Smith, edited by Margaret Rose Gladney (1993).

Entitled to Power: Farm Women and Technology, 1913–1963, by Katherine Jellison (1993).

Revising Life: Sylvia Plath's Ariel Poems, by Susan R. Van Dyne (1993).

Made From This Earth: American Women and Nature, by Vera Norwood (1993).

Unruly Women: The Politics of Social and Sexual Control in the Old South, by Victoria E. Bynum (1992).

The Work of Self-Representation: Lyric Poetry in Colonial New England, by Ivy Schweitzer (1991).

Labor and Desire: Women's Revolutionary Fiction in Depression America, by Paula Rabinowitz (1991).

Community of Suffering and Struggle: Women, Men, and the Labor Movement in Minneapolis, 1915–1945, by Elizabeth Faue (1991).

All That Hollywood Allows: Re-reading Gender in 1950s Melodrama, by Jackie Byars (1991).

Doing Literary Business: American Women Writers in the Nineteenth Century, by Susan Coultrap-McQuin (1990).

Ladies, Women, and Wenches: Choice and Constraint in Antebellum Charleston and Boston, by Jane H. Pease and William H. Pease (1990).

The Secret Eye: The Journal of Ella Gertrude Clanton Thomas, 1848–1889, edited by Virginia Ingraham Burr, with an introduction by Nell Irvin Painter (1990).

Second Stories: The Politics of Language, Form, and Gender in Early American Fictions, by Cynthia S. Jordan (1989).

Within the Plantation Household: Black and White Women of the Old South, by Elizabeth Fox-Genovese (1988).

The Limits of Sisterhood: The Beecher Sisters on Women's Rights and Woman's Sphere, by Jeanne Boydston, Mary Kelley, and Anne Margolis (1988).